SANDOWN PUBLIC LIBRARY
305 MAIN STREET, P.O. BOX 580
SANDOWN, NH 03873
603-887-3428

Korean Battle Chronology

Korean Battle Chronology

*Unit-by-Unit United States
Casualty Figures and
Medal of Honor Citations*

Richard E. Ecker

McFarland & Company, Inc., Publishers
Jefferson, North Carolina, and London

LIBRARY OF CONGRESS CATALOGUING-IN-PUBLICATION DATA

Ecker, Richard E., 1930–
Korean battle chronology : unit-by-unit United States casualty figures
and medal of honor citations / Richard E. Ecker.
p.   cm.
Includes bibliographical references and index.

ISBN 0-7864-1980-6 (illustrated case binding : 50# alkaline paper) ∞

1. Korean War, 1950–1953 — Biography.
2. Medal of Honor.
3. United States — Armed Forces — Biography.
4. Soldiers — United States — Biography.
5. Heroes — United States — Biography.
I. Title.
DS918.A553E25   2005   951.904'24'0202 — dc22   2004021871

British Library cataloguing data are available

©2005 Richard E. Ecker. All rights reserved

*No part of this book may be reproduced or transmitted in any form
or by any means, electronic or mechanical, including photocopying
or recording, or by any information storage and retrieval system,
without permission in writing from the publisher.*

Cover photograph courtesy National Park Service,
U.S. Department of the Interior, Washington, D.C.

Manufactured in the United States of America

*McFarland & Company, Inc., Publishers
Box 611, Jefferson, North Carolina 28640
www.mcfarlandpub.com*

To my friend, Charlie ... fellow scientist, fellow combat infantryman, Purple Heart veteran of "The Big War" and, for the last seven years, esteemed accomplice in our Wednesday afternoon brain games.

Contents

Preface
1

I. The Peninsular War
5

II. Active Defense
128

III. The War of the Hills
136

IV. The End of Hostilities
185

V. Summary Statistics
192

Appendix: Data Sources
201

Index
205

PREFACE

On June 28, 1950, five U.S. airmen, 1st Lt. Remer L. Harding (age 26) of Ft. Worth, TX, 1st Lt Raymond J Cyborski (age 25) of Chicago, IL, 1st Lt. Derrell B. Sayre (age 27) of Racine, OH, SSgt William J. Goodwin (age 28) of Tacoma, WA, and SSgt Jose C. Campos, Jr. (age 31) of Miami, AZ, died when their aircraft were shot down over Korea. They became the first U. S. casualties in a war that started three days earlier, when the North Korean People's Army (NKPA) crossed the 38th parallel and invaded the Republic of South Korea. The losses of U.S. military personnel that began with these five airmen would continue for 37 months and would ultimately total 33,985* American fatalities and more than 100,000 other American casualties. This is a history of U.S. involvement in the Korean War as told by those casualties— not in person, of course, but by the dates they occurred, their causes, their numbers and the units in which they served.

The primary source of the information from which this history is compiled is *The Adjutant General's Korean War Casualty File— U.S. Army* (AGCF), a database listing by name 109,933 U.S. Army Korean War combat casualties, both fatal and non-fatal. Regrettably, no data source is currently available that identifies both fatal and non-fatal combat casualties for the other U.S. armed services. Another database, *The Korean Conflict Casualty File from the Office of the Secretary of Defense* (KCCF), lists fatalities for all services, but the information in this database for Army and Marine Corps casualties has been found to contain significant errors and omissions. This book draws information on U.S. Army casualties exclusively from AGCF.

Recently, the Marine Corps Casualty Section in Washington amended and supplemented its original contribution to KCCF. With these modifications, the database provides significantly more reliable records. A database containing these modifications was used to document USMC fatalities recorded in this book. About 2 percent of the KCCF records still do not contain a usable date of occurrence and cannot be used to assign these casualties to a specific date, but the majority of the data appear

---

*U.S. Army, 27,709; U.S. Marine Corps, 4,610; U.S. Air Force, 1,200; U.S. Navy, 466. These numbers, which may or may not agree with figures available from other sources, were determined by calculating every combat fatality for which an available official record identifies the individual combatant by name.

to be sufficiently accurate to show the general pattern of Marine Corps losses in the war. The original KCCF database is used here to document U.S. Navy and U.S. Air Forces fatalities.*

Casualty statistics for presentation here were developed by simply adding the number of individual records in the data files that meet certain selection criteria: unit, date, casualty type and disposition, service branch, etc.

The Korean War began on June 25, 1950, and continued for 37 months. In many ways, it was not a single war, but two very different wars. The first of these wars was a 17-month give-and-take conflict over occupation of the Korean countryside, as first one side and then the other prevailed in the action. Then, when peace negotiations in Panmunjom began in earnest late in 1951, this war gave way to a different kind of conflict. Popularly known as "The War of the Hills," this conflict was carried on as trench warfare with each side hunkered down, sniping at one another with artillery and mortars, and battling for the right to occupy certain strategic hills. The two conflicts were separated by a period of almost six months, in which active engagement was limited and casualties were light. The narrative that follows is subdivided into three sections, corresponding to these three phases of the conflict: (I) The Peninsular War; (II) Active Defense; and (III) The War of the Hills.

The AGCF data for U.S. Army casualties identify five different types of casualty and eleven different ultimate dispositions of the casualty. For simplicity, most of the tables in this book reduce to six the many possible combinations of type and disposition. The six categories are: (1) **KIA**— Killed in action, including individuals who died of injuries and those who were initially reported missing and later were found dead; (2) **WIA**— Wounded in action, including individuals who sustained injuries other than wounds (e.g., paratroopers who were injured in the drop); (3) **POW returned**— Captured and later returned to military control; (4) **POW died**— Captured and died in captivity; (5) **MIA returned**— Missing in action and later returned to military control; and (6) **MIA died**— Missing in action, never found and later declared dead — most often after the end of hostilities. In some cases, a more detailed accounting of casualty type and disposition will be used to better describe the outcome of a particular battle.†

The KCCF database of combat fatalities in other services uses different categories than AGCF for recording casualty type and cause. Because Air Force and Navy casualties are included in this database, each fatality is categorized as either a *Ground Casualty*, a *Sea Casualty* or one of six categories of *Air Casualty*: either *Fixed Wing* or *Helicopter*, and either *Pilot*, *Other Aircrew*, or *Non-Aircrew*. The KCCF data include a more detailed accounting of cause of death than that used in AGCF. In most cases, these details (e.g., small arms vs. artillery or mortar vs. explosive device) do not con-

---

*Readers interested in more information on how records in the databases were evaluated and organized for use in this project will find a detailed explanation in the Appendix.

†Included in the AGCF data are 298 casualties that use two records to document the circumstances. All of these casualties are instances in which the individual was both wounded and either captured or reported missing. One record was used to record the occurrence and disposition relative to the disappearance. The second was used to record the occurrence and disposition relative to the wound(s). To avoid having these duplicate records inflate the accounting of losses reported here, those individuals who were captured and wounded will be accounted as POW. Those who were reported as missing and were later found wounded will be accounted as WIA.

tribute significantly to the descriptions of battle losses and are not included in this book's statistics. However, if specific causes of death help clarify what took place in a particular battle, they are noted.

In my research to find a reference work to guide me through the key battles of the Korean War, and to provide an accurate timeline of events in the conflict, I could find no more reliable resource than *Battles of the Korean War* (Richard K. Kolb, Editor, VFW Publications, 2003). Battle descriptions in this resource were invaluable in helping me build the historical foundations needed to give significance to the casualty statistics. Included in *Battles of the Korean War* is *The Korean War Combat Chronology 1950–53*, which provides details of significant events in the war (other than just major battles), including reported losses. In many cases, my calculations of those losses from the databases—and sometimes the dates those losses were reported to have occurred—do not agree with the information reported in the chronology. Whenever these differences are significant, I point them out in the book.

Medal of Honor citations were obtained from the U.S. Army Center of Military History and were reproduced verbatim from their website.

I

THE PENINSULAR WAR

Delaying Action

The first 35 U.S. ground forces arrived in Korea on June 29, 1950 — members of the 507th Anti-aircraft Artillery Weapons Battalion, code named Detachment X. That day, at Suwan airfield, they shot down one enemy airplane and sustained the first two American ground casualties of the war: Pfc. Thomas Merante, AAA Weapons Crewman from Columbia county, New York, and artillery officer, 1st Lt. Joseph V. Bailey from Salt Lake county, Utah, whose reported unit was the 7th Cavalry Regiment. Both were wounded in action. The next day, the first fatalities of U.S. ground forces occurred when a U.S. troop carrier was shot down over Korea. Eighteen Army personnel — all Signal Corps specialists — and five aircrew members lost their lives in the crash.

On July 1, the first U.S. infantry and artillery units arrived on the Korean peninsula. Code named Task Force Smith, this contingent included the 1st Battalion of the 24th Division's 21st Infantry Regiment and A Battery of the 52nd Field Artillery Battalion. By then, the South Korean capital, Seoul, was already in the hands of the attacking forces. Task Force Smith took up positions in an attempt to block the advance of the enemy along western access routes to cities in the south. Casualties were light for the next four days. Then, on July 5, with Task Force Smith joined on the ground by elements of the 1st Cavalry Division and the 25th Infantry Division, the battle to delay the enemy advance began in earnest. That day, at Osan, the Task Force sustained 171 casualties, the majority killed, captured or missing.

Table 1— Battle of Osan

	KIA	WIA	POW Returned	POW Died	MIA Returned	MIA Died	Unit Total
21st Inf, 24th Inf Div	46	16	43	27	4	7	143
52nd FA Bn, 24th Inf Div	7	5	7	5	4		28
Task Force Smith Totals	53	21	50	32	8		171
6 other units	1	6		1			8
Total casualties 7/5/50	54	27	50	33	8	7	179

For the next month, a costly losing battle raged as U.S. forces grudgingly gave ground to superior numbers of enemy. At Chochiwon, between July 10 and 12, the 21st Infantry of the 24th Division continued to take a pounding, sustaining the majority of 665 total casualties in the battle, again mostly killed, captured or missing in action.

Table 2 — Battle of Chochiwon

	KIA	WIA	POW Returned	POW Died	MIA Returned	MIA Died	Unit Total
21st Inf, 24th Inf. Div.	228	61	85	130	7	20	531
23 other units that period	31	79	5	10	9	0	134
Total casualties 7/10–7/12/50	259	140	90	140	16	20	665

Two days later, the 63rd Field Artillery Battalion was overrun and suffered catastrophic losses, almost half of them captured.

Table 3 — 63rd FA Battalion

	KIA	WIA	POW Returned	POW Died	MIA Returned	MIA Died	Unit Total
63rd FA Bn, 24th Inf Div	31	13	24	24	12	1	105
13 other units that day	6	19	3	1	2	0	31
Total casualties 7/14/50	37	32	27	25	14	1	136

Then, on July 16th, as beleaguered U.S. troops dug in to make a stand at the Kum River, the 19th Infantry of the 24th Division, along with three of the division's supporting units, took the brunt of the enemy onslaught, suffering more than 90 percent of 617 U.S. ground casualties that day.

Table 4 — Kum River

	KIA	WIA	POW Returned	POW Died	MIA Returned	MIA Died	Unit Total
19th Inf, 24th Inf Div	279	72	22	50	9	34	466
52nd, FA Bn, 24th Inf Div	13	42				1	56
3rd Engr Bn, 24th Inf Div	17	4					21
13th FA Bn, 24th Inf Div	8	6	1		1		16
Unit Totals 7/16/50	317	124	23	50	10	35	559

By July 19th, the NKPA had occupied almost half of the territory between the 38th Parallel and the southern coast of the peninsula. In west-central Korea, the city of Taejon was the next major objective of their advancing armies. There the U.S. 24th Infantry Division made a gallant stand at great cost to further delay the advancing enemy. In the two days of the battle, units of the division reported 1087 out of 1146 total casualties reported on those days. The majority of these losses were in the 34th Infantry Regiment.

Table 5 — Battle of Taejon

	KIA	WIA	POW Returned	POW Died	MIA Returned	MIA Died	Unit Total
19th Inf, 24th Inf Div	76	72	10	12		9	179
34th Inf, 24th Inf Div	280	146	48	73	23	46	616
3rd Engr Bn, 24th Inf Div	44	26	5	6	2	6	89
63rd FA Bn, 24th Inf Div	7	15		3	13	4	42
11th FA Bn, 24th Inf Div	29	16	5	1	2	2	55
24th QM Co, 24th Inf Div	9	14	4	2	5	1	35
13 other 24th Div units	20	38	2	4	3	4	71
Total 24th Div 7/19–7/20/50	465	325	74	101	48	72	1085

In this battle, the first two of 131 Korean War Medals of Honor were awarded.

MEDAL OF HONOR: WILLIAM F. DEAN

Awarded to: Major General William F. Dean, Alameda County, California, U.S. Army, Commanding General, 24th Infantry Division, Taejon, Korea, 20 July 1950

> Maj. Gen. Dean distinguished himself by conspicuous gallantry and intrepidity at the repeated risk of his life above and beyond the call of duty. In command of a unit suddenly relieved from occupation duties in Japan and as yet untried in combat, faced with a ruthless and determined enemy, highly trained and overwhelmingly superior in numbers, he felt it his duty to take action which to a man of his military experience and knowledge was clearly apt to result in his death. He personally and alone attacked an enemy tank while armed only with a hand grenade. He also directed the fire of his tanks from an exposed position with neither cover nor concealment while under observed artillery and small-arm fire. When the town of Taejon was finally overrun he refused to insure his own safety by leaving with the leading elements but remained behind organizing his retreating forces, directing stragglers, and was last seen assisting the wounded to a place of safety. These actions indicate that Maj. Gen. Dean felt it necessary to sustain the courage and resolution of his troops by examples of excessive gallantry committed always at the threatened portions of his frontlines. The magnificent response of his unit to this willing and cheerful sacrifice, made with full knowledge of its certain cost, is history. The success of this phase of the campaign is in large measure due to Maj. Gen. Dean's heroic leadership, courageous and loyal devotion to his men, and his complete disregard for personal safety.

Gen. Dean, a brigadier general at the time, was captured by the NKPA that day and remained in captivity for more than three years. He was released on September 4, 1953.

MEDAL OF HONOR: GEORGE D. LIBBY

Awarded to: Sergeant George D. Libby, Cumberland County, ME, U.S. Army, Company C, 3d Engineer Combat Battalion, 24th Infantry Division. Near Taejon, Korea, 20 July 1950.

Sgt. Libby distinguished himself by conspicuous gallantry and intrepidity above and beyond the call of duty in action. While breaking through an enemy encirclement, the vehicle in which he was riding approached an enemy roadblock and encountered devastating fire which disabled the truck, killing or wounding all the passengers except Sgt. Libby. Taking cover in a ditch Sgt. Libby engaged the enemy and despite the heavy fire crossed the road twice to administer aid to his wounded comrades. He then hailed a passing M-5 artillery tractor and helped the wounded aboard. The enemy directed intense small-arms fire at the driver, and Sgt. Libby, realizing that no one else could operate the vehicle, placed himself between the driver and the enemy thereby shielding him while he returned the fire. During this action he received several wounds in the arms and body. Continuing through the town the tractor made frequent stops and Sgt. Libby helped more wounded aboard. Refusing first aid, he continued to shield the driver and return the fire of the enemy when another roadblock was encountered. Sgt. Libby received additional wounds but held his position until he lost consciousness. Sgt. Libby's sustained, heroic actions enabled his comrades to reach friendly lines. His dauntless courage and gallant self-sacrifice reflect the highest credit upon himself and uphold the esteemed traditions of the U.S. Army.

Sgt. Libby, a combat construction specialist, was initially reported as missing in action and was later discovered dead from his wounds.

By this time, the 1st Cavalry Division and the 25th Infantry Division were established in force a few miles to the east of Taejon and were beginning to take a greater share of the punishment from enemy units pushing toward Pusan. Casualties for these divisions had been light since they first arrived in Korea some three weeks earlier. However, in the days following the battle of Taejon — and as the battle lines began to collapse into a perimeter around Taegu and Pusan — their casualties increased. On July 24 and 25, the 1st Cav. was hit particularly hard, and on July 27 and 28, the 25th Division took its highest casualties in this first phase of the war.

Table 6 — Late July Losses

	KIA	WIA	POW Returned	POW Died	MIA Returned	MIA Died	Unit Total
1st Cavalry Division 7/24/50–7/25/50	204	248	7	1	7	22	489
25th Infantry Division 7/27/50–7/28/50	53	283	1		1	5	343

These casualties were dwarfed, however, by the losses sustained by the 3rd Battalion of the 29th Infantry Regiment* when it was ambushed at Hadong on July 27.

---

*Some sources list the 29th Infantry as a unit integral to the 24th Infantry Division. The AGCF database, however, identifies it as an independent regiment or Regimental Combat Team (RCT). Thus, although it was attached to the 24th Division in some of the operations reported here, it is identified in this report as an independent unit.

I. The Peninsular War

Table 7 — Ambush at Hadong

	KIA	WIA	POW Returned	POW Died	MIA Returned	MIA Died	Unit Total
29th Infantry/RCT 7/27/50	242	135	49	2	4	63	495

Then, on July 31, the 19th Regiment of the 24th Division and the 29th Regt/RCT engaged the enemy in the Battle of the Notch. These units reported 117 casualties that day, the majority killed, captured or missing.

Table 8 — Battle of the Notch

	KIA	WIA	POW Returned	POW Died	MIA Returned	MIA Died	Unit Total
19th Inf, 24th Inf Div	32	26	1	1	1	9	70
29th Infantry/RCT	25	11	2	2	1	6	47

By August 3, the three U.S. divisions had established a line of defense along the Naktong River in south-central Korea, from Woegwan, 15 miles northwest of Taegu, extending to the southern coast of the peninsula, a few miles west of Mason. This line became the western rim of the Pusan perimeter, the last line of defense in the battle to keep South Korea from being totally overrun by the NKPA. The northern rim of the perimeter was being held by units of the ROK army.

The first phase of the Peninsular War was over. The delaying action had succeeded in preventing the total occupation of South Korea by the NKPA, but it had been a costly operation for the defending armies. U.S. casualties during the action are summarized in Table 9.

Table 9 — Total U. S. Army Casualties
29 June 1950 to 3 August 1950

1st Cavalry Division	KIA	WIA	POW Returned	POW Died	MIA Returned	MIA Died	Unit Total
5th Cav, 1st Cav Div	171	243	8	1	5	27	455
7th Cav, 1st Cav Div	36	122	2	2	5	3	170
8th Cav, 1st Cav Div	102	245	3	2	1	5	358
16th Recon Co, 1st Cav Div	14	12				3	29
8th Engr Bn, 1st Cav Div	8	33			1		42
61st FA Bn, 1st Cav Div	10	26			1		37
77th FA Bn, 1st Cav Div	2	24					26
99th FA Bn, 1st Cav Div	9	29					38
71st Med Tk Bn, 1st Cav Div	9	19	1			1	30
Other 1st Cav Div units (10)	6	20					26
Total 1st Cav casualties	367	773	14	5	13	39	1211
24th Infantry Division							
19th Inf, 24th Inf Div	449	337	39	66	13	60	964
21st Inf, 24th Inf Div	284	127	129	159	11	27	737
34th Inf, 24th Inf Div	397	351	63	110	44	69	1034
24th QM Co, 24th Inf Div	6	12	4	2	5	1	30
24th Sig Co, 24th Inf Div	12	7		1		1	21

(continued on next page)

Table 9 (*cont.*)

24th Infantry Division	KIA	WIA	POW Returned	POW Died	MIA Returned	MIA Died	Unit Total
24th Recon Co, 24th Inf Div	7	11		3		1	22
3rd Engr Bn, 24th Inf Div	71	56	5	6	2	11	151
13th FA Bn, 24th Inf Div	10	27	1		1		39
52nd FA Bn, 24th Inf Div	24	60	7	7	6	1	105
63rd FA Bn, 24th Inf Div	43	38	24	27	25	5	162
11th FA Bn, 24th Inf Div	35	41	5	2	2	2	87
26th AAA Bn, 24th Inf Div	7	20			1		28
Other 24th Inf Div Units (9)	15	36	4	2	2	2	61
Total 24th Div casualties	1360	1123	281	385	112	180	3441
29th Inf Regt/RCT	297	219	59	5	7	75	662
25th Infantry Division							
24th Inf, 25th Inf Div	70	355	1	1	3	6	436
27th Inf, 25th Inf Div	99	293	3	6	5	3	409
35th Inf, 25th Inf Div	32	68	3	5	2	10	120
65th Engr Bn, 25th Inf Div	16	8				1	25
8th FA Bn, 25th Inf Div	5	24					29
Other 25th Div Units (12)	9	49			1	3	62
Total 25th Div casualties	231	797	7	12	11	23	1081
Total other units (52)	50	108	4		10	2	167
Total U.S. Army Casualities 06/29/50 to 08/03/50	2305	3013	365	407	153	319	6562

In the same period, the U.S. Air Force lost 19 airmen in action against the enemy. The causes and dispositions of these fatalities are summarized in Table 10.

Table 10 — Air Force Losses 06/29/50 to 08/03/50

Fixed Wing Crash Over Land	
Pilot, Killed in Action	1
Pilot, Died of Wounds	1
Pilot, Died in Captivity	1
Aircrew, Died While Missing	8
Non-Aircrew, Killed in Action	4
Non-Aircrew, Died While Missing	1
Non-Aircrew, Died in Captivity	1
Fixed Wing Crash At Sea	
Pilot, Killed in Action	1
Ground Casualty	
Small-arms Fire, Killed in Action	1
Total 06/29–08/03/50	**19**

The U.S. Navy lost two men in this period, one pilot lost in a fixed-wing crash over land and one reported ground casualty KIA from small-arms fire. Most ground casualties of Navy personnel are hospital corpsmen serving with the marines. As the U.S. Marine Corps was not yet in the war, it is very possible that his record has a bad date.

Now, with U.N. forces consolidated in positions around the Pusan perimeter, the next stage of the Peninsular War began.

The Pusan Perimeter

By early August 1950, the three American divisions that had succeeded in delaying the advance of the NKPA were joined in the conflict by the U.S. 2nd Infantry Division, the 5th Regimental Combat Team and the First Provisional Marine Brigade. For the next month and a half, the defense of the Pusan Perimeter became a bloody give-and-take affair with a total of more than 3,600 combat fatalities among U.S. forces. Although some observers refer to this six-week period as a single battle, the perimeter was some over 100 miles in length as this phase of the conflict began and the casualties of each of the American units committed to the conflict had their own individual stories to tell.

On the northern rim of the perimeter, ROK divisions continued to give ground slowly through much of the month of August, but the NKPA was only able to push back the battle line in this region about 20 miles during that time. Along the Naktong River, U.S. forces held their positions, allowing only minor and temporary penetrations by the enemy and continuing to consolidate their hold on the western rim of the perimeter.

Meanwhile, the U.S. Air Force continued to increase its commitment to the support of the troops on the ground. No better example of that commitment can be found than that described in the first USAF award of the Medal of Honor in the war.

Medal of Honor: Louis J. Sebille

Awarded to: Major Louis J. Sebille, Chicago, IL, U.S. Air Force, 67th Fighter-Bomber Squadron, 18th Fighter-Bomber Group, 5th Air Force. Near Hanchang, Korea, 5 August 1950.

> Maj. Sebille, distinguished himself by conspicuous gallantry and intrepidity at the risk of his life above and beyond the call of duty. During an attack on a camouflaged area containing a concentration of enemy troops, artillery, and armored vehicles, Maj. Sebille's F-51 aircraft was severely damaged by antiaircraft fire. Although fully cognizant of the short period he could remain airborne, he deliberately ignored the possibility of survival by abandoning the aircraft or by crash landing, and continued his attack against the enemy forces threatening the security of friendly ground troops. In his determination to inflict maximum damage upon the enemy, Maj. Sebille again exposed himself to the intense fire of enemy gun batteries and dived on the target to his death. The superior leadership, daring, and selfless devotion to duty which he displayed in the execution of an extremely dangerous mission were an inspiration to both his subordinates and superiors and reflect the highest credit upon himself, the U.S. Air Force, and the armed forces of the United Nations.

For U.S. forces, the battle to defend the Pusan Perimeter was the longest and bloodiest sustained conflict of the war. The story of this battle as told by its casualties was substantially different than the one they had told in the first month of the war. The first month had been a chaotic affair, with the badly outnumbered defending forces being frequently overrun as they doggedly attempted to hold critical positions against the enemy onslaught. Now, even though the battle line was little, if any, shorter than it had been during the earlier delaying action, reinforcement of the defending divisions—and extension of enemy supply lines—leveled the playing field sufficiently that they could now battle the NKPA on more even terms. Obviously, the large number of casualties in the period indicate that the fighting remained intense, but for the most part the proportions that were killed, captured or missing were substantially reduced.

Because there was little net change in the line of resistance along the Naktong River over the six weeks the perimeter was being defended, it is difficult to identify by location specific battles during this time. Some chronologies of the war identify a couple of extended periods of conflict during that time as battles of the "Naktong Bulge," the first from August 8 to 18 and the second from August 31 to September 16. Indeed, as Figure 1 indicates, total casualty patterns for U.S. forces during the battle do show two extended periods of elevated conflict separated by a reduced level of fighting during the later weeks in August.

However, the casualties of each fighting unit have their own unique stories to tell and those stories suggest that the battle was considerably more complex. This is clearly demonstrated by the patterns of casualties during the battle by the different units that were involved.

These graphs demonstrate not only the different experiences of the different units in the battle, but also help identify those dates on which losses were particularly high or on which the proportion of fatalities were unusually large. Some of these dates will now be selected for a more detailed look at casualty patterns in the units involved.

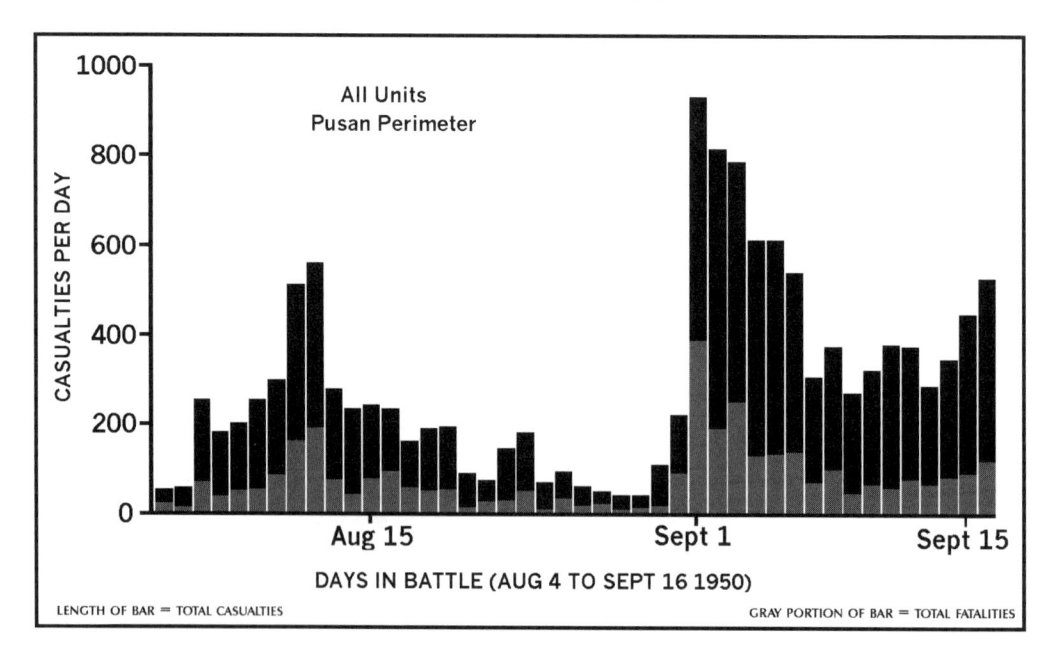

Figure 1. Daily casualties for all units during the battle of the Pusan Perimeter. The length of each bar indicates total casualties for the day. The gray portion of each bar represents the total number of fatalities.

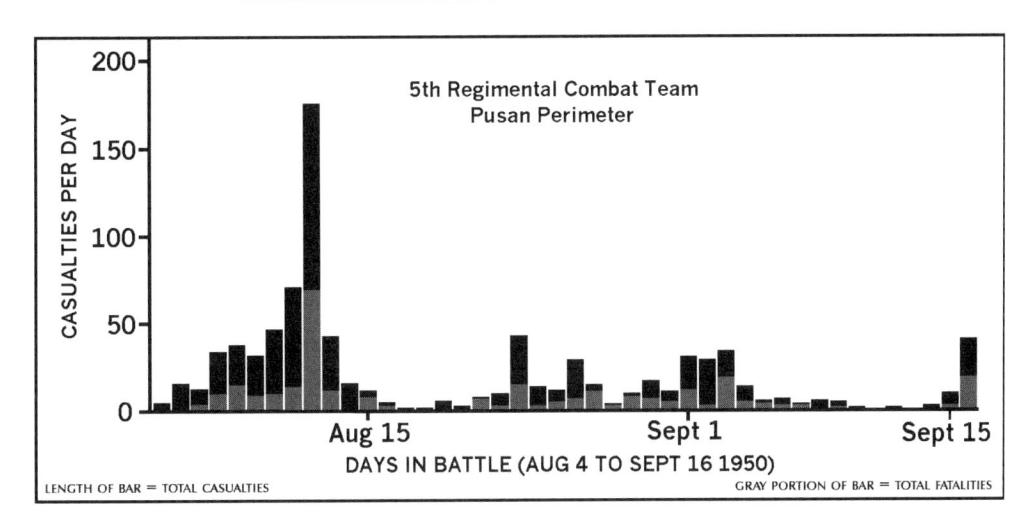

Figure 2. Daily casualties for the 5th Regiment Combat Team during the battle of the Pusan Perimeter.

5th Regimental Combat Team (RCT)

Figure 2 shows particularly high casualties and a very high proportion of fatalities in the 5th RCT on Aug. 12, 1950. A closer look at the casualty figures reveals that of 175 total casualties the RCT sustained that day, 103 of them (including 45 fatalities) were in the 555th Field Artillery Battalion, one of the regiment's supporting units. Unfortunately, this was the beginning of a pattern of losses that tended to plague the "Triple Nickel" throughout the rest of the war.

For the remainder of the battle for the Pusan Perimeter, losses in the 5th RCT were not extraordinary, although on some dates, as Figure 2 indicates, the proportion of fatalities was very high. The kinds of actions this unit experienced as it sustained these losses can be seen in the narrative describing the award of its first Medal of Honor in the war.

MEDAL OF HONOR: MELVIN O. HANDRICH

Awarded to: Master Sergeant Melvin O. Handrich, Manawa, Wis, U.S. Army, Company C, 5th Regimental Combat Team. Near Sobuk San Mountain, Korea, 25 and 26 August 1950.

> M/Sgt. Handrich, Company C, distinguished himself by conspicuous gallantry and intrepidity above and beyond the call of duty in action. His company was engaged in repulsing an estimated 150 enemy who were threatening to overrun its position. Near midnight on 25 August, a hostile group over 100 strong attempted to infiltrate the company perimeter. M/Sgt. Handrich, despite the heavy enemy fire, voluntarily left the comparative safety of the defensive area and moved to a forward position where he could direct mortar and artillery fire upon the advancing enemy. He remained at this post for 8 hours directing fire against the enemy who often approached to within 50 feet of his position. Again, on the morning of 26 August,

another strong hostile force made an attempt to overrun the company's position. With complete disregard for his safety, M/Sgt. Handrich rose to his feet and from this exposed position fired his rifle and directed mortar and artillery fire on the attackers. At the peak of this action he observed elements of his company preparing to withdraw. He perilously made his way across fire-swept terrain to the defense area where, by example and forceful leadership, he reorganized the men to continue the fight. During the action M/Sgt. Handrich was severely wounded. Refusing to take cover or be evacuated, he returned to his forward position and continued to direct the company's fire. Later a determined enemy attack overran M/Sgt. Handrich's position and he was mortally wounded. When the position was retaken, over 70 enemy dead were counted in the area he had so intrepidly defended. M/Sgt. Handrich's sustained personal bravery, consummate courage, and gallant self-sacrifice reflect untold glory upon himself and the heroic traditions of the military service.

There is probably no better testimony to the significance of MSgt. Handrich's valiant efforts in defense of his unit's position than the statistics on total casualties in all 5th RCT units that day (8/26/50): only 6 KIA (including MSgt. Handrich) and 17 WIA.

For the entire period of the battle in defense of the Pusan Perimeter, total casualties for the 5th RCT and its supporting units are summarized in Table 11.

Table 11—5th Regimental Combat Team

	KIA	WIA	POW Returned	POW Died	MIA Returned	MIA Died	Unit Total
5th RCT	204	463			1	2	670
555th FA Bn.	53	93			3	6	155
2nd Combat Engr. Co.	4	18					22
Total 8/4–9/16/50	261	574			4	8	847

1st Cavalry Division

For the most part, casualties in the 1st Cavalry Division during the first month of the battle were minimal. As Fig 3 indicates, the 8th Cavalry Regiment had almost no casualties at all during that time and obviously was not significantly committed to the action. The 7th Cavalry Regiment had a few days with significant losses early in the month, but with the exception of those days, their casualties in August were minimal.

Like the 7th Cav., the 5th Cav. had relatively few days in August in which numbers of casualties were significant. On those days, however, the losses were anything but routine. It is impossible to determine in detail from the database the exact cause of every one of those casualties, but we do know from other sources that a number of 5th Cavalry troops were captured on August 15 when their positions on Hill 303 were overrun by the NKPA. A number of these captives were subsequently massacred by enemy soldiers. The database can give us some insight into the details of those fatalities.

Accounts of the massacre tend to be sketchy and somewhat conflicting. There were reported to have been five of the captives who were wounded but survived.

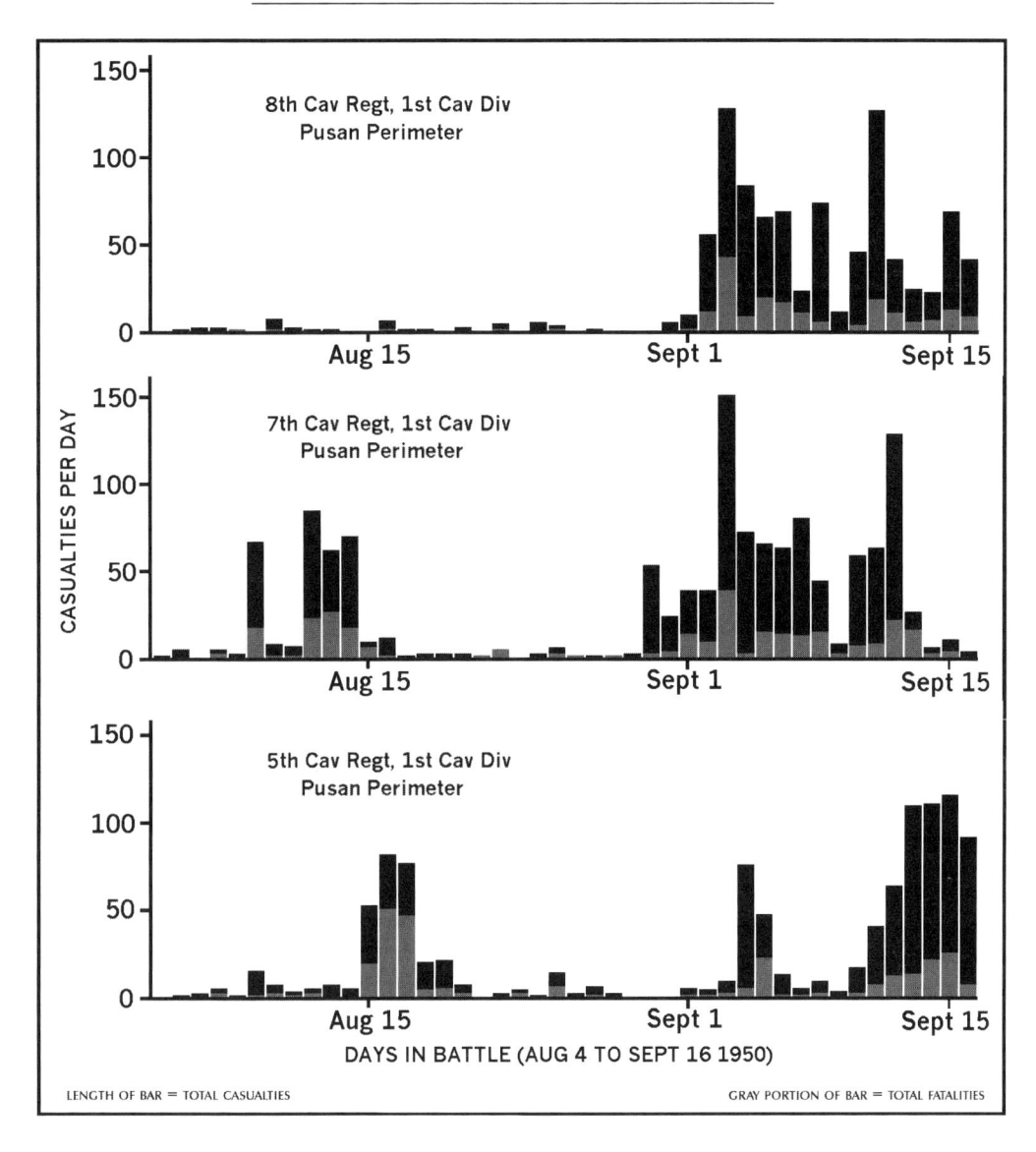

Figure 3. Daily casualties for the 1st Cavalry Division during the battle of the Pusan Perimeter.

Their stories have helped piece together what happened on those days. And, as news of the massacre began to appear in the public media, the survivors received a great deal of attention. However, dozens of others who were captured will never be able to tell their stories because they did not survive the slaughter. In fact, even their names have never become a matter of public record. So, as much as is possible from the available data, those individuals will be identified and honored here.

Because the known survivors were all members of H Company's mortar platoon, most of the first-hand information about the massacre details information about men from that unit. Indeed, the database indicates that three of the five survivors and 31 of the fatalities had the Military Occupation Specialty (MOS) 4812: Heavy Weapons Infantryman. The mortar platoon (and possibly some other units) was overrun by the enemy on August 15 and the men were taken prisoner. There were reported to be 42 captives from the mortar platoon and, according to one eyewitness account, a total of 67 prisoners held by NKPA over the three-day period. Executions began that night and continued through the following two days, with the majority bound and massacred on August 17, just prior to the hill being retaken by other 5th Cav. units. The 1st Cavalry Division's official history of the war recounts that 36 executed GIs were found by the units that recaptured the hill that day.

According to the database, there were 115 fatalities in the 5th Cavalry Regiment on August 15 to 17, 1950. Certainly, not all of these records represented executed prisoners. The majority MOS among these fatalities was 4745: Light Weapons Infantryman. It can be assumed that some of the executed soldiers had this (or another) MOS, but there is no way from the available data to determine which ones they might be. So, recognizing that it will only be a partial accounting at best, we can list the most likely known victims of the Hill 303 massacre—five survivors and 31 fatalities with MOS 4812.

As *survivors*, we can list individuals recorded in the database as having been captured on Aug. 15, then both wounded and returned to military control on Aug. 17. They are as follows (Home of record is by county only.

Pfc Trenton E Purser, Tuscaloosa AL
Pvt2 Frederick M Ryan, Campbell KY
Pvt2 Roy Manring, Cook IL

Cpl Roy L Day, Jr, El Paso TX
Sgt Melvin Rudd, Magoffin KY

We list as *executed* the following individuals, all heavy weapons infantrymen. With the exception of the Jones and Vogeli, all were reported as simply killed in action. Except as noted, all were reported to have been killed on Aug. 17. (Home of record is by county only.)

Cpl Emerson L Jones, Montgomery OH (Reported wounded Aug. 17 and died of wounds Aug. 18)
Cpl Delbert E Vogeli, Leavenworth KS (Reported wounded and died of wounds Aug. 17)
Pvt2 Robert J O'Brien, Hudson NJ
Pvt2 Charles Hastings, Worcester MD
Cpl Ernest Regney, Jr, Beaver PA
Pvt2 George Semosky, Jr, FayettE PA
Pfc John T Kerchinsky, Jefferson PA (Reported KIA Aug 16)
Cpl George P Gunkel, Lehigh PA (Reported KIA Aug 15)
Pvt2 Stewart C Lewis, Jr, Northumberland VA

Pvt2 Billy J Causey, Elmore AL
Pvt1 William D Trammell, Greenville SC
Pvt2 Joe C Sisk, Montgomery TN (Reported KIA Aug 15)
Pfc Benjamin F Bristow, Campbell KY
Pfc Brook Powell, Clay KY
Pvt2 Leroy Abbott, Muhlenberg KY
Cpl Robert A Humes, Franklin OH
Pvt1 John W Collins, Miami OH
Pvt2 Glenn E Huffman, Seneca OH
Pvt1 John J Hilgerson, Hillsborough FL
Pvt2 Melvin W Morden, Luce MI
Pvt2 Milton J Mlaskac, Cook IL
Cpl Ray A Briley, Wayne MI
Pvt2 Kenneth C Fletke, Wayne MI

I. The Peninsular War

Pfc Richard Jahnke, Milwaukee WI
Pvt2 Herbert McKenzie, Kiowa OK
Pvt2 Buford Coleson, Jasper TX
 (Reported KIA Aug 15)
Pvt2 Cecil C Edwards, Garland AR
Pvt2 Houston E Montfort, Ouachita LA
Pvt1 Arthur S Garcia, Los Angeles CA
Pfc Antonio Hernandez, Los Angeles CA
Pvt2 John W Simmons, Solona CA

There is no way of knowing for sure that each of these individuals was in fact among those who were executed. All that can be said is that the dates and the MOSs fit with the information reported by survivors.

Among the 84 other fatalities reported for these dates, there are 32 which were initially recorded as missing and then, on the same day, declared to have been KIA. Eleven were recorded as missing and never found. Nine were recorded as captured and then declared either KIA or dead from wounds. Regrettably, it is not possible to determine solely from these data which, if any, of them might have been victims of the massacre.

Following two weeks of minimal casualties during the last half of August, the 1st Cavalry Division began to report more significant losses through the end of the battle. As Figure 3 indicates, those losses tended to be sporadic, reflecting the ebb-and-flow nature of the conflict during that time. What Figure 3 doesn't reflect are the losses in that period sustained by supporting units of the 1st Cav., two of which are worthy of note, the 8th Combat Engineer Battalion and the 16th Reconnaissance Company. In both of these units, the losses would certainly have been much greater were it not for the valiant sacrifice of two men Pfc Melvin Brown of the 8th Engineers and Cpl Gordon Craig of the 16th Recon Company, who gave their own lives to help achieve their units' missions and defend their comrades. Both were awarded the Medal of Honor.

The 8th Engr. Bn. had a very bad day on September 4. In fact, on that day, this battalion suffered more fatalities than all three regimental units combined. Table 12 documents those losses.

Table 12 — 8th Engineer Battalion

	KIA	WIA	POW Returned	POW Died	MIA Returned	MIA Died	Unit Total
8th Engr Bn, 1st Cav Div 09/04/50	11	19	2	1	1	4	38

MEDAL OF HONOR: MELVIN L. BROWN

Awarded to: Private First Class, Melvin L. Brown, Mahaffey, PA, U.S. Army, Company D, 8th Engineer Combat Battalion, 1st Cavalry Division. Near Kasan, Korea, 4 September 1950.

> Pfc. Brown, Company D distinguished himself by conspicuous gallantry and intrepidity above and beyond the call of duty in action against the enemy. While his platoon was securing Hill 755 (the Walled City), the enemy, using heavy automatic weapons and small arms, counterattacked. Taking a position on a 50-foot-high wall he delivered heavy rifle fire on the enemy. His ammunition was soon expended and although wounded, he remained at his post and threw his few grenades into the attackers causing many casu-

alties. When his supply of grenades was exhausted his comrades from nearby foxholes tossed others to him and he left his position, braving a hail of fire, to retrieve and throw them at the enemy. The attackers continued to assault his position and Pfc. Brown weaponless, drew his entrenching tool from his pack and calmly waited until they 1 by 1 peered over the wall, delivering each a crushing blow upon the head. Knocking 10 or 12 enemy from the wall, his daring action so inspired his platoon that they repelled the attack and held their position. Pfc. Brown's extraordinary heroism, gallantry, and intrepidity reflect the highest credit upon himself and was in keeping with the honored traditions of the military service. He was initially reported as missing in action and then officially killed in action, September 5, 1950.

As the following MOH award suggests, the 16th Reconnaissance Company had its toughest encounter in the battle on August 9 and 10.

Medal of Honor: Gordon M. Craig

Awarded to: Corporal Gordon M. Craig, Brockton, MA, U.S. Army, 16th Reconnaissance Company, 1st Cavalry Division, Near Kasan, Korea, 10 September 1950.

Cpl. Craig, 16th Reconnaissance Company, distinguished himself by conspicuous gallantry and intrepidity above and beyond the call of duty in action against the enemy. During the attack on a strategic enemy-held hill his company's advance was subjected to intense hostile grenade, mortar, and small-arms fire. Cpl. Craig and four comrades moved forward to eliminate an enemy machine gun nest that was hampering the company's advance. At that instant, an enemy machine gunner hurled a hand grenade at the advancing men. Without hesitating or attempting to seek cover for himself, Cpl. Craig threw himself on the grenade and smothered its burst with his body. His intrepid and selfless act, in which he unhesitatingly gave his life for his comrades, inspired them to attack with such ferocity that they annihilated the enemy machine gun crew, enabling the company to continue its attack. Cpl. Craig's noble self-sacrifice reflects the highest credit upon himself and upholds the esteemed traditions of the military service.

Total casualties for the 1st Cavalry Division during the battle for the Pusan Perimeter are shown in Table 13.

Table 13 — Pusan Perimeter, 1st Cavalry Division

	KIA	WIA	POW Returned	POW Died	MIA Returned	MIA Died	Unit Total
7th Cav, 1st Cav Div	245	880			10	9	1144
5th Cav, 1st Cav Div	243	754	7	4	28	18	1054
8th Cav, 1st Cav Div	167	736	1		11	12	927
8th Engr Bn, 1st Cav Div	18	62	2	1	1	4	88
99th FA Bn, 1st Cav Div	15	19				2	36
16th Recon Co, 1st Cav Div	14	51					65
61st FA Bn, 1st Cav Div	6	31					37
71st Med Tk Bn, 1st Cav Div	6	14					20
13 Other Units	7	65			2		74
Total casualties 8/4–9/16/50	720	2613	10	5	52	45	3445

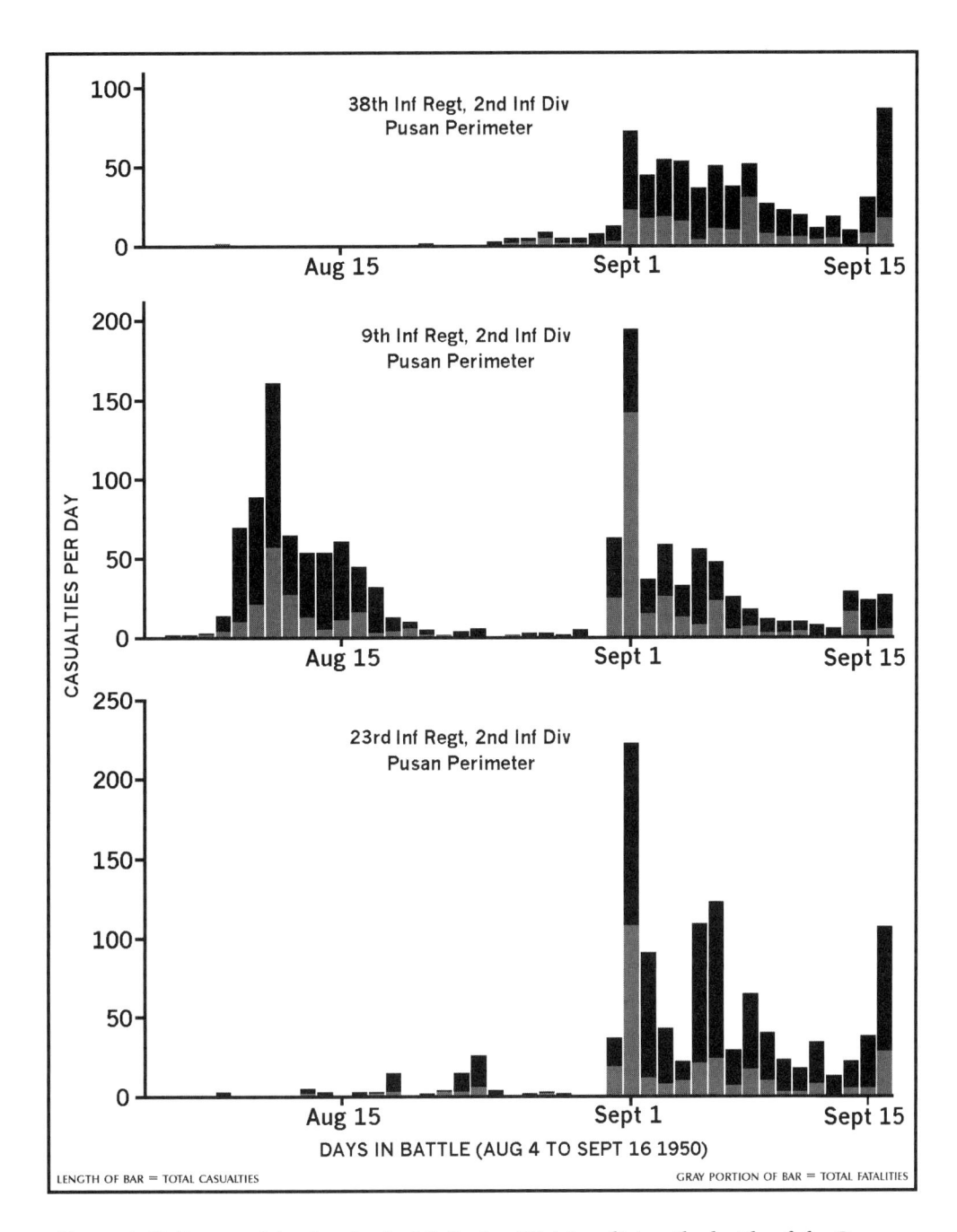

Figure 4. Daily casualties for the 2nd Infantry DIvision diring the battle of the Pusan Perimeter.

2nd Infantry Division

The 2nd Division, new to action in the war as battle lines were being consolidated around the Pusan Perimeter, ultimately suffered the greatest number of casualties in the battle. As Figure 4 indicates, the majority of those casualties were sustained beginning in September.

Neither the 23rd Infantry nor the 38th Infantry suffered any serious losses until September. The 9th Infantry, on the other hand, was significantly engaged in early August and sustained substantial casualties in that engagement. On August 11, in particular, the 9th and one supporting unit, the 15th FA Battalion, suffered both substantial losses and a high percentage of fatalities. Table 14 describes the losses on that day by these units.

Table 14 — 9th Infantry and 15th FA Battalion

	KIA	WIA	POW Returned	POW Died	MIA Returned	MIA Died	Unit Total
9th Inf, 2nd Div	49	102			2	7	160
15th FA Bn, 2nd Inf Div	8	4	2			6	20
8/11/50	57	106	2		2	13	180

Total casualties for the 2nd Division through the 29th of August were 896. Of these, 724 were in the 9th Infantry and the 15th FA Bn.

Beginning the last day of August, casualties in the 2nd Division began to evidence a substantial increase in the level of fighting in their sector. In particular, as Figure 4 indicates, losses were exceptionally high on September 1. Table 15 shows how those casualties were distributed among the various 2nd Division units that day.

Table 15 — 2nd Division, September 1

	KIA	WIA	POW Returned	POW Died	MIA Returned	MIA Died	Unit Total
9th Inf, 2nd Div	125	42	5		6	16	194
23rd Inf, 2nd Div	90	66	30		19	17	222
38th Inf, 2nd Div	15	48	1	1	1	6	72
2nd RP Co, 2nd Inf Div	6	23			2	4	35
2nd Recon Co, 2nd Inf Div	4	12					16
2nd Engr Bn, 2nd Inf Div	1	8					9
82nd AAA Bn, 2nd Inf Div	1	3	2				6
72nd Tank Bn, 2nd Inf Div	2	3					5
15th FA Bn, 2nd Inf Div		4					4
37th FA Bn, 2nd Inf Div	2	2					4
38th FA Bn, 2nd Inf Div	1						1
Hq, 2nd Inf Div	1						1
HHC, 2nd Inf Div		2					2
Total casualties 9/1/50	248	213	38	1	28	43	571

The ferocity of fighting by the 2nd Division on this day, and the days immediately following, can best be seen in the number of Medals of Honor (8) awarded to members of the division for their valor during the battle.

MEDAL OF HONOR: ERNEST R. KOUMA

Awarded to: Master Sergeant (then Sfc.) Ernest R. Kouma, Penobscot Co., ME, U.S. Army, Company A, 72d Tank Battalion, 2nd Infantry Division. Vicinity of Agok, Korea, 31 August to 1 September 1950.

> M/Sgt. Kouma, a tank commander in Company A, distinguished himself by conspicuous gallantry and intrepidity at the risk of his life above and beyond the call of duty in action against the enemy. His unit was engaged in supporting infantry elements on the Naktong River front. Near midnight on 31 August, a hostile force estimated at 500 crossed the river and launched a fierce attack against the infantry positions, inflicting heavy casualties. A withdrawal was ordered and his armored unit was given the mission of covering the movement until a secondary position could be established. The enemy assault overran 2 tanks, destroyed 1 and forced another to withdraw. Suddenly M/Sgt. Kouma discovered that his tank was the only obstacle in the path of the hostile onslaught. Holding his ground, he gave fire orders to his crew and remained in position throughout the night, fighting off repeated enemy attacks. During one fierce assault, the enemy surrounded his tank and he leaped from the armored turret, exposing himself to a hail of hostile fire, manned the .50 caliber machinegun mounted on the rear deck, and delivered pointblank fire into the fanatical foe. His machinegun emptied, he fired his pistol and threw grenades to keep the enemy from his tank. After more than 9 hours of constant combat and close-in fighting, he withdrew his vehicle to friendly lines. During the withdrawal through 8 miles of hostile territory, M/Sgt. Kouma continued to inflict casualties upon the enemy and exhausted his ammunition in destroying 3 hostile machinegun positions. During this action, M/Sgt. Kouma killed an estimated 250 enemy soldiers. His magnificent stand allowed the infantry sufficient time to reestablish defensive positions. Rejoining his company, although suffering intensely from his wounds, he attempted to resupply his tank and return to the battle area. While being evacuated for medical treatment, his courage was again displayed when he requested to return to the front. M/Sgt. Kouma's superb leadership, heroism, and intense devotion to duty reflect the highest credit on himself and uphold the esteemed traditions of the U.S. Army.

M/Sgt. Kouma was returned to duty three days later.

MEDAL OF HONOR: JOSEPH R. OUELLETTE

Private First Class Joseph R. Ouellette, Lowell, MA, U.S. Army, Company H, 9th Infantry Regiment, 2d Infantry Division. Near Yongsan, Korea, from 31 August to 3 September 1950.

> Pfc. Ouellette distinguished himself by conspicuous gallantry and intrepidity in action against the enemy in the Makioug-Chang River salient. When an enemy assault cut off and surrounded his unit he voluntarily made a reconnaissance of a nearby hill under intense enemy fire to locate friendly troop positions and obtain information of the enemy's strength and location. Finding that friendly troops were not on the hill, he worked his way back to his unit under heavy fire. Later, when an airdrop of water was made outside the perimeter, he again braved enemy fire in an attempt to retrieve water for his unit. Finding the dropped cans broken and devoid of water, he returned to his unit. His heroic attempt greatly increased his comrades' morale. When ammunition and grenades ran low, Pfc. Ouellette again slipped out of the perimeter to collect these from the enemy dead. After collecting grenades he was attacked by an enemy soldier. He killed this enemy in hand-to-hand combat, gathered up the ammunition, and

returned to his unit. When the enemy attacked on 3 September, they assaulted his position with grenades. On 6 occasions Pfc. Ouellette leaped from his foxhole to escape exploding grenades. In doing so, he had to face enemy small-arms fire. He continued his resistance, despite a severe wound, until he lost his life. The extraordinary heroism and intrepidity displayed by Pfc. Ouellette reflect the highest credit on himself and are in keeping with the esteemed traditions of the military service.

MEDAL OF HONOR: TRAVIS E. WATKINS

Awarded to: Master Sergeant Travis E. Watkins , Gregg Co., TX, U.S. Army, Company H, 9th Infantry Regiment, 2d Infantry Division Near Yongsan, Korea, 31 August through 3 September 1950.

> M/Sgt. Watkins distinguished himself by conspicuous gallantry and intrepidity above and beyond the call of duty in action against the enemy. When an overwhelming enemy force broke through and isolated 30 men of his unit, he took command, established a perimeter defense and directed action which repelled continuous, fanatical enemy assaults. With his group completely surrounded and cut off, he moved from foxhole to foxhole exposing himself to enemy fire, giving instructions and offering encouragement to his men. Later when the need for ammunition and grenades became critical he shot 2 enemy soldiers 50 yards outside the perimeter and went out alone for their ammunition and weapons. As he picked up their weapons he was attacked by 3 others and wounded. Returning their fire he killed all 3 and gathering up the weapons of the 5 enemy dead returned to his amazed comrades. During a later assault, 6 enemy soldiers gained a defiladed spot and began to throw grenades into the perimeter making it untenable. Realizing the desperate situation and disregarding his wound he rose from his foxhole to engage them with rifle fire. Although immediately hit by a burst from an enemy machinegun he continued to fire until he had killed the grenade throwers. With this threat eliminated he collapsed and despite being paralyzed from the waist down, encouraged his men to hold on. He refused all food, saving it for his comrades, and when it became apparent that help would not arrive in time to hold the position ordered his men to escape to friendly lines. Refusing evacuation as his hopeless condition would burden his comrades, he remained in his position and cheerfully wished them luck. Through his aggressive leadership and intrepid actions, this small force destroyed nearly 500 of the enemy before abandoning their position. M/Sgt. Watkins' sustained personal bravery and noble self-sacrifice reflect the highest glory upon himself and is in keeping with the esteemed traditions of the U.S. Army.

M/Sgt. Watkins, a heavy weapons infantry leader, had been wounded in action earlier in the defense of the perimeter and was returned to duty on August 19. In this engagement, he was initially reported as missing in action and then confirmed to have died.

MEDAL OF HONOR: FREDERICK F. HENRY

Awarded to: First Lieutenant Frederick F. Henry, Clinton, OK, U.S. Army, Company F, 38th Infantry Regiment, 2nd Infantry Division. Vicinity of Am-Dong, Korea, 1 September 1950.

1st Lt. Henry, Company F, distinguished himself by conspicuous gallantry and intrepidity above and beyond the call of duty in action. His platoon was holding a strategic ridge near the town when they were attacked by a superior enemy force, supported by heavy mortar and artillery fire. Seeing his platoon disorganized by this fanatical assault, he left his foxhole and moving along the line ordered his men to stay in place and keep firing. Encouraged by this heroic action the platoon reformed a defensive line and rained devastating fire on the enemy, checking its advance. Enemy fire had knocked out all communications and 1st Lt. Henry was unable to determine whether or not the main line of resistance was altered to this heavy attack. On his own initiative, although severely wounded, he decided to hold his position as long as possible and ordered the wounded evacuated and their weapons and ammunition brought to him. Establishing a l-man defensive position, he ordered the platoon's withdrawal and despite his wound and with complete disregard for himself remained behind to cover the movement. When last seen he was single-handedly firing all available weapons so effectively that he caused an estimated 50 enemy casualties. His ammunition was soon expended and his position overrun, but this intrepid action saved the platoon and halted the enemy's advance until the main line of resistance was prepared to throw back the attack. 1st Lt. Henry's outstanding gallantry and noble self-sacrifice above and beyond the call of duty reflect the highest honor on him and are in keeping with the esteemed traditions of the U.S. Army.

Medal of Honor: Luther H. Story

Awarded to: Private First Class, Luther H. Story, U.S. Army, Buena Vista, GA, Company A, 9th Infantry Regiment, 2d Infantry Division. Near Agok, Korea, 1 September 1950

Pfc. Story distinguished himself by conspicuous gallantry and intrepidity above and beyond the call of duty in action. A savage daylight attack by elements of 3 enemy divisions penetrated the thinly held lines of the 9th Infantry. Company A beat off several banzai attacks but was bypassed and in danger of being cut off and surrounded. Pfc. Story, a weapons squad leader, was heavily engaged in stopping the early attacks and had just moved his squad to a position overlooking the Naktong River when he observed a large group of the enemy crossing the river to attack Company A. Seizing a machinegun from his wounded gunner he placed deadly fire on the hostile column killing or wounding an estimated 100 enemy soldiers. Facing certain encirclement the company commander ordered a withdrawal. During the move Pfc. Story noticed the approach of an enemy truck loaded with troops and towing an ammunition trailer. Alerting his comrades to take cover he fearlessly stood in the middle of the road, throwing grenades into the truck. Out of grenades he crawled to his squad, gathered up additional grenades and again attacked the vehicle. During the withdrawal the company was attacked by such superior numbers that it was forced to deploy in a rice field. Pfc. Story was wounded in this action, but, disregarding his wounds, rallied the men about him and repelled the attack. Realizing that his wounds would hamper his comrades he refused to retire to the next position but remained to cover the company's withdrawal. When last seen he was firing every weapon available and fighting off another hostile assault.

Private Story's extraordinary heroism, aggressive leadership, and supreme devotion to duty reflect the highest credit upon himself and were in keeping with the esteemed traditions of the military service.

MEDAL OF HONOR: CHARLES W. TURNER

Awarded to: Sergeant First Class Charles W. Turner, Suffolk Co., MA, U.S. Army, 2d Reconnaissance Company, 2nd Infantry Division. Near Yongsan, Korea, 1 September 1950.

Sfc. Turner distinguished himself by conspicuous gallantry and intrepidity above and beyond the call of duty in action against the enemy. A large enemy force launched a mortar and automatic weapon supported assault against his platoon. Sfc. Turner, a section leader, quickly organized his unit for defense and then observed that the attack was directed at the tank section 100 yards away. Leaving his secured section he dashed through a hail of fire to the threatened position and, mounting a tank, manned the exposed turret machinegun. Disregarding the intense enemy fire he calmly held this position delivering deadly accurate fire and pointing out targets for the tank's 75mm. gun. His action resulted in the destruction of 7 enemy machinegun nests. Although severely wounded he remained at the gun shouting encouragement to his comrades. During the action the tank received over 50 direct hits; the periscopes and antenna were shot away and 3 rounds hit the machinegun mount. Despite this fire he remained at his post until a burst of enemy fire cost him his life. This intrepid and heroic performance enabled the platoon to withdraw and later launch an attack which routed the enemy. Sfc. Turner's valor and example reflect the highest credit upon himself and are in keeping with the esteemed traditions of the U.S. Army.

MEDAL OF HONOR: DAVID M. SMITH

Awarded to: Private First Class, David M. Smith, Livingston, KY, U.S. Army, Company E, 9th Infantry Regiment, 2d Infantry Division. Near Yongsan, Korea, 1 September 1950.

Pfc. Smith, distinguished himself by conspicuous gallantry and outstanding courage above and beyond the call of duty in action. Pfc. Smith was a gunner in the mortar section of Company E, emplaced in rugged mountainous terrain and under attack by a numerically superior hostile force. Bitter fighting ensued and the enemy overran forward elements, infiltrated the perimeter, and rendered friendly positions untenable. The mortar section was ordered to withdraw, but the enemy had encircled and closed in on the position. Observing a grenade lobbed at his emplacement, Pfc. Smith shouted a warning to his comrades and, fully aware of the odds against him, flung himself upon it and smothered the explosion with his body. Although mortally wounded in this display of valor, his intrepid act saved 5 men from death or serious injury. Pfc. Smith's inspirational conduct and supreme sacrifice reflect lasting glory on himself and are in keeping with the noble traditions of the infantry of the U.S. Army.

Medal of Honor: Loren R. Kaufman

Awarded to: Sergeant First Class Loren R. Kaufman, The Dalles, OR, U.S. Army, Company G, 9th Infantry Regiment, 2nd Infantry Division. Near Yongsan, Korea, 4 and 5 September 1950

Sfc. Kaufman distinguished himself by conspicuous gallantry and intrepidity above and beyond the call of duty in action. On the night of 4 September the company was in a defensive position on 2 adjoining hills. His platoon was occupying a strong point 2 miles away protecting the battalion flank. Early on 5 September the company was attacked by an enemy battalion and his platoon was ordered to reinforce the company. As his unit moved along a ridge it encountered a hostile encircling force. Sfc. Kaufman, running forward, bayoneted the lead scout and engaged the column in a rifle and grenade assault. His quick vicious attack so surprised the enemy that they retreated in confusion. When his platoon joined the company he discovered that the enemy had taken commanding ground and pinned the company down in a draw. Without hesitation Sfc. Kaufman charged the enemy lines firing his rifle and throwing grenades. During the action, he bayoneted 2 enemy and seizing an unmanned machinegun, delivered deadly fire on the defenders. Following this encounter the company regrouped and resumed the attack. Leading the assault he reached the ridge, destroyed a hostile machinegun position, and routed the remaining enemy. Pursuing the hostile troops he bayoneted 2 more and then rushed a mortar position shooting the gunners. Remnants of the enemy fled to a village and Sfc. Kaufman led a patrol into the town, dispersed them, and burned the buildings. The dauntless courage and resolute intrepid leadership of Sfc. Kaufman were directly responsible for the success of his company in regaining its positions, reflecting distinct credit upon himself and upholding the esteemed traditions of the military service.

Sfc. Kaufman was not wounded in this action, but he received the award posthumously after he was killed in action on February 2, 1951.

Total casualties in the 2nd Infantry Division during the battle for the Pusan Perimeter are shown in Table 16.

Table 16 — Pusan Perimeter, 2nd Infantry Division

	KIA	WIA	POW Returned	POW Died	MIA Returned	MIA Died	Unit Total
9th Inf, 2nd Div	419	841	14		20	33	1327
23rd Inf, 2nd Div	265	734	40		36	21	1096
38th Inf, 2nd Div	171	475	3	1	3	12	665
2nd RP Co, 2nd Inf Div	45	149	2		7	7	210
2nd Engr Bn, 2nd Inf Div	19	55					74
82nd AAA Bn, 2nd Inf Div	23	38	5		3	2	71
15th FA Bn, 2nd Inf Div	14	32	2			6	54
37th FA Bn, 2nd Inf Div	9	41					50
38th FA Bn, 2nd Inf Div	7	35	1				43
2nd Recon Co, 2nd Inf Div	11	26					37
12 other units	10	37					47
Total casualties 8/4–9/16/50	1038	2563	67	1	69	81	3819

A brief comment needs to be made concerning the very high casualty count in the 2nd Replacement (RP) Company in this battle. It seems most unlikely that the company itself was involved in the fighting. It is more likely that the individuals who were listed as RP Company casualties were actually fighting with combat units and simply overtook their paperwork as they were rushed into the fray. There were 343 total 2nd RP Company casualties in the war, most of them with MOS 4745 (Light Weapons Infantryman) and none of them after December 8, 1950. By then, apparently, replacements into the 2nd Division were able to become officially assigned to their units before they became casualties.

24th Infantry Division

Among American units, the 24th Division had taken the brunt of the early losses as UN forces fought to delay the advance of the NKPA toward Pusan. Yet now, even with additional manpower committed to the defense of the perimeter, the 24th had

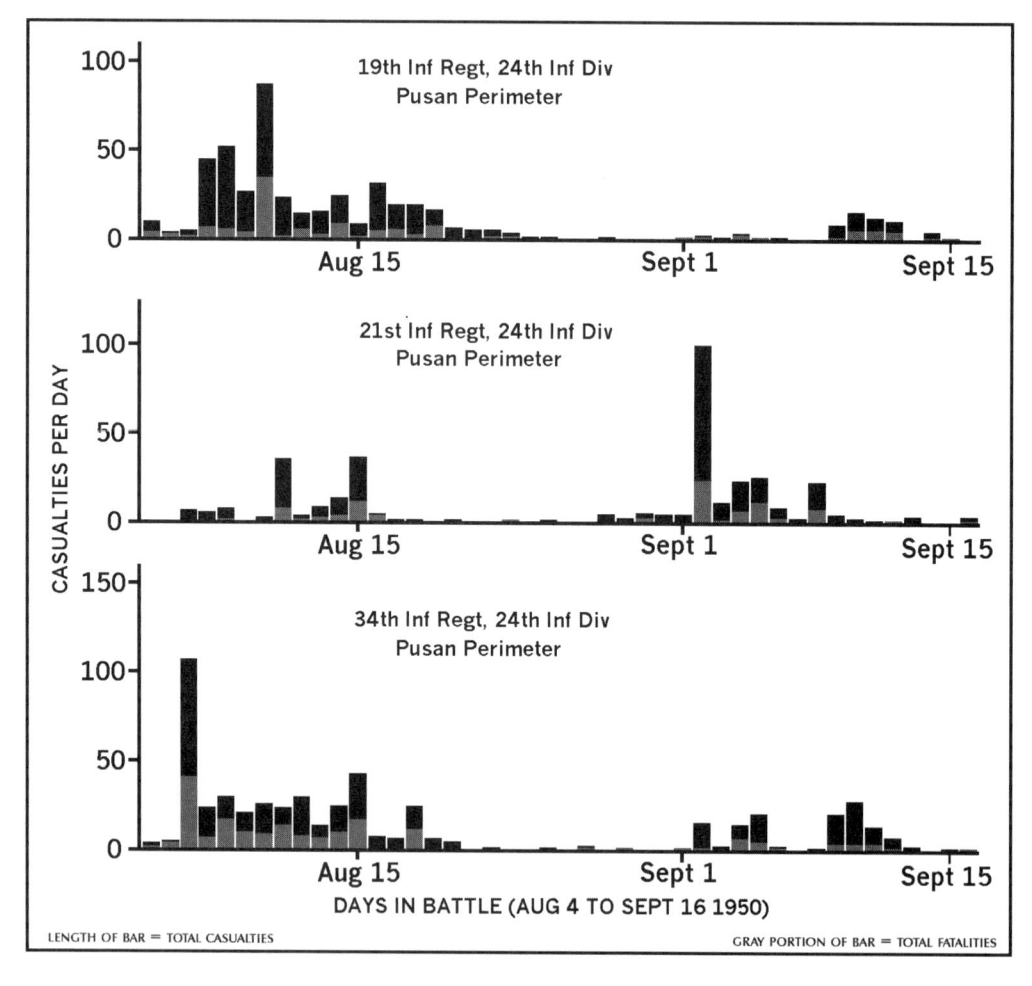

Figure 5. Daily casualties for the 24th Infantry Division during the battle of the Pusan Perimeter.

little opportunity to lick its wounds. As Figure 5 indicates, casualties in the division were lower in this battle than they had been earlier in the war, and fewer in total than the other divisions involved in the defense, but they were by no means trivial, particularly in the early weeks of the battle.

One feature in particular stands out from the data in Figure 5 that requires closer inspection. This is the consistency of losses and the very high percentage of fatalities in the 34th Regiment between the 5th and 15th of August. In that period, only the 2nd Division's 23rd Regiment had more casualties (and only slightly more fatalities) than the 34th, but none of the other units in the battle came close to the 34th in percentage of fatalities. Following is a summary of the 34th Regiment's losses during this time.

Table 17 — 34th Infantry Regiment

	KIA	WIA	POW Returned	POW Died	MIA Returned	MIA Died	Unit Total
34th Infantry 8/5–8/15/50	119	193		2	12	12	338

Percentage of fatalities in the 34th was 39 percent (compared, for example, with the 23rd, which had 25 percent fatalities in the same period).

Total losses in the 24th Division during the battle for the Pusan Perimeter are shown in the Table 18.

Table 18 — Pusan Perimeter, 24th Infantry Division

	KIA	WIA	POW Returned	POW Died	MIA Returned	MIA Died	Unit Total
19th Inf, 24th Inf Div	106	348	2		10	7	473
34th Inf, 24th Inf Div	155	334	1	2	13	14	519
21st Inf, 24th Inf Div	75	260			4	8	347
3rd Engr Bn, 24th Inf Div	10	20				9	39
26th AAA Bn, 24th Inf Div	9	11	2		1	4	27
13th FA Bn, 24th Inf Div	5	19			1		25
13 other 24th Div Units	6	94					100
Total 08/04–09/16/50	366	1086	5	2	29	42	1530

29th Infantry Regiment/RCT

As Figure 6 indicates, most of the losses experienced by the 29th Infantry in defense of the Pusan Perimeter occurred in September.

Although the unit experienced no episodes of extraordinary losses in the battle, its total casualties were by no means insignificant. A summary of these losses is shown in the Table 19.

Table 19 — Pusan Perimeter, 29th Infantry Regiment/RCT

	KIA	WIA	POW Returned	POW Died	MIA Returned	MIA Died	Unit Total
29th Infantry/RCT Total 8/4–9/16/50	81	341	1		7	5	435

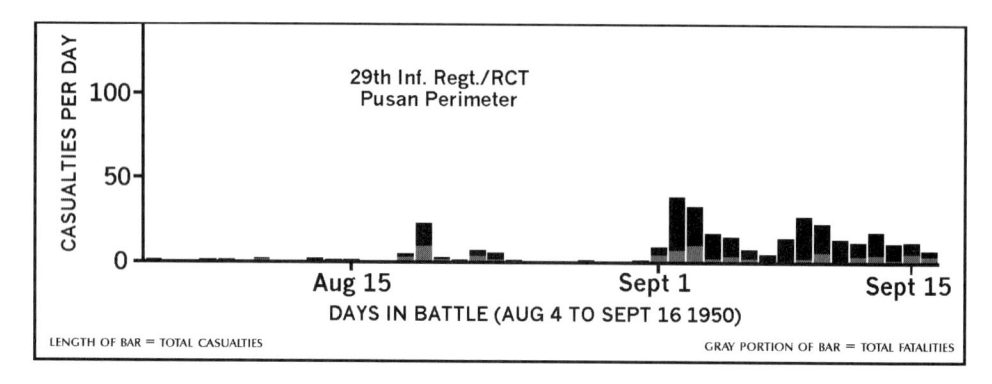

Figure 6. Daily casualties for the 29th Infantry Regiment/RCT during the battle of the Pusan Perimeter.

25th Infantry Division

As Figure 7 indicates, although daily losses by the 25th Division in defense of the Pusan Perimeter tended to be less than some other units in the battle, they were more constant.

There were few days in this battle when the men of the 25th could depend on relief from combat. Perhaps no better testimony to that fact can be found than the description of the action that earned PFC William Thompson the Medal of Honor.

MEDAL OF HONOR: WILLIAM THOMPSON

Awarded to: Private First Class William Thompson, Bronx, NY, U.S. Army, Company M, 24th Infantry Regiment, 25th Infantry Division. Near Haman, Korea, 6 August 1950.

> Pfc. Thompson, distinguished himself by conspicuous gallantry and intrepidity above and beyond the call of duty in action against the enemy. While his platoon was reorganizing under cover of darkness, fanatical enemy forces in overwhelming strength launched a surprise attack on the unit. Pfc. Thompson set up his machinegun in the path of the onslaught and swept the enemy with withering fire, pinning them down momentarily thus permitting the remainder of his platoon to withdraw to a more tenable position. Although hit repeatedly by grenade fragments and small-arms fire, he resisted all efforts of his comrades to induce him to withdraw, steadfastly remained at his machinegun and continued to deliver deadly, accurate fire until mortally wounded by an enemy grenade. Pfc. Thompson's dauntless courage and gallant self-sacrifice reflect the highest credit on himself and uphold the esteemed traditions of military service.

To measure the importance of PFC Thompson's sacrifice in terms of battle losses, we have to take a look at the MOSs of those who were casualties that day. Thompson was a member of a weapons company, so we would expect that most of the losses from that company would have MOS 4812, Heavy Weapons Infantryman. Only five men from the 24th Regiment with that MOS were casualties that day, and among them PFC Thompson was the only fatality.

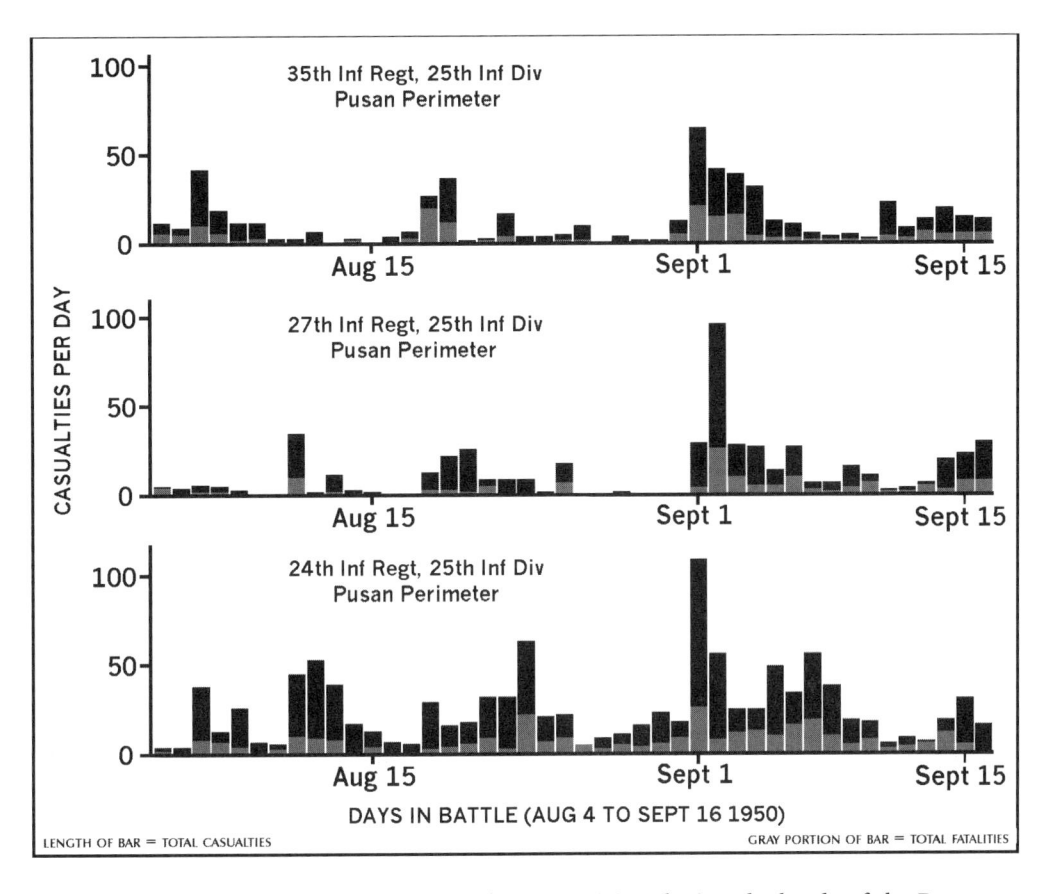

Figure 7. Daily casualties for the 25th Infantry Division during the battle of the Pusan Perimeter.

Table 20 summarizes 25th Infantry Division losses in defense of the Pusan Perimeter

Table 20 — Pusan Perimeter, 25th Infantry Division

	KIA	WIA	POW Returned	POW Died	MIA Returned	MIA Died	Unit Total
24th Inf, 25th Inf Div	258	796	1	1	2	8	1066
27th Inf, 25th Inf Div	117	382	1			1	501
35th Inf, 25th Inf Div	154	381			2		537
65th Engr Bn, 25th Inf Div	27	75					102
8th FA Bn, 25th Inf Div	16	26				2	44
64th FA Bn, 25th Inf Div	15	27	1		5	1	49
159th FA Bn, 25th Inf Div	18	41					59
90th FA Bn, 25th Inf Div	14	54			1	1	70
25th Recon Co, 25th Inf Div	5	12					17
79th Tank Bn, 25th Inf Div	2	20					22
77th Cmbt Engr Bn, 25th Inf Div	4	15					19
Other 25th Div Units (10)	6	37	1				44
Total 8/04–09/16/50	636	1866	4	1	10	13	2530

The Battle of the Bowling Alley

In an operation that endured for six weeks and accounted for more than 13,000 U.S. casualties, it is gratifying to report at least one skirmish in which enemy losses were abundant and U.S. casualties were few. Such was the Battle of the Bowling Alley, fought by the 23rd Infantry of the 2nd Division and the 27th Infantry of the 25th Division on August 15–20 along the Naktong River west of Taegu. Reports suggest that the NKPA was "mauled" by these U.S. units in the battle and, as the following table confirms, friendly losses were minimal.

Table 21— Battle of the Bowling Alley

	KIA	WIA	POW Returned	POW Died	MIA Returned	MIA Died	Unit Total
27th Inf, 25th Inf Div	5	54					59
23rd Inf, 2nd Div	3	16					19
Totals 08/15–08/20/50	8	70					78

Other Army Units with Casualties in the Battle of the Pusan Perimeter

Obviously, not all of the casualties sustained in the battle were assigned to the infantry divisions (or RCTs) and their supporting units. In fact, casualties were reported for 114 additional units. Of these, 22 were reported to be from the 7th Infantry Division and 19 from the 3rd Infantry Division. Neither of these units was known to be in the war at this time, yet the reported numbers are too large to be simply written off as data-entry errors. No other explanation is available at this time.

Table 22 is an accounting of the casualties in these 114 additional units. Several of the units are identified specifically in the table either because of the number and/or type of their casualties or because of the unique type of the unit.

Table 22 — Pusan Perimeter, Non-divisional Units

	KIA	WIA	POW Returned	POW Died	MIA Returned	MIA Died	Unit Total
14th Combat Engr Bn	25	10				1	36
89th Arm Cav Bn	2	29				1	32
70th Arm Cav Bn	9	27					36
1st Ord Bomb Dist Det	3	14					17
2nd Ord Bomb Dist Det		9					9
8035th Intelligence Detachments	5	2					7
8036th Intelligence Detachments	2	4				3	9
8050th Photo Center Library	5	2					7
8076th Sub Command HQ/MASH						1	1
121st Med Hosp, Evac S-Mbl			1				1
Other Units (104)	36	187			3	1	227
Total 08/04–09/16/50	87	284	1		3	7	382

Table 23 summarizes U.S. Army casualties in the Battle of the Pusan Perimeter.

Table 23 — Pusan Perimeter, All U.S. Army Units

	KIA	WIA	POW Returned	POW Died	MIA Returned	MIA Died	Unit Total
5th RCT	261	573			4	8	846
1st Cavalry Division	720	2613	10	5	52	45	3445
2nd Infantry Division	1038	2563	67	1	69	81	3819
24th Infantry Division	366	1086	5	2	29	42	1530
29th Infantry Regiment/RCT	81	341	1		7	5	435
25th Infantry Division	636	1866	4	1	10	13	2530
Other units (114)	87	284	1		3	7	382
Total 08/04–09/16/50	3189	9326	88	9	174	201	12987

The First Provisional Marine Brigade

The general pattern of casualties among members of the Marine Brigade followed that of other units in the battle. The marines experienced sporadic losses during the first two weeks in August, few casualties from then till the beginning of September and then increased losses until the unit was relieved on September 13 to join the 1st Marine Division for the invasion of Inchon.

There were 185 marine fatalities during the battle. Among these deaths there were no extraordinary causes. Two marine pilots were lost in fixed-wing plane crashes over land.

U.S. Air Force

There were a total of 53 Air Force fatalities in the period of the Battle of the Pusan Perimeter, the majority in September. However, because there is a slight overlap of dates in the chronology for this battle and the Invasion of Inchon, the four Air Force casualties that occurred on September 15 and 16 cannot be unambiguously identified with a specific battle. They will be included here. Following is an accounting of these fatalities by type of casualty.

Table 24 — Pusan Perimeter, U.S. Air Force

Fixed Wing Crash Over Land	
Pilot, Killed in Action	5
Pilot, Died While Missing	24
Aircrew, Killed in Action	2
Air Crew, Died of Wounds	1
Aircrew, Died While Missing	11
Non-Aircrew, Killed in Action	1
Non-Aircrew, Died While Missing	2
Fixed Wing Crash At Sea	
Pilot, Died While Missing	1
Aircrew, Killed in Action	1
Aircrew, Died While Missing	2
Non-Aircrew, Died While Missing	1
Ground Casualty	
Small-arms Fire, Killed in Action	2
Total	53

U.S. Navy

Of the 14 U.S. Navy fatalities during the battle, half were ground casualties, all of these the result of small-arms fire. Although the database listing Navy fatalities does not specifically identify the MOS of the casualty, it is most likely that these ground casualties were hospital corpsmen attached to marine fighting units.

Among the seven remaining Navy fatalities, five were Navy pilots who died in fixed-wing crashes over land. Four of these were listed as KIA and the other as missing and never found. The other two fatalities were both losses at sea, one from drowning and the other from multiple fragmentation wounds.

Turning the Tide: The Inchon Invasion and the Liberation of Seoul

With the Pusan defenders continuing to be reinforced (including a brigade of British troops, the first non–American units in the UN force) and with supplies to UN units becoming more abundant and air superiority becoming more clearly established, the defense of the perimeter was no longer in question. Now, military planning became focused on offensive strategies for recovering the ground that had been lost in the first 40 days of the war.

NKPA supply lines had been stretched to their limit and interdiction of their supplies by relentless air attacks continued to further constrain their abilities to wage effective combat. The time was ripe for a major UN offensive. That offensive took place on two fronts, coordinated to surprise and overwhelm the overextended NKPA forces: the Inchon Invasion and the liberation of Seoul.

On September 15, 1950, the First Marine Division, followed by the 7th Infantry Division, mounted a surprise amphibious assault on the port city of Inchon on the west coast of Korea. Resistance was light and, by the next day, the objective was secured with few U.S. casualties. Those two days the marines lost 24 men, 22 KIA from enemy action, one by drowning (who was listed as missing and never found), and one marine pilot who was lost in a fixed-wing plane crash over land. In that assault, the first Marine Corps Medal of Honor of the war was awarded.

MEDAL OF HONOR: BALDOMERO LOPEZ

Awarded to: First Lieutenant Baldomero Lopez, Tampa, FL, U.S. Marine Corps, Company A, 1st Battalion, 5th Marines, 1st Marine Division (Rein.). During Inchon invasion in Korea, 15 September 1950.

> For conspicuous gallantry and intrepidity at the risk of his life above and beyond the call of duty as a marine platoon commander of Company A, in action against enemy aggressor forces. With his platoon 1st Lt. Lopez was engaged in the reduction of immediate enemy beach defenses after landing with the assault waves. Exposing himself to hostile fire, he moved forward alongside a bunker and prepared to throw a handgrenade into the next pillbox whose fire was pinning down that sector of the beach. Taken

under fire by an enemy automatic weapon and hit in the right shoulder and chest as he lifted his arm to throw, he fell backward and dropped the deadly missile. After a moment, he turned and dragged his body forward in an effort to retrieve the grenade and throw it. In critical condition from pain and loss of blood, and unable to grasp the handgrenade firmly enough to hurl it, he chose to sacrifice himself rather than endanger the lives of his men and, with a sweeping motion of his wounded right arm, cradled the grenade under him and absorbed the full impact of the explosion. His exceptional courage, fortitude, and devotion to duty reflect the highest credit upon 1st Lt. Lopez and the U.S. Naval Service. He gallantly gave his life for his country.

On the first day of the Invasion of Inchon, three sailors also lost their lives. Two were ground casualties and are assumed to be corpsmen. The third was a sea casualty who was reported to have been killed by artillery.

Twenty miles east of Inchon lay the city of Seoul, capital of South Korea. Three months earlier, it had been overrun by the NKPA. Now, facing minimum resistance, and with the Han River as the only natural obstacle in the intervening territory, the marines moved quickly to liberate the capital city. Meanwhile the 7th Division moved south to cut off any possible NKPA reinforcements from their forces around Pusan.

The marines captured Kimpo Airfield on September 17 and began crossing the Han on September 20. Both of these achievements were possible, in part, because of the valor of PFC Walter Monegan and 2nd Lt. Walter A. Commiskey, both of whom were awarded the Medal of Honor for their actions.

MEDAL OF HONOR: WALTER C. MONEGAN, JR.

Awarded to: Private First Class Walter C. Monegan, Jr., Seattle, WA, U.S. Marine Corps, Company F, 2d Battalion, 1st Marines, 1st Marine Division (Rein.). Near Sosa-ri, Korea, 17 and 20 September 1950.

> For conspicuous gallantry and intrepidity at the risk of his life above and beyond the call of duty while serving as a rocket gunner attached to Company F, and in action against enemy aggressor forces. Dug in on a hill overlooking the main Seoul highway when 6 enemy tanks threatened to break through the battalion position during a predawn attack on 17 September, Pfc. Monegan promptly moved forward with his bazooka, under heavy hostile automatic weapons fre and engaged the lead tank at a range of less than 50 yards. After scoring a direct hit and killing the sole surviving tankman with his carbine as he came through the escape hatch, he boldly fired 2 more rounds of ammunition at the oncoming tanks, disorganizing the attack and enabling our tank crews to continue blasting with their 90-mm guns. With his own and an adjacent company's position threatened by annihilation when an overwhelming enemy tank-infantry force bypassed the area and proceeded toward the battalion command post during the early morning of September 20, he seized his rocket launcher and, in total darkness, charged down the slope of the hill where the tanks had broken through. Quick to act when an illuminating shell lit the area, he scored a direct hit on one of the tanks as hostile rifle and automatic-weapons fire raked the area at close range. Again exposing himself, he fired another round to destroy a second tank and, as the rear tank turned to retreat, stood

upright to fire and was fatally struck down by hostile machinegun fire when another illuminating shell silhouetted him against the sky. Pfc. Monegan's daring initiative, gallant fighting spirit and courageous devotion to duty were contributing factors in the success of his company in repelling the enemy, and his self-sacrificing efforts throughout sustain and enhance the highest traditions of the U.S. Naval Service. He gallantly gave his life for his country .

MEDAL OF HONOR: HENRY A. COMMISKEY, SR.

Awarded to: First Lieutenant (then 2d Lt.) Henry A. Commiskey, Sr., Hattiesburg, MS, U.S. Marine Corps, Company C, 1st Battalion, 1st Marines, 1st Marine Division (Rein.). Near Yongdungp'o, Korea, 20 September 1950.

> For conspicuous gallantry and intrepidity at the risk of his life above and beyond the call of duty while serving as a platoon leader in Company C, in action against enemy aggressor forces. Directed to attack hostile forces well dug in on Hill 85, 1st Lt. Commiskey, spearheaded the assault, charging up the steep slopes on the run. Coolly disregarding the heavy enemy machinegun and small arms fire, he plunged on well forward of the rest of his platoon and was the first man to reach the crest of the objective. Armed only with a pistol, he jumped into a hostile machinegun emplacement occupied by 5 enemy troops and quickly disposed of 4 of the soldiers with his automatic pistol. Grappling with the fifth, 1st Lt. Commiskey knocked him to the ground and held him until he could obtain a weapon from another member of his platoon and killed the last of the enemy gun crew. Continuing his bold assault, he moved to the next emplacement, killed 2 more of the enemy and then led his platoon toward the rear nose of the hill to rout the remainder of the hostile troops and destroy them as they fled from their positions. His valiant leadership and courageous fighting spirit served to inspire the men of his company to heroic endeavor in seizing the objective and reflect the highest credit upon 1st Lt. Commiskey and the U.S. Naval Service.

The battle for Seoul required more than a week of house-to-house combat before the marines raised the Stars and Stripes over Government House on September 27. For action in this battle, and the continuing fighting required to completely pacify the city, two more Medals of Honor were awarded to gallant marines.

MEDAL OF HONOR: EUGENE ARNOLD OBREGON

Awarded to: Private First Class Eugene Arnold Obregon, U.S. Marine Corps, Los Angeles, CA, Company G, 3d Battalion, 5th Marines, 1st Marine Division (Rein.). Seoul, Korea, 26 September 1950.

> For conspicuous gallantry and intrepidity at the risk of his life above and beyond the call of duty while serving with Company G, in action against enemy aggressor forces. While serving as an ammunition carrier of a machinegun squad in a marine rifle company which was temporarily pinned down by hostile fire, Pfc. Obregon observed a fellow marine fall

wounded in the line of fire. Armed only with a pistol, he unhesitating dashed from his covered position to the side of the casualty. Firing his pistol with 1 hand as he ran, he grasped his comrade by the arm with his other hand and, despite the great peril to himself dragged him to the side of the road. Still under enemy fire, he was bandaging the man's wounds when hostile troops of approximately platoon strength began advancing toward his position. Quickly seizing the wounded marine's carbine, he placed his own body as a shield in front of him and lay there firing accurately and effectively into the hostile group until he himself was fatally wounded by enemy machinegun fire. By his courageous fighting spirit, fortitude, and loyal devotion to duty, Pfc. Obregon enabled his fellow marines to rescue the wounded man and aided essentially in repelling the attack, thereby sustaining and enhancing the highest traditions of the U.S. Naval Service. He gallantly gave his life for his country.

Medal of Honor: Stanley R. Christianson

Awarded to: Private First Class Stanley R. Christianson, Mindoro, WI, U.S. Marine Corps, Company E, 2d Battalion, 1st Marines, 1st Marine Division (Rein.). Seoul, Korea, 29 September 1950.

> For conspicuous gallantry and intrepidity at the risk of his life above and beyond the call of duty while serving with Company E, in action against enemy aggressor forces at Hill 132, in the early morning hours. Manning 1 of the several listening posts covering approaches to the platoon area when the enemy commenced the attack, Pfc. Christianson quickly sent another marine to alert the rest of the platoon. Without orders, he remained in his position and, with full knowledge that he would have slight chance of escape, fired relentlessly at oncoming hostile troops attacking furiously with rifles, automatic weapons, and incendiary grenades. Accounting for 7 enemy dead in the immediate vicinity before his position was overrun and he himself fatally struck down, Pfc. Christianson, by his superb courage, valiant fighting spirit, and devotion to duty, was responsible for allowing the rest of the platoon time to man positions, build up a stronger defense on that flank, and repel the attack with 41 of the enemy destroyed, many more wounded, and 3 taken prisoner. His self-sacrificing actions in the face of overwhelming odds sustain and enhance the finest traditions of the U.S. Naval Service. Pfc. Christianson gallantly gave his life for his country.

Figure 8 shows the pattern of U.S. Marine Corps losses in the period following the invasion of Inchon.

Total Marine fatalities in the period September 17 to October 3 were 400. Three of these were pilots lost in fixed-wing crashes over land, one each on the 22nd, 23rd and 24th. As Figure 8 indicates, 18 Navy personnel were lost as ground casualties in this action and are assumed to have been corpsmen assigned to the marines. Following the period shown in Figure 8, marine losses diminished substantially for some time, with only 14 fatalities in the next three weeks.

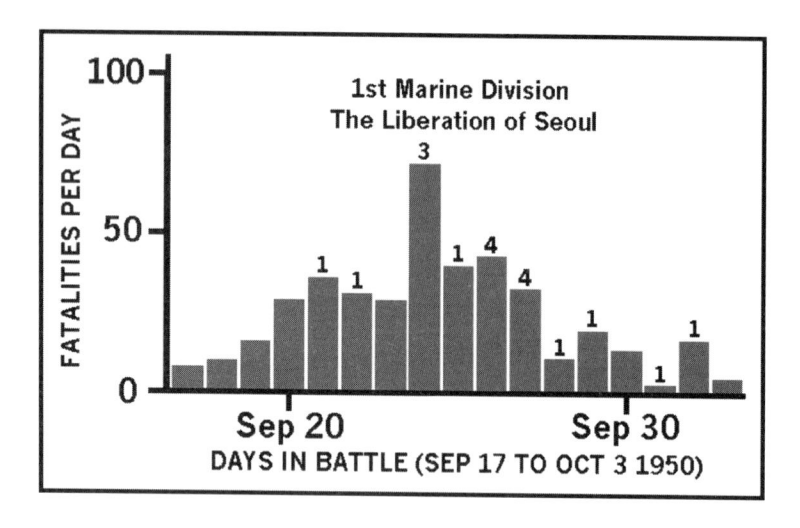

Figure 8. Daily fatalities for the 1st Marine Division following the invasion at Inchon, and including the liberation of Seoul. The numbers over the bars on some dates indicate the number of presumed Navy corpsmen killed in ground action on those days.

Breakout from the Pusan Perimeter

With the U.S. 7th Division following the same route south as the NKPA had in its onslaught in July, and appreciating many of the same numerical advantages, the invaders now found themselves facing UN forces on two fronts. Because of the length of the perimeter and the different tactical situations facing the various defending units, it is difficult to pinpoint a date on which the breakout can be said to have begun. Somewhat arbitrarily, it will be assumed here that it began on September 17.

The four U.S. divisions and two RCTs (plus the ROK divisions on the north perimeter and the British brigade) that had so successfully kept the NKPA from occupying the whole of South Korea now mounted a major offensive to push back the attacking forces. It took them one-fourth the time the invaders required to occupy the territory originally. In eleven days, the NKPA was put to flight. Short as it was, however, it was still a costly endeavor, with more than 700 fatalities and more than 3,600 total casualties. Figure 9 shows how those casualties accrued during the course of the battle. The breakout is reported to have essentially ended on September 27, and as the figure indicates, the majority of the casualties were sustained between the 17th and the 27th. Also apparent from the figure is the fact that the percentage of fatalities was significantly lower than in earlier engagements.

The worst day of this battle was September 19. Of some interest is the fact that there was a very even distribution of casualties among the different units in the battle that day. It was obviously a day of maximum, coordinated effort on the part of UN forces, and this clearly was the day that broke the back of the invading army.

I. The Peninsular War

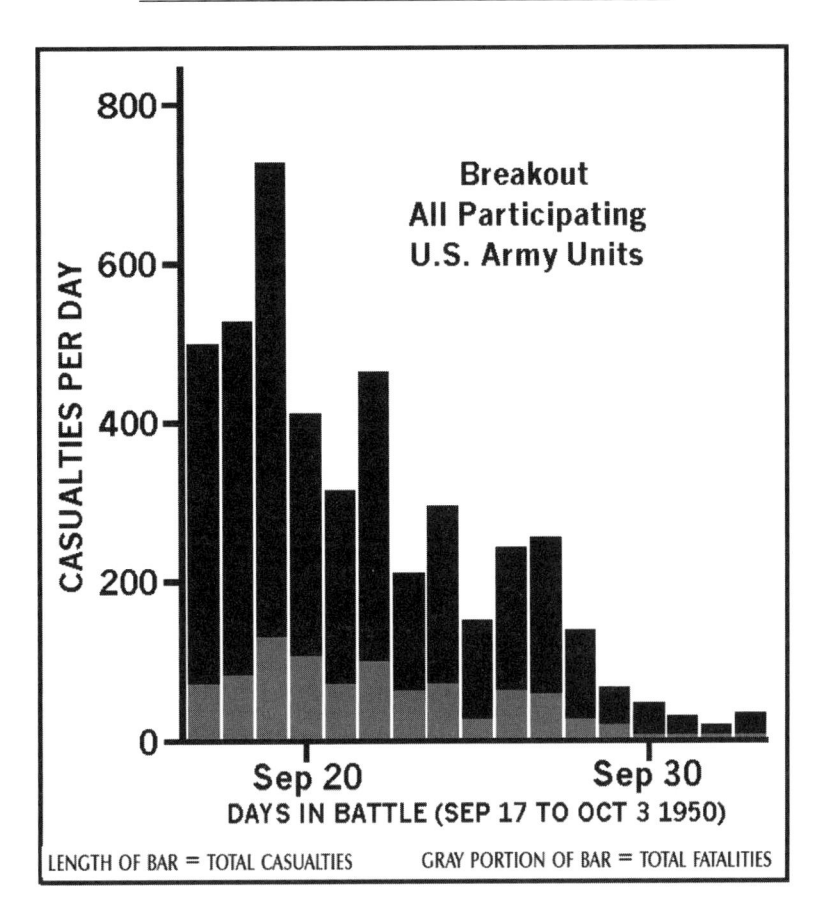

Breakout — All Participating U.S. Army Units

(Casualties per day, Sep 17 to Oct 3 1950. Length of bar = total casualties; gray portion of bar = total fatalities.)

Figure 9. Daily casualties for all units engaged in the breakout from the Pusan Perimeter.

Fighting continued, of course, and casualties continued to occur, but they diminished steadily and did not achieve these kinds of levels again until early November, after the Chinese Communist Forces (CCF) entered the war. This was also the day that two men from the 25th Division earned the Medal of Honor for their heroic actions.

MEDAL OF HONOR: WILLIAM R. JECELIN

Awarded to: Sergeant William R. Jecelin, Baltimore, MD, U.S. Army, Company C, 35th Infantry Regiment, 25th Infantry Division. Near Saga, Korea, 19 September 1950.

> Sgt. Jecelin, Company C, distinguished himself by conspicuous gallantry and intrepidity above and beyond the call of duty in action against the enemy. His company was ordered to secure a prominent, saw-toothed ridge from a well-entrenched and heavily armed enemy. Unable to capture the

objective in the first attempt, a frontal and flanking assault was launched. He led his platoon through heavy enemy fire and bursting shells, across rice fields and rocky terrain, in direct frontal attack on the ridge in order to draw fire away from the flanks. The unit advanced to the base of the cliff, where intense, accurate hostile fire stopped the attack. Realizing that an assault was the only solution, Sgt. Jecelin rose from his position firing his rifle and throwing grenades as he called on his men to follow him. Despite the intense enemy fire this attack carried to the crest of the ridge where the men were forced to take cover. Again he rallied his men and stormed the enemy strongpoint. With fixed bayonets they charged into the face of antitank fire and engaged the enemy in hand-to-hand combat. After clubbing and slashing this force into submission the platoon was forced to take cover from direct frontal fire of a self-propelled gun. Refusing to be stopped he leaped to his feet and through sheer personal courage and fierce determination led his men in a new attack. At this instant a well-camouflaged enemy soldier threw a grenade at the remaining members of the platoon. He immediately lunged and covered the grenade with his body, absorbing the full force of the explosion to save those around him. This incredible courage and willingness to sacrifice himself for his comrades so imbued them with fury that they completely eliminated the enemy force. Sgt. Jecelin's heroic leadership and outstanding gallantry reflect the highest credit upon himself and uphold the esteemed traditions of the military service.

MEDAL OF HONOR: JOHN W. COLLIER

Awarded to: Corporal John W. Collier, Worthington, KY, U.S. Army, Company C, 27th Infantry Regiment. Place and date: Near Chindong-ni, Korea, 19 September 1950.

Cpl. Collier, Company C, distinguished himself by conspicuous gallantry and intrepidity above and beyond the call of duty in action. While engaged in an assault on a strategic ridge strongly defended by a fanatical enemy, the leading elements of his company encountered intense automatic weapons and grenade fire. Cpl. Collier and 3 comrades volunteered and moved forward to neutralize an enemy machinegun position which was hampering the company's advance, but they were twice repulsed. On the third attempt, Cpl. Collier, despite heavy enemy fire and grenade barrages, moved to an exposed position ahead of his comrades, assaulted and destroyed the machinegun nest, killing at least 4 enemy soldiers. As he returned down the rocky, fire-swept hill and joined his squad, an enemy grenade landed in their midst. Shouting a warning to his comrades, he, selflessly and unhesitatingly, threw himself upon the grenade and smothered its explosion with his body. This intrepid action saved his comrades from death or injury. Cpl. Collier's supreme, personal bravery, consummate gallantry, and noble self-sacrifice reflect untold glory upon himself and uphold the honored traditions of the military service.

Table 25 shows how casualties were distributed among the various units in the breakout from the Pusan Perimeter.

I. The Peninsular War

Table 25 — Pusan Perimeter Breakout, All Participating Units

	KIA	WIA	POW Returned	POW Died	MIA Returned	MIA Died	Unit Total
5th RCT	61	290			2		353
1st Cavalry Division	201	678			2	3	884
2nd Infantry Division	198	816			5	3	1022
24th Infantry Division	81	305					386
29th Infantry Regiment/RCT	29	93					122
25th Infantry Division	138	646			3	2	789
Other units (68)	20	91					111
Total 09/17–09/27/50	728	2919			12	8	3667

Because the U.S. Army was now involved in battles on two fronts, it is impossible to determine definitively which of the non-divisional supporting units should be included in the category defined in the above table as "Other units." In this case, the determination was made by identifying which of the non-divisional units had sustained casualties during the defense of the Pusan Perimeter. This list was then matched against all the units that had sustained casualties in the period 9/17 to 9/27. Only those units that were in both lists were included among the 68 listed in the table. The remainder was assumed to have been in support of the 7th Division in its march south from Inchon.

In that move south, the element of surprise probably gave UN forces more tactical advantage than anywhere on any other battle fronts of the time. The 32nd Infantry was the primary assault unit in the initial stages of the action, and as the table below indicates, this unit took the majority of the casualties. The 31st Infantry sustained most of its casualties during the final days of the campaign, with 62 of its 104 casualties September 27th.

Table 26 — Post Inchon Invasion, 7th Infantry Division

	KIA	WIA	POW Returned	POW Died	MIA Returned	MIA Died	Unit Total
32nd Inf, 7th Inf Div	55	211			3	2	271
31st Inf, 7th Inf Div	27	77					104
17th Inf, 7th Inf Div	2	19					21
7th MP Co, 7th Inf Div	2	5					7
7th Recon Co, 7th Inf Div	1	4					5
13th Engr Bn, 7th Inf Div		5					5
Hq, 7th Inf Div	1	3					4
57th FA Bn, 7th Inf Div		3					3
31st FA Bn, 7th Inf Div		3					3
77th Med Tk Bn, 7th Inf Div		3					3
48th FA Bn, 7th Inf Div		3					3
HHB, 7th Inf Div Fld Arty	1						1
7th Sig Co, 7th Inf Div		1					1
7th Sig Co, 7th Inf Div		1					1
Total 7th Division	87	290			3	2	382
Other units (32)	2	47					49
Total 09/17–09/27/50	89	337			3	2	431

Like the marines and the units in the perimeter breakout, the 7th Division and its supporting units sustained few casualties in the weeks following the 27th. The advantage now lay with the UN forces, which had the badly battered NKPA on the run.

U.S. Air Force

In the period September 17 through September 30, 1950, the U.S. Air Force lost 17 men, all in fixed-wing air crashes. The details are listed below.

Table 27 — Breakout/Inchon Invasion, U.S. Air Force

Fixed Wing Crash Over Land	
Pilot, Died While Missing	12
Aircrew, Died While Missing	2
Non-Aircrew, Killed in Action	1
Fixed Wing Crash At Sea	
Aircrew, Died While Missing	2
Total 09/17–09/30/50	17

U.S. Navy

The chronology specifies that, on September 26, 1950, the USS *Brush* hit a mine off the city of Tanchon on the east coast of North Korea sustaining significant losses. The database confirms Navy casualties on the 26th, indicating 10 fatalities from an explosive device at sea. Five of these were missing and never found.

On September 29, the minesweeper *Magpie* was reported to have hit a mine and sunk with significant loss of life. The next day, according to reports, the USS *Mansfield* struck a mine and sustained additional losses. The chronology indicates that there were 21 KIA in the *Magpie* incident and 5 MIA from the *Mansfield*. The database, however, does not confirm these losses. There were no casualties at sea indicated on either the 29th or the 30th. The data do show 2 KIAs at sea from an explosive device on September 28 and 16 fatalities on October 1, four of these listed as KIA and the remainder as missing and never found. There was also one record showing a KIA at sea from burns on October 2. If the MIAs from the *Mansfield* were later found, they would not be in the database, which only lists fatalities. In any case, only 19 Navy fatalities at sea can be confirmed in this time period.

On September 20, one U.S. Navy pilot was lost in a fixed-wing plane crash over land.

Pursuit

On October 9, 1950, elements of I Corps, led by the 1st Cavalry Division, crossed the 38th Parallel in western Korea, just north of Kaesong, pushing back the NKPA toward the North Korean capital city of Pyongyang. Resistance, however, continued to be significant, as indicated by an accounting of casualties in the 1st Cavalry Division in the week of this action.

It should be noted that, of the heavy losses indicated for the 77th FA Battalion, all but one were sustained on one day, October 13.

Table 28 — Fall of Pyongyang, 1st Cavalry Division

	KIA	WIA	POW Returned	POW Died	MIA Returned	MIA Died	Unit Total
5th Cav, 1st Cav Div	8	47					55
7th Cav, 1st Cav Div	23	101	1		1	2	128
8th Cav, 1st Cav Div	25	96				1	122
77th FA Bn, 1st Cav Div	32	22	1				55
8th Engr Bn, 1st Cav Div	1	5					6
525th MP Co, 1st Cav Div		3					3
99th FA Bn, 1st Cav Div	1	2					3
82nd FA Bn, 1st Cav Div		1					1
6th Tank Bn, 1st Cav Div		1					1
AG Bnd, 1st Cav Div		1					1
HHB, 1st Cav Div Fld Arty	1						1
27th Ord Co, 1st Cav Div		1					1
Total 10/09–10/15/50	91	280	2		1	3	377

The intense nature of this conflict is further revealed by the following descriptions of two Medals of Honor awarded to members of the 1st Cav for their selfless contributions to the success of the operation.

MEDAL OF HONOR: ROBERT H. YOUNG

Awarded to: Private First Class Robert H. Young, Vallejo, CA, U.S. Army, Company E, 8th Cavalry Regiment, 1st Cavalry Division. North of Kaesong, Korea, 9 October 1950.

> Pfc. Young distinguished himself by conspicuous gallantry and intrepidity above and beyond the call of duty in action. His company, spearheading a battalion drive deep in enemy territory, suddenly came under a devastating barrage of enemy mortar and automatic weapons crossfire which inflicted heavy casualties among his comrades and wounded him in the face and shoulder. Refusing to be evacuated, Pfc. Young remained in position and continued to fire at the enemy until wounded a second time. As he awaited first aid near the company command post the enemy attempted an enveloping movement. Disregarding medical treatment he took an exposed position and firing with deadly accuracy killed 5 of the enemy. During this action he was again hit by hostile fire which knocked him to the ground and destroyed his helmet. Later when supporting tanks moved forward, Pfc. Young, his wounds still unattended, directed tank fire which destroyed 3 enemy gun positions and enabled the company to advance. Wounded again by an enemy mortar burst, and while aiding several of his injured comrades, he demanded that all others be evacuated first. Throughout the course of this action the leadership and combative instinct displayed by Pfc. Young exerted a profound influence on the conduct of the company. His aggressive example affected the whole course of the action and was responsible for its success. Pfc. Young's dauntless courage and intrepidity reflect the highest credit upon himself and uphold the esteemed traditions of the U.S. Army.

Medal of Honor: Samuel S. Coursen

Awarded to: First Lieutenant Samuel S. Coursen, Madison, NJ, U.S. Army, Company C, 5th Cavalry Regiment. Near Kaesong, Korea, 12 October 1950.

> 1st Lt. Coursen distinguished himself by conspicuous gallantry and intrepidity above and beyond the call of duty in action. While Company C was attacking Hill 174 under heavy enemy small-arms fire, his platoon received enemy fire from close range. The platoon returned the fire and continued to advance. During this phase one of his men moved into a well-camouflaged emplacement, which was thought to be unoccupied, and was wounded by the enemy who were hidden within the emplacement. Seeing the soldier in difficulty he rushed to the man's aid and, without regard for his personal safety, engaged the enemy in hand-to-hand combat in an effort to protect his wounded comrade until he himself was killed. When his body was recovered after the battle, 7 enemy dead were found in the emplacement. As the result of 1st Lt. Coursen's violent struggle several of the enemies' heads had been crushed with his rifle. His aggressive and intrepid actions saved the life of the wounded man, eliminated the main position of the enemy roadblock, and greatly inspired the men in his command. 1st Lt. Coursen's extraordinary heroism and intrepidity reflect the highest credit on himself and are in keeping with the honored traditions of the military service.

On October 19, 1950, the 1st Cavalry Division and the 1st ROK Division captured the North Korean capital city of Pyongyang.

Airborne Operation

On October 20, the war's first airborne assault was conducted by the 187th Airborne RCT (187th Airborne Infantry Regiment, the 674th FA Battalion and at least three other support units) in the vicinity of the cities of Sukchon and Sunchon, about 25 miles north of Pyongyang. Over 2,800 paratroopers were reported to have been involved in the assault. The table below shows the distribution of casualties among these units during the first three days of the operation. Thereafter, casualties in these units were very light.

Table 29 — Airborne Assault, 187th Airborne RCT

	KIA	WIA	POW Returned	POW Died	MIA Returned	MIA Died	Unit Total
10/20/05							
187th Abn Inf/RCT	3	40					43
674th FA Bn, 187th RCT	1	1					2
11th Med Det, 11th Abn Div Hq		1					1
127th (Engr?), 11th Abn Div		1					1
Day Total 10/20/50	4	43					47

(continued on next page)

Table 29 (*cont.*)

	KIA	WIA	POW Returned	POW Died	MIA Returned	MIA Died	Unit Total
10/21/50							
187th Abn Inf/RCT	36	38				2	76
674th FA Bn, 187th RCT		1					1
88th (AAA?), 11th Abn Div		2					2
Day Total 10/21/50	36	41				2	79
10/22/50							
187th Abn Inf/RCT	8	42					50
674th FA Bn, 187th RCT						1	1
127th (Engr?), 11th Abn Div		2					2
Day Total 10/22/50	8	44				1	53
Total 10/20–10/22/50	48	128				3	179

The units shown in the table above with (?) after the type of unit were identified in the database with a code that could not be unambiguously interpreted. The types indicated were assumed by elimination from a listing of all the units that served in Korea.

Various reports have suggested that as many as 100 of the troopers were injured in the drop on October 20. However, the database, which has a casualty type titled "injured in action other than wounds," lists only 35 of the injured that day with that casualty type. As the table suggests, that number was still a very large percentage of the 43 listed as WIA on the drop day.

Given the kinds of casualty figures reported so far for early actions in the war, the total number of casualties among the paratroopers in this operation seems rather small. Yet, it is significant commentary on the way the tide had turned in the conflict that the 179 casualties in the operation was a major percentage of the total (235, including 2 marines) among all U.S. units in Korea on those three days.

However, as few as their casualties were by comparison other units on earlier days, combat for the men of the 187th in this operation was by no means a walk in the park. This is aptly confirmed by the following description of the action that earned medic Richard Wilson the Medal of Honor.

MEDAL OF HONOR: RICHARD G. WILSON

Awarded to: Private First Class Richard G. Wilson, Cape Girardeau, MO, U.S. Army, Medical Company, Company I, 187th Airborne Infantry Regiment. Opari, Korea, 21 October 1950.

> Pfc. Wilson distinguished himself by conspicuous gallantry and intrepidity above and beyond the call of duty in action. As medical aid man attached to Company I, he accompanied the unit during a reconnaissance in force through the hilly country near Opari. The main body of the company was passing through a narrow valley flanked on 3 sides by high hills when the enemy laid down a barrage of mortar, automatic-weapons and small-arms fire. The company suffered a large number of casualties from the intense hostile fire while fighting its way out of the ambush. Pfc. Wilson proceeded at once to move among the wounded and administered aid

to them oblivious of the danger to himself, constantly exposing himself to hostile fire. The company commander ordered a withdrawal as the enemy threatened to encircle and isolate the company. As his unit withdrew Private Wilson assisted wounded men to safety and assured himself that none were left behind. After the company had pulled back he learned that a comrade previously thought dead had been seen to be moving and attempting to crawl to safety. Despite the protests of his comrades, unarmed and facing a merciless enemy, Pfc. Wilson returned to the dangerous position in search of his comrade. Two days later a patrol found him Iying beside the man he returned to aid. He had been shot several times while trying to shield and administer aid to the wounded man. Pfc. Wilson's superb personal bravery, consummate courage and willing self-sacrifice for his comrades reflect untold glory upon himself and uphold the esteemed traditions of the military service.

More Reports of Executions

The chronology suggests that, during September and October, as NKPA units were being routed by UN forces, very significant numbers of American POWs were recovered that had been executed by their captors. Following is a listing of these accounts.

Late September 1950—In Taejon, 42 U. S. soldiers are found executed.
October 9, 1950—As U.S. forces cross the 38th parallel and push toward Pyongyang, 86 GIs are found massacred.
October 20, 1950—In Suchon, 75 GIs are found executed.
October 23, 1950—In Kunsang, 128 GIs are found executed.

To attempt to confirm these accounts, we will first need to look at the available data in the records of individuals that were reported to have been captured.

Each record in the database contains two dates relative to the circumstances of the casualty. The first is the date of occurrence. The second is the date of disposition; that is, the date when the final outcome is determined and the record can be closed. Regrettably, the exact meaning of the disposition date is not always clear, particularly in the cases of individuals that were captured and died in captivity. How was information of the death obtained? Is the disposition date in the record the date the information was received, the date it was recorded or the actual date of death?

In the database records for captured individuals, four possible dispositions are specified. These are (1) returned to military control (RMC), (2) died of wounds (DOW), (3) killed in action (KIA) and (4) died non-battle (DNB). In the tables used here to account for casualties, the final three of these four are all included in the designation **POW Died**. In none of these cases, however, is it possible to determine the circumstances of the death from the type of disposition alone.

All of this is further complicated by the fact that some individuals who were reported as missing in action may not have been missing, but captured. This possibility is supported by the observation that the records of many deceased MIAs had their dispositions listed as KIA with disposition dates some months after the occurrence. Presumably, their bodies were recovered. Otherwise they would have been recorded as missing and presumed dead. Where were they in the intervening months? Conversely, some individuals that were reported as captured were then recorded as KIA within a week of their reported capture (presumably after the body was recovered). Were these individuals in fact POWs or were they simply missing in action and then found dead?

With these questions in mind, we can look at the records of those individuals that were reported as captured or missing early in the war, and were then reported to have died in captivity or found dead, and then see if we can make any sense of them, particularly in regard to the above reports of mass executions. Of particular interest will be those records of individuals that showed disposition dates between September 17 (the beginning of the breakout from the Pusan Perimeter) and October 23 (the last date on which the discovery of executed GIs was reported).

Among reported POWs, only 131 records meet these criteria. As the reports of executions account for a total of 331 victims, the selection criteria are obviously inadequate—at least to account for all of the executed GIs. However, among these 131 records, there is a group that appears to account for one of the discoveries listed in the chronology. This is the report of 75 executed GIs discovered in Suchon on October 20. In the data are 73 records of deceased POWs all with the disposition date October 20, 1950. Of these records, 68 list the disposition as KIA, one as DOW (died of wounds) and four as DNB (died non-battle).

Among reported MIAs, only 31 records meet the criteria. However, all of these records have the same disposition date (September 26) and disposition type (KIA). Were some or all of these among those that were reported to have been found executed in late September?

Except for these two possibilities, reports of mass executions cannot be confirmed from the records in the database. Certainly there are a large number records of deceased POWs that show disposition dates early in the war (over 300 with disposition dates between September 17 and December 31, 1950). These could very possibly include some or all of the executed individuals in the reports cited above. However, other than those dated October 20, these records show no pattern in either the date or the type of disposition; that is, no more than 25 reported on any single date (and only one on October 9; none on October 23) and the disposition type generally alternating randomly between KIA and DNB—and even a few DOW.

The Offensive Stalls

With its army being rapidly decimated by now superior UN forces, the NKPA was able to offer little resistance to its pursuers. However, this disadvantage was about to disappear, as reinforcing units from the People's Republic of China began to enter the conflict.

Table 30 summarizes of all U.S. Army casualties from the end of the perimeter breakout until the CCF (Chinese Communist Forces) entered the war.

Table 30—Pursuit, All U.S. Army Units

	KIA	WIA	POW Returned	POW Died	MIA Returned	MIA Died	Unit Total
5th RCT	6	10					16
1st Cavalry Division	117	399	3		2	3	524
2nd Infantry Division	29	113					142
3rd Infantry Division	16	29					45
7th Infantry Division	23	120			1	1	145
24th Infantry Division	9	60	1			1	71
29th Inf Regt/RCT	5	14					19
25th Infantry Division	35	54				5	94
11th Airborne (187th RCT)	49	147				3	199
Other Units (59)	12	92	1			2	107
TOTAL 09/28–10/24/50	301	1038	5		3	15	1362

U.S. Navy

On October 12, the minesweepers *Pirate* and *Pledge* were reported to have been sunk by mines in Wonsan harbor with six fatalities. The database indicates 13 losses at sea from an explosive device on that day, seven listed as KIA and the other six as missing, never found and declared dead. One additional KIA from the same cause was recorded on the following day.

U.S. Marines

As indicated in the preceding chapter, Marine losses in the period October 4–24 were minimal, with only 14 KIA and one Navy KIA from ground action that most likely represents a corpsman.

U.S. Air Force

Regrettably, the Air Force did not fare as well in roughly the same time period, losing 46 airmen between October 1st and 24th. All of the losses were the result of fixed-wing crashes over land. Most could not be associated with any specific ground action, with at least one fatality on 19 of the 24 days in the period. There were 11 airmen (4 pilots and 7 aircrew) lost on the 19th, when the 1st Cav. began its push into North Korea, and 5 airmen (3 pilots, 1 aircrew and 1 non-aircrew) lost the next day, as the 187th RCT made its airborne drop north of Pyongyang. However, there is no way of knowing if the ground actions and the air losses were related.

Total Air Force losses in the period are summarized in Table 31.

Table 31—October 1950 Losses, U.S. Air Force

Fixed Wing Crash Over Land	
Pilot, Killed in Action	5
Aircrew, Killed in Action	10
Pilot, Died While Missing	25
Aircrew, Died While Missing	5
Non-Aircrew, Died While Missing	1
Total 10/01–10/24/50	46

A New Enemy: UN Forces Meet the Chinese at Unsan and Sudong

On October 25, 1950, the Chinese Communist Forces (CCF) entered the conflict. For the next week their presence was not evident in the level of combat. Casualties remained light, even though elements of the 24th Division's 21st Regiment penetrated to within a few miles of Sinuiju near the mouth of the Yalu River, the border between North Korea and China.

Then, on November 1 and 2 came the first real confrontation between UN forces and the CCF. The U.S. 1st Cavalry Division met the CCF at Unsan. The consequences for the 1st Cav, particularly the 8th Regiment, as the table below indicates, were severe.

Table 32 — Battle of Unsan, 1st Cavalry Division

	KIA	WIA	POW Returned	POW Died	MIA Returned	MIA Died	Unit Total
5th Cav, 1st Cav Div	23	151	5	1		11	191
7th Cav, 1st Cav Div		2		1			3
8th Cav, 1st Cav Div	59	197	257	116	15	199	843
99th FA Bn, 1st Cav Div	4	18	18	4		19	63
8th Engr Bn, 1st Cav Div	2	18	3	1		5	29
525th MP Co, 1st Cav Div		2	2			1	5
92nd AAA Bn, 1st Cav Div		4					4
61st FA Bn, 1st Cav Div		3				1	4
13th Sig Co, 1st Cav Div		1		1			2
6th Tank Bn, 1st Cav Div		1					1
15th Med Bn, 1st Cav Div		1					1
77th FA Bn, 1st Cav Div						1	1
8th MP Co, 1st Cav Div			1				1
HHC, 1st Cav Div		1					1
Total 11/01–11/02/50	88	399	286	124	15	237	1149

The casualty count in the 8th Cavalry Regiment on those two days of battle was staggering. The number of KIAs was not extraordinary, but more than two-thirds of all the casualties reported in the regiment were either captured or were reported missing, never found and declared dead. It may be significant to note that, among those GIs that were captured in this encounter, the proportion that died in captivity was much lower than in earlier actions. This may have been due to a difference between the NKPA and the CCF in the way they treated their prisoners.

Except for one day of elevated losses (29 fatalities, including two Navy corpsmen, on October 27), the U.S. 1st Marine Division had reported very few casualties for almost a month. Then, on November 2–4, they encountered the CCF at Sudong and lost 67 marines KIA, plus three Navy corpsmen, in the three days. One of these was a marine pilot lost in a fixed-wing crash over land.

This action earned three marines the Medal of Honor for their heroism under fire.

MEDAL OF HONOR: ARCHIE VAN WINKLE

Awarded to: Staff Sergeant Archie Van Winkle, Arlington, WA, U.S. Marine Corps Reserve, Company B, 1st Battalion, 7th Marines, 1st Marine Division (Rein.). Vicinity of Sudong, Korea, 2 November 1950.

For conspicuous gallantry and intrepidity at the risk of his life above and beyond the call of duty while serving as a platoon sergeant in Company B, in action against enemy aggressor forces. Immediately rallying the men in his area after a fanatical and numerically superior enemy force penetrated the center of the line under cover of darkness and pinned down the platoon with a devastating barrage of deadly automatic weapons and grenade fire, S/Sgt. Van Winkle boldly spearheaded a determined attack through withering fire against hostile frontal positions and, though he and all the others who charged with him were wounded, succeeded in enabling his platoon to gain the fire superiority and the opportunity to reorganize. Realizing that the left flank squad was isolated from the rest of the unit, he rushed through 40 yards of fierce enemy fire to reunite his troops despite an elbow wound which rendered 1 of his arms totally useless. Severely wounded a second time when a direct hit in the chest from a hostile hand grenade caused serious and painful wounds, he staunchly refused evacuation and continued to shout orders and words of encouragement to his depleted and battered platoon. Finally carried from his position unconscious from shock and from loss of blood, S/Sgt. Van Winkle served to inspire all who observed him to heroic efforts in successfully repulsing the enemy attack. His superb leadership, valiant fighting spirit, and unfaltering devotion to duty in the face of heavy odds reflect the highest credit upon himself and the U.S. Naval Service.

MEDAL OF HONOR: LEE H. PHILLIPS

Awarded to: Corporal Lee H. Phillips, Ben Hill, GA, U.S. Marine Corps, Company E, 2d Battalion, 7 Marines, 1st Marine Division (Rein.). Korea, 4 November 1950.

For conspicuous gallantry and intrepidity at the risk of his life above and beyond the call of duty while serving as a squad leader of Company E, in action against enemy aggressor forces. Assuming the point position in the attack against a strongly defended and well-entrenched numerically superior enemy force occupying a vital hill position which had been unsuccessfully assaulted on 5 separate occasions by units of the Marine Corps and other friendly forces, Cpl. Phillips fearlessly led his men in a bayonet charge up the precipitous slope under a deadly hail of hostile mortar, small-arms, and machinegun fire. Quickly rallying his squad when it was pinned down by a heavy and accurate mortar barrage, he continued to lead his men through the bombarded area and, although only 5 members were left in the casualty ridden unit, gained the military crest of the hill where he was immediately subjected to an enemy counterattack. Although greatly outnumbered by an estimated enemy squad, Cpl. Phillips boldly engaged the hostile force with handgrenades and rifle fire and, exhorting his gallant group of marines to follow him, stormed forward to completely overwhelm the enemy. With only 3 men now left in his squad, he proceeded to spearhead an assault on the last remaining strongpoint which was defended by 4 of the enemy on a rocky and almost inaccessible portion of the hill position. Using 1 hand to climb up the extremely hazardous precipice, he hurled grenades with the other and, with 2 remaining comrades, succeeded in annihilating the pocket of resistance and in consolidating the position. Immediately subjected to a sharp counterattack by an estimated enemy squad, he skillfully directed the fire of his men and employed his own weapon with deadly effectiveness to repulse the numerically superior hostile force. By his valiant leadership, indomitable fighting spirit and resolute determination in the face of heavy odds, Cpl. Phillips served to inspire all who observed him and was directly responsible for the destruction of the enemy stronghold. His great personal valor reflects the highest credit upon himself and enhances and sustains the finest traditions of the U.S. Naval Service.

Medal of Honor: James I. Poynter

Awarded to: Sergeant James I. Poynter, Downey, CA, U.S. Marine Corps Reserve, Company A, 1st Battalion, 7th Marines, 1st Marine Division (Rein.). Near Sudong, Korea, 4 November 1950.

>For conspicuous gallantry and intrepidity at the risk of his life above and beyond the call of duty while serving as a squad leader in a rifle platoon of Company A, in action against enemy aggressor forces during the defense of Hill 532, south of Sudong, Korea. When a vastly outnumbering, well-concealed hostile force launched a sudden, vicious counterattack against his platoon's hasty defensive position, Sgt. Poynter displayed superb skill and courage in leading his squad and directing its fire against the onrushing enemy. With his ranks critically depleted by casualties and he himself critically wounded as the onslaught gained momentum and the hostile force surrounded his position, he seized his bayonet and engaged in bitter hand-to-hand combat as the breakthrough continued. Observing 3 machineguns closing in at a distance of 25 yards, he dashed from his position and, grasping handgrenades from fallen marines as he ran, charged the emplacements in rapid succession, killing the crews of 2 and putting the other out of action before he fell, mortally wounded. By his self-sacrificing and valiant conduct, Sgt. Poynter inspired the remaining members of his squad to heroic endeavor in bearing down upon and repelling the disorganized enemy, thereby enabling the platoon to move out of the trap to a more favorable tactical position. His indomitable fighting spirit, fortitude, and great personal valor maintained in the face of overwhelming odds sustain and enhance the finest traditions of the U.S. Naval Service. He gallantly gave his life for his country.

Only seven fatalities were reported for the 1st Marine Division on November 6, 1950. Perhaps this was due, at least in part, to the actions of one marine officer, who was awarded the Medal of Honor for his sacrifice on behalf of his men.

Medal of Honor: Robert Dale Reem

Awarded to: Second Lieutenant Robert Dale Reem, Elizabethtown, PA, U.S. Marine Corps, Company H, 3d Battalion, 7th Marines, 1st Marine Division (Rein.). Vicinity Chinhung-ni, Korea, 6 November 1950.

> For conspicuous gallantry and intrepidity at the risk of his life above and beyond the call of duty as a platoon commander in Company H, in action against enemy aggressor forces. Grimly determined to dislodge a group of heavy enemy infantry units occupying well-concealed and strongly fortified positions on commanding ground overlooking unprotected terrain. 2d Lt. Reem moved slowly forward up the side of the ridge with his platoon in the face of a veritable hail of shattering hostile machinegun, grenade, and rifle fire. Three times repulsed by a resolute enemy force in achieving his objective, and pinned down by the continuing fury of hostile fire, he rallied and regrouped the heroic men in his depleted and disorganized platoon in preparation for a fourth attack. Issuing last-minute orders to his noncommissioned officers when an enemy grenade landed in a depression of the rocky ground in which the group was standing, 2d Lt. Reem unhesitatingly chose to sacrifice himself and, springing upon the deadly missile, absorbed the full impact of the explosion in his body, thus protecting others from serious injury and possible death. Stouthearted and indomitable, he readily yielded his own chance of survival that his subordinate leaders might live to carry on the fight against a fanatic enemy. His superb courage, cool decisiveness, and valiant spirit of self-sacrifice in the face of certain death reflect the highest credit upon 2d Lt. Reem and the U.S. Naval Service. He gallantly gave his life for his country.

After the major confrontations at Unsan and Sudong, the level of conflict diminished. All U.S. units were sustaining significant casualties, but with the exception of the obviously intense engagement noted below, none reported exceptionally large numbers in any specific operation throughout most of the rest of November. In fact, on November 21, the 7th Division's 17th Infantry even advanced to the Yalu River at Hyesan, north of the 41st Parallel, with almost no losses.

Table 33 — 19th Infantry Regiment, near Chonghyon

	KIA	WIA	POW Returned	POW Died	MIA Returned	MIA Died	Unit Total
19th Inf, 24th Inf Div 11/04/–11/05/50	69	79	58	22	1	4	233

The intensity of this engagement is graphically illustrated in the Medal of Honor award to Cpl. Mitchell Red Cloud, Jr. of the 19th Infantry.

MEDAL OF HONOR: MITCHELL RED CLOUD

Awarded to: Corporal Mitchell Red Cloud, Jr., Merrilan WI, U S. Army, Company E, 19th Infantry Regiment, 24th Infantry Division. Near Chonghyon, Korea, 5 November 1950.

> Cpl. Red Cloud, Company E, distinguished himself by conspicuous gallantry and intrepidity above and beyond the call of duty in action against the enemy. From his position on the point of a ridge immediately in front of the company command post he was the first to detect the approach of the Chinese Communist forces and give the alarm as the enemy charged from a brush-covered area less than 100 feet from him. Springing up he delivered devastating pointblank automatic rifle fire into the advancing enemy. His accurate and intense fire checked this assault and gained time

I. The Peninsular War

for the company to consolidate its defense. With utter fearlessness he maintained his firing position until severely wounded by enemy fire. Refusing assistance he pulled himself to his feet and wrapping his arm around a tree continued his deadly fire again, until he was fatally wounded. This heroic act stopped the enemy from overrunning his company's position and gained time for reorganization and evacuation of the wounded. Cpl. Red Cloud's dauntless courage and gallant self-sacrifice reflects the highest credit upon himself and upholds the esteemed traditions of the U.S. Army.

Total U.S. Army casualties for the period October 25 through November 24 are shown in Table 34.

Table 34 — Before the CCF Counteroffensive, All U.S. Army Units

	KIA	WIA	POW Returned	POW Died	MIA Returned	MIA Died	Unit Total
1st Cavalry Division	119	546	307	132	16	243	1363
2nd Infantry Division	65	252	6	1	1	7	332
3rd Infantry Division	25	83	6			3	117
7th Infantry Division	39	179		1	1	4	224
24th Infantry Division	95	221	67	27	3	10	423
25th Infantry Division	84	81	6	5	3	6	185
29th Inf. Regt./RCT	10	19	4	2		1	36
5th RCT	24	134		1		2	161
Other units							
2nd Chem Bn Mortar	3	18	7	5		15	48
96th FA Bn	8	17				3	28
70th Arm Cav Bn	4	9	1		2	5	21
Others (83)	36	96	8	5	2	5	152
Totals 10/25–11/24/50	521	1684	412	179	28	304	3128

U.S. Marines

Total marine fatalities in the period were 162, plus 7 Navy ground casualties that are assumed to have been corpsmen. Three of the marine fatalities were pilots lost in fixed-wing air crashes over land. In the case of three others (one officer on November 14 and two enlisted men on November 21), the cause was identified simply as "aircraft loss/crash not at sea, ground casualty."

U.S. Navy

All Navy losses in the period, with the exception of the corpsmen listed with the marines, were the result of air crashes. These are summarized in Table 35.

Table 35 — Before the CCF Counteroffensive, U.S. Navy

Fixed Wing Crash Over Land	
Pilot, Killed in Action	3
Aircrew, Killed in Action	1
Aircrew, Died While Missing	5
Fixed Wing Crash At Sea	
Pilot, Killed in Action	2
Aircrew, Died While Missing	1
Total 10/25–11/24/50	12

U.S. Air Force

Air Force fatalities in the period totaled 31. They are summarized in Table 36.

Table 36 — Before the CCF Counteroffensive, U.S. Air Force

Fixed Wing Crash Over Land	
Pilot, Killed in Action	7
Pilot, Died While Missing	8
Pilot, Died of Wounds	1
Pilot, Died in Captivity	2
Aircrew, Killed in Action	7
Aircrew, Died While Missing	3
Aircrew, Died in Captivity	3
Total 10/25–11/24/50	31

Difficult as the times had been for UN forces in the month since the CCF entered the war, things were about to get worse — much worse.

CCF Counteroffensive in North Korea

On November 25, 1950, the Chinese mounted an all-out effort to push the "invaders" out of North Korea. Placed once again on the defensive, UN forces found themselves badly outnumbered and badly unprepared for the onslaught they encountered. For the next three weeks, seven U.S. divisions (and two RCTs*) struggled in a losing battle to hold on to the territory they had so rapidly occupied the previous two months. Battle losses in these units were substantial. Casualties in U.S. Army units are shown in Figure 10.

Particularly noteworthy in this figure, in addition to the their very high totals, is the large proportion of fatalities among the casualties, even when total casualties were relatively low.

In a repeat of the first 40 days of the war, American units were being overrun and GIs were being captured and left unaccounted for in very large numbers. Among the 9,127 total casualties sustained by Army units in this battle, 2,262 were captured and 1,301 were reported missing, never found and declared dead. Following are the stories these fallen GIs have to tell about the part each of their units played in this battle.

2nd Infantry Division

Among the nine major U.S. units in this battle, the Army's 2nd Infantry Division sustained by far the greatest number of casualties, reporting almost half the total number recorded for all Army units. Figure 11 shows the pattern of casualties in this division during the three weeks of the battle.

Comparing Figure 11 with Figure 10, it can be seen that, on several of the highest casualty days in the battle, 2nd Division units accounted for a majority of all the

---

*According to information available in the database, the 29th Infantry Regt/RCT experienced its last reported losses on 11/11/50. Thereafter, it ceased to exist as a fighting unit in the Korea War.

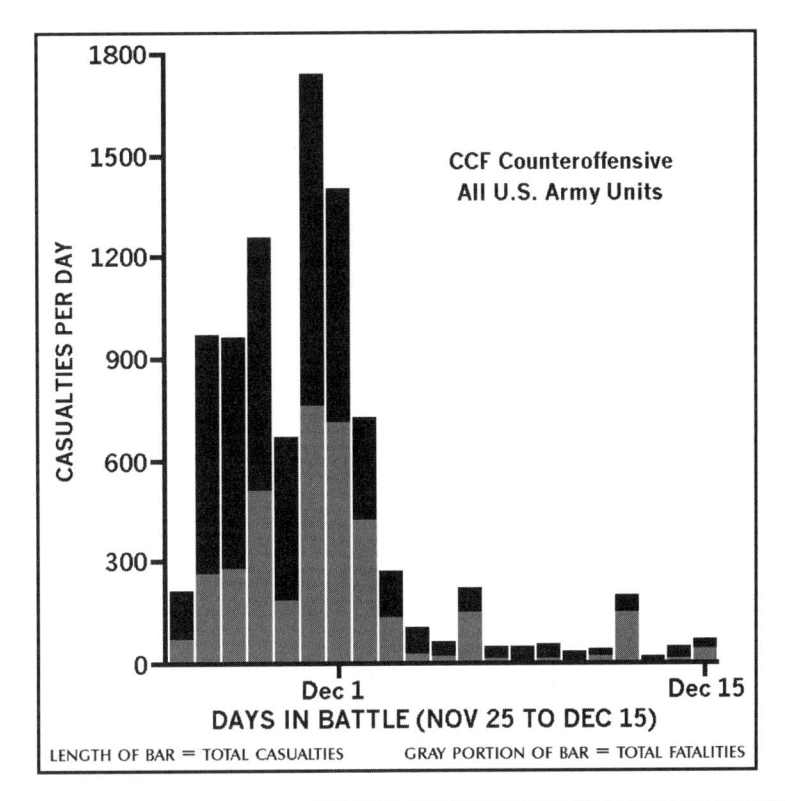

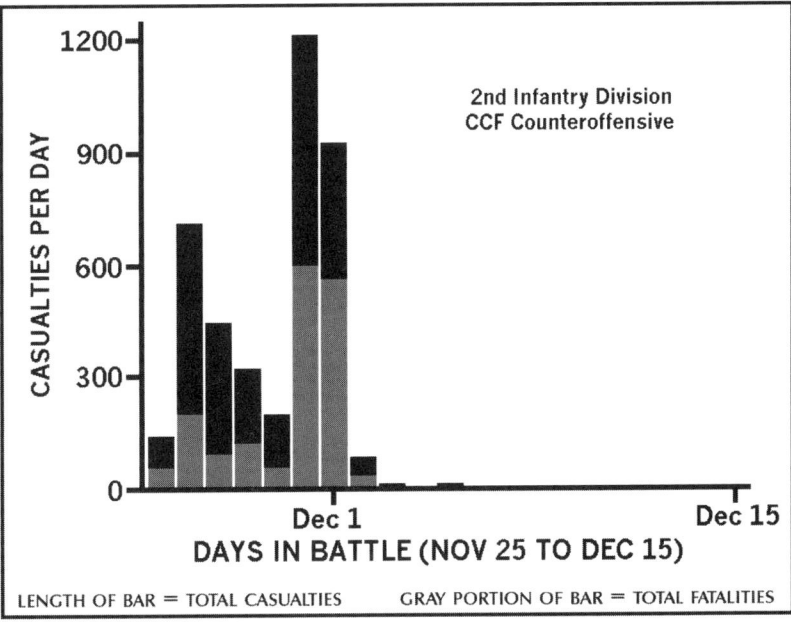

Figure 10. (*top*) Daily casualties for all U.S. Army units during the 1950 CCF counteroffensive. Figure 11. (*bottom*) Daily casualties for the 2nd Infantry Division during the 1950 CCF counteroffensive.

losses. Listed below is a summary of how those losses were distributed among division units on the three days with the largest number of casualties. Of particular interest in these table is the very high level of losses by divisional supporting units.

Table 37 — CCF Counteroffensive, 2nd Infantry Division

	KIA	WIA	POW Returned	POW Died	MIA Returned	MIA Died	Unit Total
11/26/50							
9th Inf, 2nd Div	14	156	36	46		48	300
23rd Inf, 2nd Div	31	130	2			4	167
38th Inf, 2nd Div	16	126	2	8	4	14	170
Other Units (10)	9	50	1	1		2	63
Total	70	462	41	55	4	68	700
11/30/50							
9th Inf, 2nd Div	17	70	42	40	2	51	222
23rd Inf, 2nd Div	15	43	22	14		13	107
38th Inf, 2nd Div	23	166	8	8	4	25	234
38th FA Bn, 2nd Inf Div	35	6	112	141	2	36	332
2nd Engr Bn, 2nd Inf Div	16	13	54	82		16	181
37th FA Bn, 2nd Inf Div	5	7	3	7		8	30
503rd FA Bn, 2nd Inf Div	11	15					26
Other Units (12)	9	36	7	10		7	69
Total	131	356	248	302	8	156	1201
12/1/50							
9th Inf, 2nd Div	24	8	75	117		29	253
23rd Inf, 2nd Div	2	8	1				11
38th Inf, 2nd Div	3	32	2		5	2	44
503rd FA Bn, 2nd Inf Div	22	9	98	112		40	281
82nd AAA Bn, 2nd Inf Div	13	1	78	79		16	187
2nd Engr Bn, 2nd Inf Div	6	3	36	57		18	120
Other Units (8)	5	11	2	4		1	23
Total	75	72	292	369	5	106	919

The chronology specifically identifies the last two days listed here, November 30 and December 1, as the battle of Kunu-ri, although it is quite obvious from the numbers that there had been plenty of battling taking place on the days leading up to that encounter. On one of those days, the Medal of Honor was awarded Sgt. John Pittman of the 23rd Infantry for his heroic actions. Sgt Pittman already had one Purple Heart, having been out of action for a month after being wounded in the Battle of the Pusan Perimeter.

MEDAL OF HONOR: JOHN A. PITTMAN

Awarded to: Sergeant John A. Pittman, Carrolton, MS, U.S. Army, Company C, 23d Infantry Regiment, 2d Infantry Division. Near Kujangdong, Korea, 26 November 1950.

> Sgt. Pittman, distinguished himself by conspicuous gallantry and intrepidity above and beyond the call of duty in action against the enemy. He volunteered to lead his squad in a counterattack to regain commanding terrain lost in an earlier engagement. Moving aggressively forward in the face

of intense artillery, mortar, and small-arms fire he was wounded by mortar fragments. Disregarding his wounds he continued to lead and direct his men in a bold advance against the hostile standpoint. During this daring action, an enemy grenade was thrown in the midst of his squad endangering the lives of his comrades. Without hesitation, Sgt. Pittman threw himself on the grenade and absorbed its burst with his body. When a medical aid man reached him, his first request was to be informed as to how many of his men were hurt. This intrepid and selfless act saved several of his men from death or serious injury and was an inspiration to the entire command. Sgt. Pittman's extraordinary heroism reflects the highest credit upon himself and is in keeping with the esteemed traditions of the military service.

Sgt. Pittman was not killed in the action for which he received this award, but he was wounded seriously, evacuated to the United States and separated from the service in early 1951.

A summary of 2nd Infantry Division losses during the counteroffensive is shown in Table 38.

Table 38 — CCF Counteroffensive, All 2nd Division Losses

	KIA	WIA	POW Returned	POW Died	MIA Returned	MIA Died	Unit Total
9th Inf, 2nd Div	67	473	174	233	2	161	1110
23rd Inf, 2nd Div	64	264	36	19		25	408
38th Inf, 2nd Div	94	590	86	69	22	114	975
2nd Engr Bn, 2nd Inf Div	36	92	96	148		63	435
38th FA Bn, 2nd Inf Div	48	37	113	144	2	36	380
503rd FA Bn, 2nd Inf Div	37	36	99	113		40	325
82nd AAA Bn, 2nd Inf Div	17	10	79	79		18	203
37th FA Bn, 2nd Inf Div	5	35	4	9		8	61
72nd Tank Bn, 2nd Inf Div	1	19	5	5		3	33
Other Units (13)	11	65	13	14		11	114
Total 2nd Div 11/25–12/15/50	380	1621	705	833	26	479	4044

7th Infantry Division

The 7th Division was also badly battered in this engagement. Three periods during the three weeks of the battle are of particular interest. In the first, between November 28 and December 3, elements of the 31st and 32nd Regiments, and a number of supporting units, engaged the CCF in a costly battle east of the Chosin Reservoir. A summary of 7th Division losses in this battle is shown in the Table 39.

Table 39 — Chosin Reservoir, 7th Infantry Division

	KIA	WIA	POW Returned	POW Died	MIA Returned	MIA Died	Unit Total
17th Inf, 7th Inf Div	1	4					5
31st Inf, 7th Inf Div	175	271	121	35		118	720
32nd Inf, 7th Inf Div	120	196	51	24	2	234	627
57th FA Bn, 7th Inf Div	36	82	8				126
7th Med Bn, 7th Inf Div	3	2	1	1	1	2	10
Other 7th Div Units (6)	4	10	2		1	1	18
Total 11/28–12/03/50	339	565	183	60	4	355	1506

A measure of the intensity of the fighting in this battle can be found in the description of the actions of Lt. Col. Don Faith, for which he was awarded the Medal of Honor.

MEDAL OF HONOR: DON C. FAITH

Awarded to: Lieutenant Colonel Don C. Faith, Jr., Washington, IN, U.S. Army, commanding officer, 1st Battalion, 32d Infantry Regiment, 7th Infantry Division. Vicinity Hagaru-ri, Northern Korea, 27 November to 1 December 1950.

>Lt. Col. Faith, commanding 1st Battalion, distinguished himself conspicuously by gallantry and intrepidity in action above and beyond the call of duty in the area of the Chosin Reservoir. When the enemy launched a fanatical attack against his battalion, Lt. Col. Faith unhesitatingly exposed himself to heavy enemy fire as he moved about directing the action. When the enemy penetrated the positions, Lt. Col. Faith personally led counterattacks to restore the position. During an attack by his battalion to effect a junction with another U.S. unit, Lt. Col. Faith reconnoitered the route for, and personally directed, the first elements of his command across the ice-covered reservoir and then directed the movement of his vehicles which were loaded with wounded until all of his command had passed through the enemy fire. Having completed this he crossed the reservoir himself. Assuming command of the force his unit had joined he was given the mission of attacking to join friendly elements to the south. Lt. Col. Faith, although physically exhausted in the bitter cold, organized and launched an attack which was soon stopped by enemy fire. He ran forward under enemy small-arms and automatic weapons fire, got his men on their feet and personally led the fire attack as it blasted its way through the enemy ring. As they came to a hairpin curve, enemy fire from a roadblock again pinned the column down. Lt. Col. Faith organized a group of men and directed their attack on the enemy positions on the right flank. He then placed himself at the head of another group of men and in the face of direct enemy fire led an attack on the enemy roadblock, firing his pistol and throwing grenades. When he had reached a position approximately 30 yards from the roadblock he was mortally wounded, but continued to direct the attack until the roadblock was overrun. Throughout the 5 days of action Lt. Col. Faith gave no thought to his safety and did not spare himself. His presence each time in the position of greatest danger was an inspiration to his men. Also, the damage he personally inflicted firing from his position at the head of his men was of material assistance on several occasions. Lt. Col. Faith's outstanding gallantry and noble self-sacrifice above and beyond the call of duty reflect the highest honor on him and are in keeping with the highest traditions of the U.S. Army.

The second significant period of loss by a 7th Division unit was by the 57th FA Battalion on December 6. Obviously overrun in this encounter with the enemy, losses in the battalion were devastating, as indicated in Table 40.

Table 40 — 57th FA Battalion Overrun

12/06/50	KIA	WIA	POW Returned	POW Died	MIA Returned	MIA Died	Unit Total
57th FA Bn, 7th Inf Div	25	4	25	17		93	164
All other 7th Div units (5)	3	16				5	24
Total 7th Division	28	20	25	17		98	188

The 57th sustained three-fourths of all U.S. Army casualties that day and almost 90 percent of all fatalities.

The third engagement with significant 7th Division losses was on December 12, when one battalion of the 31st Infantry was decimated at Koto-ri.

Table 41 — Koto-ri, 31st Infantry Regiment

12/12/50	KIA	WIA	POW Returned	POW Died	MIA Returned	MIA Died	Unit Total
31st Inf, 7th Inf Div	22		27	10	1	111	171
All other 7th Div units (2)	1	2	1			3	7
Total 7th Division	23	2	28	10	1	114	178

To show how much of a disaster this engagement was for the men of the 31st, we need to look in more detail at the casualty types and dispositions indicated in the database for these records. Recall that, to limit the number of categories listed, some types and dispositions have been combined in the tables (see page 2). If we inspect the December 12th data in their full available detail, the following description emerges: Of 171 regimental casualties that day, all but one were either captured or reported missing. Among the missing, 111 were later declared dead (after the war was over), another 18 were recovered and confirmed as killed in action and one was found alive. Among the captured, 27 were later repatriated and 13 died in captivity, 3 of them as a result of their battle injuries and 10 listed simply as "died, non-battle." The one casualty that was neither captured nor missing, died later of his injuries.

Table 42 is an accounting of all 7th Division casualties during the three weeks of the 1950 CCF counteroffensive.

Table 42 — CCF Counteroffensive, All 7th Division Losses

	KIA	WIA	POW Returned	POW Died	MIA Returned	MIA Died	Unit Total
17th Inf, 7th Inf Div	1	9					10
31st Inf, 7th Inf Div	210	307	156	45	1	239	958
32nd Inf, 7th Inf Div	130	232	60	25	2	237	686
57th FA Bn, 7th Inf Div	63	98	36	17		93	307
48th FA Bn, 7th Inf Div	5	6		2		5	18
13th Engr Bn, 7th Inf Div	4	7				3	14
7th Med Bn, 7th Inf Div	3	2	1	1	1	2	10
Other 7th Div Units (7)	5	11	2		1	2	20
Total 7th Div 11/25–12/15/50	421	672	255	90	5	581	2024

25th Infantry Division

The majority of 25th Division casualties occurred in the first few days of the offensive, with three-fourths of them sustained in just three days, November 26–28. The kind of action the division experienced during those days is graphically recounted in the award of the Medal of Honor to Captain Reginald Desiderio of the 27th Infantry.

MEDAL OF HONOR: REGINALD B. DESIDERIO

Awarded to: Captain Reginald B. Desiderio, Gilroy, CA, U.S. Army, commanding officer, Company E, 27th Infantry Regiment, 25th Infantry Division. Near Ipsok, Korea, 27 November 1950.

> Capt. Desiderio distinguished himself by conspicuous gallantry and intrepidity at the repeated risk of his life above and beyond the call of duty. His company was given the mission of defending the command post of a task force against an enemy breakthrough. After personal reconnaissance during darkness and under intense enemy fire, he placed his men in defensive positions to repel an attack. Early in the action he was wounded, but refused evacuation and despite enemy fire continued to move among his men checking their positions and making sure that each element was prepared to receive the next attack. Again wounded, he continued to direct his men. By his inspiring leadership he encouraged them to hold their position. In the subsequent fighting when the fanatical enemy succeeded in penetrating the position, he personally charged them with carbine, rifle, and grenades, inflicting many casualties until he himself was mortally wounded. His men, spurred on by his intrepid example, repelled this final attack. Capt. Desiderio's heroic leadership, courageous and loyal devotion to duty, and his complete disregard for personal safety reflect the highest honor on him and are in keeping with the esteemed traditions of the U.S. Army.

Table 43 is an accounting of 25th Division casualties during the CCF counteroffensive.

Table 43 — CCF Counteroffensive, 25th Infantry Division

	KIA	WIA	POW Returned	POW Died	MIA Returned	MIA Died	Unit Total
24th Inf, 25th Inf Div	31	239	98	118	20	82	588
27th Inf, 25th Inf Div	36	154	4	3		14	211
35th Inf, 25th Inf Div	34	144	80	60	7	52	377
65th Engr Bn, 25th Inf Div	4	8	25	5		4	46
25th Recon Co, 25th Inf Div	3	18					21
8th FA Bn, 25th Inf Div		8	1			1	10
159th FA Bn, 25th Inf Div		6	1		1		8
25th Sig Co, 25th Inf Div		4	2			1	7
Other 25th Div Units (4)	4	9	1		1		15
Total 25th Div 11/25–12/15/50	**112**	**590**	**212**	**187**	**28**	**154**	**1283**

1st Cavalry Division

The 1st Cav. did not fare as badly in this battle as those divisions listed above, but their experience was by no means a picnic, particularly for the 5th Cavalry Regiment, which suffered most of its losses on one day, November 28. A summary of all 1st Cavalry Division losses in the CCF counteroffensive is shown in Table 44.

Table 44 — CCF Counteroffensive, 1st Cavalry Division

	KIA	WIA	POW Returned	POW Died	MIA Returned	MIA Died	Unit Total
5th Cav, 1st Cav Div	13	158	13	20	3	27	234
7th Cav, 1st Cav Div	44	109	15	1	2	2	173
8th Cav, 1st Cav Div	10	69	1			3	83
61st FA Bn, 1st Cav Div	3	22	1	1	1		28
Other 1st Cav Units (9)	5	11	3			1	20
Total 1st Cav 11/25/–12/15/50	75	369	33	22	7	32	538

3rd Infantry Division

Except for two days, losses in the 3rd Division were relatively consistent throughout the three weeks of the battle. On those two days, December 3 and 15, the 7th Infantry Regiment suffered more than half of its total casualties and over three-fourths of its total fatalities. Table 45 shows all casualties in the 3rd Division during the battle.

Table 45 — CCF Counteroffensive, 3rd Infantry Division

	KIA	WIA	POW Returned	POW Died	MIA Returned	MIA Died	Unit Total
7th Inf, 3rd Inf Div	38	123	19	13		60	253
15th Inf, 3rd Inf Div	23	90	2			14	129
65th Inf, 3rd Inf Div	5	27	10	1			43
10th Engr Bn, 3rd Inf Div	16	33				6	55
3rd AAA Bn, 3rd Inf Div	1	13					14
3rd Med Bn, 3rd Inf Div	2	1				4	7
64th Tank Bn, 3rd Inf Div	1	5	1				7
Other 3rd Div Units (7)	2	10	1	2		2	17
Total 3rd Div 11/25–12/15/50	86	303	34	16		86	525

Other Major Army Units

Losses in the two RCTs and the 24th Division during the Chinese Counteroffensive were considerably less than those in the divisions detailed above. An accounting of these losses is shown Table 46.

Table 46 — CCF Counteroffensive, Other Major Units

	KIA	WIA	POW Returned	POW Died	MIA Returned	MIA Died	Unit Total
187th RCT							
187th RCT	17	80	2	1		8	108
187th Supporting Units (3)	3	10			1		14
Total 187th RCT 11/25–12/15/50	20	90	2	1	1	8	122

(continued on next page)

Table 46 (*cont.*)

	KIA	WIA	POW Returned	POW Died	MIA Returned	MIA Died	Unit Total
5th RCT							
5th RCT	3	52	9	1	1	10	76
555th FA Bn		5					5
Total 5th RCT 11/25–12/15/50	3	57	9	1	1	10	81
24th Infantry Division							
21st Inf, 24th Inf Div	13	44					57
19th Inf, 24th Inf Div	2	31				1	34
34th Inf, 24th Inf Div		1				1	2
24th Med Bn, 24th Inf Div	5	12					17
70th Med Tk Bn, 24th Inf Div	5	11					16
Other 24th Div Units (5)	6	4					10
Total 24th Div 11/25–12/15/50	31	103				2	136

Non-divisional U.S. Army Units

A total of 73 non-divisional units reported casualties during the CCF Counteroffensive. Among those units was the headquarters of X Corps, which reported 22 casualties, including 16 fatalities. One of those fatalities was Lt. Col. John Page, whose exploits in delaying enemy advances earned him the Medal of Honor.

MEDAL OF HONOR: JOHN U.D. PAGE

Awarded to: Lieutenant Colonel John U. D. Page, St. Paul, MN, U.S. Army, X Corps Artillery, while attached to the 52d Transportation Truck Battalion. Near Chosin Reservoir, Korea, 29 November to 10 December 1950.

Lt. Col. Page, a member of X Corps Artillery, distinguished himself by conspicuous gallantry and intrepidity in action above and beyond the call of duty in a series of exploits. On 29 November, Lt. Col. Page left X Corps Headquarters at Hamhung with the mission of establishing traffic control on the main supply route to 1st Marine Division positions and those of some Army elements on the Chosin Reservoir plateau. Having completed his mission Lt. Col. Page was free to return to the safety of Hamhung but chose to remain on the plateau to aid an isolated signal station, thus being cut off with elements of the marine division. After rescuing his jeep driver by breaking up an ambush near a destroyed bridge Lt. Col. Page reached the lines of a surrounded marine garrison at Koto-ri. He then voluntarily developed and trained a reserve force of assorted army troops trapped with the marines. By exemplary leadership and tireless devotion he made an effective tactical unit available. In order that casualties might be evacuated, an airstrip was improvised on frozen ground partly outside of the Koto-ri defense perimeter which was continually under enemy attack. During 2 such attacks, Lt. Col. Page exposed himself on the airstrip to direct fire on the enemy, and twice mounted the rear deck of a tank, manning the machinegun on the turret to drive the enemy back into a no-man's-land. On 3 December while being flown low over enemy lines in a light observation plane, Lt. Col. Page dropped hand grenades on Chinese positions and sprayed foxholes with automatic fire from his carbine. After 10 days of constant fighting the marine and army units in the vicinity of the Chosin Reservoir had succeeded in gathering at the edge of the plateau and Lt. Col. Page was flown to Hamhung to arrange for artillery support of the beleaguered troops attempting to break out. Again Lt. Col. Page refused an opportunity to remain in safety and returned to give every assistance to his comrades. As the column slowly moved south Lt. Col. Page joined the rear guard. When it neared the entrance to a narrow pass it came under frequent attacks on both flanks. Mounting an abandoned tank Lt. Col. Page manned the machinegun, braved heavy return fire, and covered the passing vehicles until the danger diminished. Later when another attack threatened his section of the convoy, then in the middle of the pass, Lt. Col. Page took a machinegun to the hillside and delivered effective counterfire, remaining exposed while men and vehicles passed through the ambuscade. On the night of 10 December the convoy reached the bottom of the pass but was halted by a strong enemy force at the front and on both flanks. Deadly small-arms fire poured into the column. Realizing the danger to the column as it lay motionless, Lt. Col. Page fought his way to the head of the column and plunged forward into the heart of the hostile position. His intrepid action so surprised the enemy that their ranks became disordered and suffered heavy casualties. Heedless of his safety, as he had been throughout the preceding 10 days, Lt. Col. Page remained forward, fiercely engaging the enemy single-handed until mortally wounded. By his valiant and aggressive spirit Lt. Col. Page enabled friendly forces to stand off the enemy. His outstanding courage, unswerving devotion to duty, and supreme self-sacrifice reflect great credit upon Lt. Col. Page and are in the highest tradition of the military service.

A summary of total losses in U.S. Army non-divisional units during the CCF counteroffensive is shown in Table 47

Table 47 — CCF Counteroffensive, Non-divisional Units

	KIA	WIA	POW Returned	POW Died	MIA Returned	MIA Died	Unit Total
15th AAA Bn	18	22	8	4		20	72
2nd Chem Bn, Mortar	3	17	4	3	1	3	31
89th Arm Cav Bn	4	15	3	1		5	28
8213th Misc Units (8th Ranger Co)		14				8	22
Hq 10th Corps	3	4			2	13	22
17th FA Bn	1	18					19
377th Transp Co, Truck	3	7	5	1		1	17
4th Signal Bn, Corps	1	13					14
8668th Mil Missions Commissions		1	3	5			9
8202nd Mil Missions Commissions	1	2	1	2			6
Other units (63)	21	91	9	1	4	8	134
Total Non-div 11/25–12/15/50	55	204	33	17	7	58	374

A summary of all U.S. Army combat losses in the CCF 1950 counteroffensive is shown in the Table 48.

Table 48 — CCF Counteroffensive, All U.S. Army Units

	KIA	WIA	POW Returned	POW Died	MIA Returned	MIA Died	Unit Total
2nd Infantry Division	380	1621	705	833	26	479	4044
7th Infantry Division	421	672	255	90	5	581	2024
25th Infantry Division	112	590	212	187	28	154	1283
1st Cavalry Division	75	369	33	22	7	32	538
3rd Infantry Division	86	303	34	16		86	525
24th Infantry Division	31	103				2	136
187th RCT	20	90	2	1	1	8	122
5th RCT	3	57	9	1	1	10	81
Non-divisional Units	55	204	33	17	7	58	374
Total U.S. Army 11/25–12/15/50	1183	4009	1283	1167	75	1410	9127

1st Marine Division

The 1st Marine Division sustained a total of 763 fatalities in the three weeks of the CCF counteroffensive. Of these, three were pilots lost in fixed wing crashes over land, 23 were reported missing, never found and declared dead and two died in captivity. Figure 12 shows the pattern of marine losses by day during the action.

As Figure 12 indicates, 15 U.S. Naval personnel were killed in ground action in this period and are presumed to have been corpsmen serving with the marines. Four of these men were reported missing, never found and declared dead.

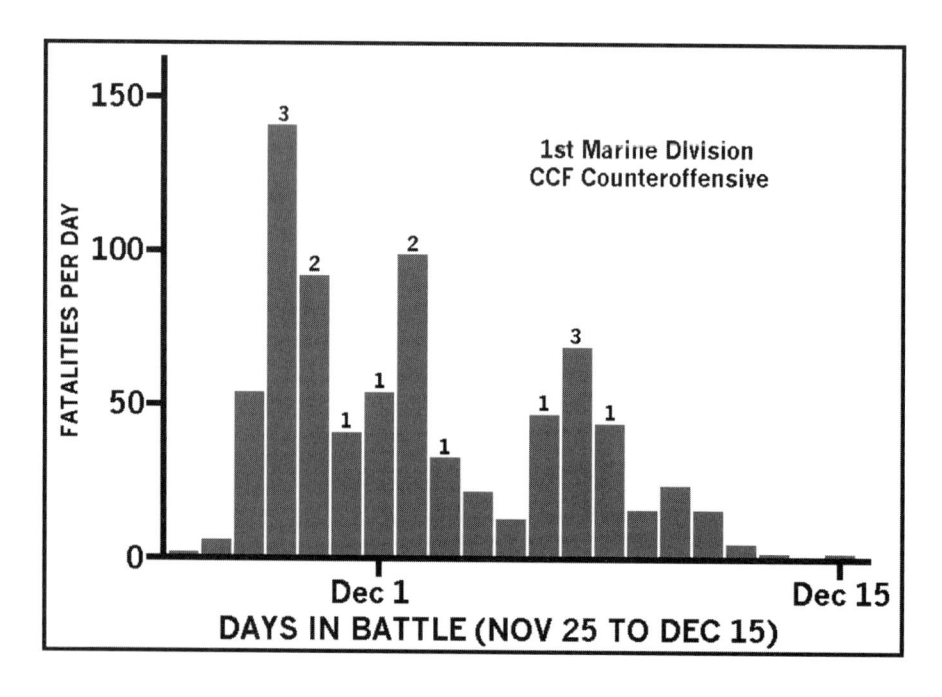

Figure 12. Daily fatalities for the 1st Marine Division during the 1950 CCF counteroffensive. The numbers over the bars on some dates indicate the number of presumed Navy corpsmen killed in ground action on those days.

Most of the losses by the 1st Marine Division were sustained as they attempted to escape encirclement by CCF forces west of the Chosin Reservoir and fight their way south to Hungnam, where they were evacuated by sea. In this battle, ten Medals of Honor were awarded to marines. Their awards help describe the intensity of the conflict.

Medal of Honor: Frank N. Mitchell

Awarded to: First Lieutenant Frank N. Mitchell, Roaring Springs, TX, U.S. Marine Corps, Company A, 1st Battalion, 7th Marines, 1st Marine Division (Rein.). Near Hansan-ni, Korea, 26 November 1950.

> For conspicuous gallantry and intrepidity at the risk of his life above and beyond the call of duty as leader of a rifle platoon of Company A, in action against enemy aggressor forces. Leading his platoon in point position during a patrol by his company through a thickly wooded and snow-covered area in the vicinity of Hansan-ni, 1st Lt. Mitchell acted immediately when the enemy suddenly opened fire at pointblank range, pinning down his forward elements and inflicting numerous casualties in his ranks. Boldly dashing to the front under blistering fire from automatic weapons and small arms, he seized an automatic rifle from one of the wounded men and effectively trained it against the attackers and, when his ammunition was expended, picked up and hurled grenades with deadly accuracy, at the same time directing and encouraging his men in driving the outnumbering enemy from his position. Maneuvering to set up a defense when the enemy furiously counterattacked to the front and left flank, 1st Lt. Mitchell, despite wounds sustained early in the action, reorganized his platoon under the devastating fire, and spearheaded a fierce hand-to-hand struggle to repulse the onslaught. Asking for volunteers to assist in searching for and evacuating the wounded, he personally led a party of litter bearers through the hostile lines in growing darkness and, although suffering intense pain from multiple wounds, stormed ahead and waged a single-handed battle against the enemy, successfully covering the withdrawal of his men before he was fatally struck down by a burst of small-arms fire. Stouthearted and indomitable in the face of tremendous odds, 1st Lt. Mitchell, by his fortitude, great personal valor and extraordinary heroism, saved the lives of several marines and inflicted heavy casualties among the aggressors. His unyielding courage throughout reflects the highest credit upon himself and the U.S. Naval Service. He gallantly gave his life for his country.

Medal of Honor: Robert S. Kennemore

Awarded to: Staff Sergeant Robert S. Kennemore, Greenville, SC, U.S. Marine Corps, Company E, 2d Battalion, 7th Marines, 1st Marine Division (Rein). North of Yudam-ni, Korea, 27 and 28 November 1950.

> For conspicuous gallantry and intrepidity at the risk of his life above and beyond the call of duty as leader of a machinegun section in Company E, in action against enemy aggressor forces. With the company's defensive perimeter overrun by a numerically superior hostile force during a savage

night attack north of Yudam-ni and his platoon commander seriously wounded, S/Sgt. Kennemore unhesitatingly assumed command, quickly reorganized the unit and directed the men in consolidating the position. When an enemy grenade landed in the midst of a machinegun squad, he bravely placed his foot on the missile and, in the face of almost certain death, personally absorbed the full force of the explosion to prevent injury to his fellow marines. By his indomitable courage, outstanding leadership and selfless efforts in behalf of his comrades, S/Sgt. Kennemore was greatly instrumental in driving the enemy from the area and upheld the highest traditions of the U.S. Naval Service.

Medal of Honor: William E. Barber

Awarded to: Captain William E. Barber, West Liberty, KY, U.S. Marine Corps, commanding officer, Company F, 2d Battalion 7th Marines, 1st Marine Division (Rein.). Chosin Reservoir area, Korea, 28 November to 2 December 1950.

For conspicuous gallantry and intrepidity at the risk of his life above and beyond the call of duty as commanding officer of Company F in action against enemy aggressor forces. Assigned to defend a 3-mile mountain pass along the division's main supply line and commanding the only route of approach in the march from Yudam-ni to Hagaru-ri, Capt. Barber took position with his battle-weary troops and, before nightfall, had dug in and set up a defense along the frozen, snow-covered hillside. When a force of estimated regimental strength savagely attacked during the night, inflicting heavy casualties and finally surrounding his position following a bitterly fought 7-hour conflict, Capt. Barber, after repulsing the enemy gave assurance that he could hold if supplied by airdrops and requested permission to stand fast when orders were received by radio to fight his way back to a relieving force after 2 reinforcing units had been driven back under fierce resistance in their attempts to reach the isolated troops. Aware that leaving the position would sever contact with the 8,000 marines trapped at Yudam-ni and jeopardize their chances of joining the 3,000 more awaiting their arrival in Hagaru-ri for the continued drive to the sea, he chose to risk loss of his command rather than sacrifice more men if the enemy seized control and forced a renewed battle to regain the position, or abandon his many wounded who were unable to walk. Although severely wounded in the leg in the early morning of the 29th, Capt. Barber continued to maintain personal control, often moving up and down the lines on a stretcher to direct the defense and consistently encouraging and inspiring his men to supreme efforts despite the staggering opposition. Waging desperate battle throughout 5 days and 6 nights of repeated onslaughts launched by the fanatical aggressors, he and his heroic command accounted for approximately 1,000 enemy dead in this epic stand in bitter subzero weather, and when the company was relieved only 82 of his original 220 men were able to walk away from the position so valiantly defended against insuperable odds. His profound faith and courage, great personal valor, and unwavering fortitude were decisive factors in the successful withdrawal of the division from the deathtrap in the Chosin Reservoir sector and reflect the highest credit upon Capt. Barber, his intrepid officers and men, and the U.S. Naval Service.

Medal of Honor: Hector A. Cafferata

Awarded To: Private Hector A. Cafferata, Jr., Dover, NJ, U.S. Marine Corps Reserve, Company F, 2d Battalion, 7th Marines, 1st Marine Division (Rein.). Korea, 28 November 1950.

>For conspicuous gallantry and intrepidity at the risk of his life above and beyond the call of duty while serving as a rifleman with Company F, in action against enemy aggressor forces. When all the other members of his fire team became casualties, creating a gap in the lines, during the initial phase of a vicious attack launched by a fanatical enemy of regimental strength against his company's hill position, Pvt. Cafferata waged a lone battle with grenades and rifle fire as the attack gained momentum and the enemy threatened penetration through the gap and endangered the integrity of the entire defensive perimeter. Making a target of himself under the devastating fire from automatic weapons, rifles, grenades, and mortars, he maneuvered up and down the line and delivered accurate and effective fire against the onrushing force, killing 15, wounding many more, and forcing the others to withdraw so that reinforcements could move up and consolidate the position. Again fighting desperately against a renewed onslaught later that same morning when a hostile grenade landed in a shallow entrenchment occupied by wounded marines, Pvt. Cafferata rushed into the gully under heavy fire, seized the deadly missile in his right hand and hurled it free of his comrades before it detonated, severing part of 1 finger and seriously wounding him in the right hand and arm. Courageously ignoring the intense pain, he staunchly fought on until he was struck by a sniper's bullet and forced to submit to evacuation for medical treatment Stouthearted and indomitable, Pvt. Cafferata, by his fortitude, great personal valor, and dauntless perseverance in the face of almost certain death, saved the lives of several of his fellow marines and contributed essentially to the success achieved by his company in maintaining its defensive position against tremendous odds. His extraordinary heroism throughout was in keeping with the highest traditions of the U.S. Naval Service.

Medal of Honor: William B. Baugh

Awarded to: Private First Class William B. Baugh, Harrison, OH, U.S. Marine Corps, Company G, 3d Battalion, 1st Marine, 1st Marine Division (Rein.). Along road from Koto-ri to Hagaru-ri, Korea, 29 November 1950.

>For conspicuous gallantry and intrepidity at the risk of his life above and beyond the call of duty while serving as a member of an antitank assault squad attached to Company G, during a nighttime enemy attack against a motorized column. Acting instantly when a hostile hand grenade landed in his truck as he and his squad prepared to alight and assist in the repulse of an enemy force delivering intense automatic-weapons and grenade fire from deeply entrenched and well-concealed roadside positions, Pfc. Baugh quickly shouted a warning to the other men in the vehicle and, unmindful of his personal safety, hurled himself upon the deadly missile, thereby saving his comrades from serious injury or possible death. Sustaining severe wounds from which he died a short time afterward, Pfc. Baugh, by his superb courage and valiant spirit of self-sacrifice, upheld

the highest traditions of the U.S. Naval Service. He gallantly gave his life for his country.

MEDAL OF HONOR: REGINALD R. MYERS

Awarded to: Major Reginald R. Myers, Boise, ID, U.S. Marine Corps, 3d Battalion, 1st Marines, 1st Marine Division, (Rein.). Near Hagaru-ri, Korea, 29 November 1950.

> For conspicuous gallantry and intrepidity at the risk of his life above and beyond the call of duty as executive officer of the 3d Battalion, in action against enemy aggressor forces. Assuming command of a composite unit of Army and Marine service and headquarters elements totaling approximately 250 men, during a critical stage in the vital defense of the strategically important military base at Hagaru-ri, Maj. Myers immediately initiated a determined and aggressive counterattack against a well-entrenched and cleverly concealed enemy force numbering an estimated 4,000. Severely handicapped by a lack of trained personnel and experienced leaders in his valiant efforts to regain maximum ground prior to daylight, he persisted in constantly exposing himself to intense, accurate, and sustained hostile fire in order to direct and supervise the employment of his men and to encourage and spur them on in pressing the attack. Inexorably moving forward up the steep, snow-covered slope with his depleted group in the face of apparently insurmountable odds, he concurrently directed artillery and mortar fire with superb skill and although losing 170 of his men during 14 hours of raging combat in subzero temperatures, continued to reorganize his unit and spearhead the attack which resulted in 600 enemy killed and 500 wounded. By his exceptional and valorous leadership throughout, Maj. Myers contributed directly to the success of his unit in restoring the perimeter. His resolute spirit of self-sacrifice and unfaltering devotion to duty enhance and sustain the highest traditions of the U.S. Naval Service.

MEDAL OF HONOR: CARL L. SITTER

Awarded to: Captain Carl L. Sitter, Pueblo, CO, U.S. Marine Corps, Company G, 3d Battalion, 1st Marines, 1st Marine Division (Rein.). Hagaru-ri, Korea, 29 and 30 November 1950.

> For conspicuous gallantry and intrepidity at the risk of his life above and beyond the call of duty as commanding officer of Company G, in action against enemy aggressor forces. Ordered to break through enemy-infested territory to reinforce his battalion the morning of 29 November, Capt. Sitter continuously exposed himself to enemy fire as he led his company forward and, despite 25 percent casualties suffered m the furious action, succeeded in driving through to his objective. Assuming the responsibility of attempting to seize and occupy a strategic area occupied by a hostile force of regiment strength deeply entrenched on a snow-covered hill commanding the entire valley southeast of the town, as well as the line of march of friendly troops withdrawing to the south, he reorganized his depleted

units the following morning and boldly led them up the steep, frozen hillside under blistering fire, encouraging and redeploying his troops as casualties occurred and directing forward platoons as they continued the drive to the top of the ridge. During the night when a vastly outnumbering enemy launched a sudden, vicious counterattack, setting the hill ablaze with mortar, machinegun, and automatic-weapons fire and taking a heavy toll in troops, Capt. Sitter visited each foxhole and gun position, coolly deploying and integrating reinforcing units consisting of service personnel unfamiliar with infantry tactics into a coordinated combat team and instilling in every man the will and determination to hold his position at all costs. With the enemy penetrating his lines in repeated counterattacks which often required hand-to-hand combat, and, on one occasion infiltrating to the command post with handgrenades, he fought gallantly with his men in repulsing and killing the fanatic attackers in each encounter. Painfully wounded in the face, arms, and chest by bursting grenades, he staunchly refused to be evacuated and continued to fight on until a successful defense of the area was assured with a loss to the enemy of more than 50 percent dead, wounded, and captured. His valiant leadership, superb tactics, and great personal valor throughout 36 hours of bitter combat reflect the highest credit upon Capt. Sitter and the U.S. Naval Service.

Medal of Honor: Raymond G. Davis

Awarded to: Lieutenant Colonel Raymond G. Davis, Atlanta, GA, U.S. Marine Corps commanding officer, 1st Battalion, 7th Marines, 1st Marine Division (Rein.). Vicinity Hagaru-ri, Korea, 1 through 4 December 1950..

For conspicuous gallantry and intrepidity at the risk of his life above and beyond the call of duty as commanding officer of the 1st Battalion, in action against enemy aggressor forces. Although keenly aware that the operation involved breaking through a surrounding enemy and advancing 8 miles along primitive icy trails in the bitter cold with every passage disputed by a savage and determined foe, Lt. Col. Davis boldly led his battalion into the attack in a daring attempt to relieve a beleaguered rifle company and to seize, hold, and defend a vital mountain pass controlling the only route available for 2 marine regiments in danger of being cut off by numerically superior hostile forces during their re-deployment to the port of Hungnam. When the battalion immediately encountered strong opposition from entrenched enemy forces commanding high ground in the path of the advance, he promptly spearheaded his unit in a fierce attack up the steep, ice-covered slopes in the face of withering fire and, personally leading the assault groups in a hand-to-hand encounter, drove the hostile troops from their positions, rested his men, and reconnoitered the area under enemy fire to determine the best route for continuing the mission. Always in the thick of the fighting Lt. Col. Davis led his battalion over 3 successive ridges in the deep snow in continuous attacks against the enemy and, constantly inspiring and encouraging his men throughout the night, brought his unit to a point within 1,500 yards of the surrounded rifle company by daybreak. Although knocked to the ground when a shell fragment struck his helmet and 2 bullets pierced his clothing, he arose and fought his way forward at the head of his men until he reached the isolated marines. On the following morning, he bravely led his battalion in securing the vital mountain pass from a strongly entrenched and numerically superior hostile force, carrying all his wounded with him, including 22 litter cases and numerous ambulatory patients. Despite repeated savage and heavy assaults by the enemy, he stubbornly held the vital terrain until the 2 regiments of the division had deployed through the pass and, on the morning of 4 December, led his battalion into Hagaru-ri intact. By his superb leadership, outstanding courage, and brilliant tactical ability, Lt. Col. Davis was directly instrumental in saving the beleaguered rifle company from complete annihilation and enabled the 2 marine regiments to escape possible destruction. His valiant devotion to duty and unyielding fighting spirit in the face of almost insurmountable odds enhance and sustain the highest traditions of the U.S. Naval Service.

Medal of Honor: William G. Windrich

Awarded to: Staff Sergeant William G. Windrich, Hammond, IN, U.S. Marine Corps, Company I, 3d Battalion, 5th Marines, 1st Marine Division (Rein.). Vicinity of Yudam-ni, Korea, 1 December 1950.

For conspicuous gallantry and intrepidity at the risk of his life above and beyond the call of duty as a platoon sergeant of Company I, in action against enemy aggressor forces the night of 1 December 1950. Promptly organizing a squad of men when the enemy launched a sudden, vicious counterattack against the forward elements of his company's position, rendering it untenable, S/Sgt. Windrich, armed with a carbine, spearheaded the assault to the top of the knoll immediately confronting the overwhelming forces and, under shattering hostile automatic-weapons, mortar, and grenade fire, directed effective fire to hold back the attackers and cover the withdrawal of our troops to commanding ground. With 7 of his men struck down during the furious action and himself wounded in the head by a bursting grenade, he made his way to his company's position and, organizing a small group of volunteers, returned with them to evacuate the wounded and dying from the frozen hillside, staunchly refusing medical attention himself. Immediately redeploying the remainder of his troops, S/Sgt. Windrich placed them on the left flank of the defensive sector before the enemy again attacked in force. Wounded in the leg during the bitter fight that followed, he bravely fought on with his men, shouting words of encouragement and directing their fire until the attack was repelled. Refusing evacuation although unable to stand, he still continued to direct his platoon in setting up defensive positions until weakened by the bitter cold, excessive loss of blood, and severe pain, he lapsed into unconsciousness and died. His valiant leadership, fortitude, and courageous fighting spirit against tremendous odds served to inspire others to heroic endeavor in holding the objective and reflect the highest credit upon S/Sgt. Windrich and the U.S. Naval Service. He gallantly gave his life for his country.

Medal of Honor: James E. Johnson

Awarded to: Sergeant James E. Johnson, Washington, DC, U.S. Marine Corps, Company J, 3d Battalion, 7th Marines, 1st Marine Division (Rein.). Yudam-ni, Korea, 2 December 1950 (declared missing in action on 2 December 1950, and killed in action as of 2 November 1953).

For conspicuous gallantry and intrepidity at the risk of his life above and beyond the call of duty while serving as a squad leader in a provisional rifle platoon composed of artillerymen and attached to Company J, in action against enemy aggressor forces. Vastly outnumbered by a well-entrenched and cleverly concealed enemy force wearing the uniforms of friendly troops and attacking his platoon's open and unconcealed positions, Sgt. Johnson unhesitatingly took charge of his platoon in the absence of the leader and, exhibiting great personal valor in the face of a heavy barrage of hostile fire, coolly proceeded to move about among his men, shouting words of encouragement and inspiration and skillfully directing their fire. Ordered to displace his platoon during the fire fight, he immediately placed himself in an extremely hazardous position from which he could provide covering fire for his men. Fully aware that his voluntary action meant either certain death or capture to himself, he courageously continued to provide effective cover for his men and was last observed in a wounded condition single-handedly engaging enemy troops in close handgrenade and hand-to-hand fighting. By his valiant and inspiring leadership, Sgt. Johnson was directly responsible for the successful completion of the platoon's displacement and the saving of many lives. His dauntless fighting spirit and unfaltering devotion to duty in the face of terrific odds reflect the highest credit upon himself and the U.S. Naval Service.

U.S. Navy

All losses of U.S. Naval personnel during the counteroffensive, other than the corpsmen listed above, were the result of air crashes over land. A summary of those losses are shown in Table 49.

Table 49 — CCF Counteroffensive, U.S. Navy

Helicopter Crash Over Land	
Pilot, Died While Missing	1
Fixed Wing Crash Over Land	
Pilot, Died While Missing	1
Aircrew, Killed in Action	1
Aircrew, Died While Missing*	1
Total 11/25–12/15/50	4

The individual above, identified with the (*) was Lt. (j.g.) Jesse L. Brown of Hattiesburg, MS, who was shot down on December 4, 1950. Because Lt. Brown was the only Navy airman lost on or near this date, it can be assumed that he was the officer whose attempted rescue was the subject of the following Medal of Honor award.

MEDAL OF HONOR: THOMAS JEROME HUDNER

Awarded to: Lieutenant (j.g.) Thomas Jerome Hudner, Jr., Fall River, MA, U.S. Navy, pilot in Fighter Squadron 32, attached to USS *Leyte*. Chosin Reservoir area of Korea, 4 December 1950.

For conspicuous gallantry and intrepidity at the risk of his life above and beyond the call of duty as a pilot in Fighter Squadron 32, while attempting to rescue a squadron mate whose plane struck by antiaircraft fire and trailing smoke, was forced down behind enemy lines. Quickly maneuvering to circle the downed pilot and protect him from enemy troops infesting the area, Lt. (j.g.) Hudner risked his life to save the injured flier who was trapped alive in the burning wreckage. Fully aware of the extreme danger in landing on the rough mountainous terrain and the scant hope of escape or survival in subzero temperature, he put his plane down skillfully in a deliberate wheels-up landing in the presence of enemy troops. With his bare hands, he packed the fuselage with snow to keep the flames away from the pilot and struggled to pull him free. Unsuccessful in this, he returned to his crashed aircraft and radioed other airborne planes, requesting that a helicopter be dispatched with an ax and fire extinguisher. He then remained on the spot despite the continuing danger from enemy action and, with the assistance of the rescue pilot, renewed a desperate but unavailing battle against time, cold, and flames. Lt. (j.g.) Hudner's exceptionally valiant action and selfless devotion to a shipmate sustain and enhance the highest traditions of the U.S. Naval Service.

U.S. Air Force

Fatalities in the Air Force during the battle are summarized in Table 50.

Table 50 — CCF Counteroffensive, U.S. Air Force

Fixed Wing Crash Over Land	
Pilot, Killed in Action	5
Pilot, Died While Missing	14
Aircrew, Killed in Action	3
Air Crew, Died of Wounds	1
Aircrew, Died While Missing	11
Air Crew, Died in Captivity	1
Non-Aircrew, Killed in Action	1
Non-Aircrew, Died While Missing	4
Ground Casualty	
Multiple Fragmentation Wounds	
Died of Wounds	1
Total 11/25–12/15/50	41

Time to Regroup

Clearly, the CCF counteroffensive had been costly for both sides, and neither side had either the resources or the opportunity for continued combat at the intensity of the past three weeks. UN forces pulled back to defensive positions along the Imjin River north of Seoul and the CCF appeared content to spend some time licking its own wounds. The level of U.S. casualties indicates that the Korean War cranked down substantially for the remainder of 1950. Table 51 summarizes the losses among U.S. Army units during the last two weeks of the year.

Table 51—Post-counteroffensive, All U.S. Army Units

	KIA	WIA	POW Returned	POW Died	MIA Returned	MIA Died	Unit Total
1st Cavalry Division		9					9
2nd Infantry Division	4	23			1		28
3rd Infantry Division	33	114					147
7th Infantry Division	7	25				3	35
24th Infantry Division	2	19	3				24
25th Infantry Division	8	22	1			2	33
187th Inf./RCT		4					4
5th RCT		5					5
Other Units (16)	1	18					19
Total 12/16–12/31/50	55	239	4		1	5	304

Activity among marine units was similarly reduced. U.S. Marine fatalities in the period totaled only nine, including one pilot lost in a fixed-wing crash over land. One sailor, presumed to be a corpsman with the marines, was also lost.

In addition, three naval airmen were lost in fixed wing crashes, two over land and one at sea. One was reported as killed in action. The other two were reported missing, never found and declared dead.

From its number of reported fatalities, it appears that only the U.S. Air Force maintained a level of combat in the final weeks of 1950 that compared with earlier periods in the war. The Air Force lost 24 men in the period. A summary of these losses is shown in Table 52.

Table 52 — Post Counteroffensive, U.S. Air Force

Fixed Wing Crash Over Land	
Pilot, Killed in Action	4
Pilot, Died While Missing	8
Aircrew, Died While Missing	9
Air Crew, Died in Captivity	1
Non-Aircrew, Killed in Action	1
Non-Aircrew, Died While Missing	1
Total 12/16–12/31/50	24

Table 53 summarizes U.S. losses in the first six months of the Korean War.

Table 53 — Year-end 1950, All U.S. Military Units

	KIA	WIA	POW Returned	POW Died	MIA Returned	MIA Died	Unit Total
U.S. Army							
1st Cavalry Division	1599	5387	367	164	92	365	7974
2nd Infantry Division	1715	5400	778	835	102	571	9401
3rd Infantry Division	160	550	40	16		89	855
7th Infantry Division	595	1365	255	91	17	594	2917
24th Infantry Division	1944	2916	357	414	144	235	6010
25th Infantry Division	1244	4056	230	205	55	205	5995
5th RCT	361	1085	9	2	7	20	1484
29th Infantry Regt/RCT	422	687	64	7	14	81	1275
187th Airborne Regt/RCT	81	292	2	1	1	11	388
Other Units (238)	255	897	51	27	17	97	1344
Total 06/28–12/31/50	8376	22635	2153	1762	449	2268	37643

(continued on next page)

Table 53 (*cont.*)

	KIA	WIA	POW Returned	POW Died	MIA Returned	MIA Died	Unit Total
U.S. Marines (fatalities)							
1st Marine Division	1511			2		26	1539
Marine Airmen	18						18
Attached Navy Corpsmen	45					7	52
Total 06/28–12/31/50	1574			2		33	1609
U.S. Navy (fatalities)							
Sailors at Sea	20					26	46
Naval Airmen	13					13	26
Total 06/28–12/31/50	33					39	72
U.S. Air Force (fatalities)							
Total 06/28–12/31/50	73			9		176	258

POWs and MIAs

Almost two thirds of all the GIs who became POWs in the Korean War were captured in the first six months of the conflict. Of these individuals, four were never accounted for further and were declared dead after the end of hostilities. These individuals were listed in the summary tables as missing and declared dead.

A few others (79) were reported to have died of wounds. Disposition dates for these individuals varied from the same day of the reported capture to several months later. The records of some other reported POWs (190) indicated their disposition as killed in action. Most of the disposition dates in these cases tended to be fairly soon after the reported capture, many of them on the same day. It is not known how information of the reported dispositions was obtained. All of these 269 individuals were listed in the summary tables as having been killed in action.

The remainder of the POWs were either returned to military control or reported to have "died non-battle." Among the 2,153 who were ultimately released, the majority (1,726) was in captivity for the duration of the war. The average tenure of their captivity was 2 years and 10 months. Others who survived captivity and were repatriated generally fell into one of two groups, depending on the length of their captivity. Some were reported to have been released within a few days of their capture. Presumably these individuals either were actually missing rather than captured, or they were captured and escaped.

The second group consisted of individuals whose length of captivity varied between 20 and 90 days. The majority of these individuals were captured during the time of the battle of the Pusan Perimeter. For example, between July 26 and September 15, there were 157 American soldiers captured and subsequently released, none of whom was in captivity for more than 90 days. Their average tenure as POWs was 48 days. Perhaps these men—and others with similarly short terms as captives—remained with NKPA tactical units after their capture and were released by advancing UN forces after their breakout from the perimeter. This suggestion is supported by the fact that there were a lot fewer of these short-term POWs reported after the CCF entered the war in late October.

Those 1,762 POWs reported to have died in captivity present a somewhat more difficult problem in interpretation. It is probably safe to assume that some kind of evidence of death was available before the disposition "died non-battle" was determined. However, available data provide no clue concerning the source of such evidence or how the individuals died. Nor is there anything in the disposition dates to establish when they died. Disposition dates for these records were distributed over a period of more than two years, although the vast majority was in 1950 and 1951. The most commonly occurring dates were the final day of most months, suggesting that information was accumulated by one side or the other—or some neutral intermediary—and recorded in batches at month end. There were only 14 deaths of 1950 POWs recorded in 1952 and none in 1953 before the end of hostilities. After the war, immediately following the repatriation of living prisoners in Operation Big Switch, 15 additional POWs from 1950 were reported to have died in captivity.

As Table 53 indicates, MIAs are classified as two types—those that survived and returned to military control and those that were never found and were declared dead. It could be argued that those that were reported as missing and were subsequently found should not be considered as casualties. After all, in most cases, these individuals were only missing for a brief time. However, the records classify them as casualties and they are reported as such here. It is no doubt an indicator of the level of battlefield chaos in these early months of the conflict that the 449 MIA/Returned individuals indicated in the table above constitute three-fourths of all reported surviving MIAs in the entire 37 months of the war.

The other type of MIA is easier, albeit more regrettable, to summarize. The fate of these 2,268 individuals is, for the most part, completely unknown. Presumably, no remains have ever been found. Disposition dates are mainly after the end of the war, most commonly December 31, 1953, and the disposition is listed simply as "Declared Dead."

Renewed CCF Counteroffensive

Beginning on January 1, 1951, the CCF juggernaut, estimated at half a million men, resumed its push southward. And again, UN forces gave ground as they struggled against an enemy with superior numbers. By January 15, the enemy had advanced 50 miles south of the 38th Parallel and had captured Seoul once again. This time, however, the retreat was more orderly and U.S. casualties were more moderate—but by no means trivial. A summary of the losses during this battle is shown in Table 54.

Table 54—Renewed Counteroffensive, All U.S. Army Units

	KIA	WIA	POW Returned	POW Died	MIA Returned	MIA Died	Unit Total
38th Inf, 2nd Div	36	104	19	13		1	173
23rd Inf, 2nd Div	18	80					98
9th Inf, 2nd Div	7	41	7			1	56
Other 2nd Div Units (5)	5	15	1	1			22
Total 2nd Division	66	244	27	14		2	353

(continued on next page)

Table 54 (*cont.*)

	KIA	WIA	POW Returned	POW Died	MIA Returned	MIA Died	Unit Total
32nd Inf, 7th Inf Div	53	63					116
17th Inf, 7th Inf Div	15	11					26
31st Inf, 7th Inf Div	4	8					12
7th Recon Co, 7th Inf Div	6	1		1		1	9
Other 7th Div Units (5)	3	8	1		1		13
Total 7th Division	81	91	1	1	1	1	176
19th Inf, 24th Inf Div	63	118	98	12	2	8	301
21st Inf, 24th Inf Div	7	9	13	5			34
Other 24th Div Units (7)	2	13		1		1	17
Total 24th Division	72	143	111	18	2	9	355
35th Inf, 25th Inf Div	2	11	18	1			32
24th Inf, 25th Inf Div	5					5	
27th Inf, 25th Inf Div	10	37	10	2		1	60
25th Recon Co, 25th Inf Div	3	7	7	3		1	21
Other 25th Div Units (5)	2	6					8
Total 25th Division	17	66	35	6		2	126
1st Cavalry Division		17		1	2		20
3rd Inantry Division	4	16					20
187th Abn Inf/RCT	1	4					5
5th RCT		7		1			8
Other Units (30)	23	70	7	4		1	105
Totals 01/01–01/15/51	264	651	181	45	5	15	1161

The first Medal of Honor of 1951 was awarded to one of the men engaged in this operation.

MEDAL OF HONOR: JUNIOR D. EDWARDS

Awarded to: Sergeant First Class Junior D. Edwards, Indianola, IA, U.S. Army, Company E, 23d Infantry Regiment, 2d Infantry Division. Near Changbong-ni, Korea, 2 January 1951.

> Sfc. Edwards, Company E, distinguished himself by conspicuous gallantry and intrepidity above and beyond the call of duty in action against the enemy. When his platoon, while assisting in the defense of a strategic hill, was forced out of its position and came under vicious raking fire from an enemy machinegun set up on adjacent high ground, Sfc. Edwards individually charged the hostile emplacement, throwing grenades as he advanced. The enemy withdrew but returned to deliver devastating fire when he had expended his ammunition. Securing a fresh supply of grenades, he again charged the emplacement, neutralized the weapon and killed the crew, but was forced back by hostile small-arms fire. When the enemy emplaced another machinegun and resumed fire, Sfc. Edwards again renewed his supply of grenades, rushed a third time through a vicious hail of fire, silenced this second gun and annihilated its crew. In this third daring assault he was mortally wounded but his indomitable courage and successful action enabled his platoon to regain and hold the vital strongpoint. Sfc. Edwards' consummate valor and gallant self-sacrifice reflect the utmost

glory upon himself and are in keeping with the esteemed traditions of the infantry and military service.

For the next 10 days, the tactical situation remained relatively static, with total U.S. casualties averaging only about 20 per day. Table 55 summarizes the U.S. Army losses in this period.

Table 55 — Post-offensive, All U.S. Army Units

	KIA	WIA	POW Returned	POW Died	MIA Returned	MIA Died	Unit Total
1st Cavalry Division	3	14					17
2nd Infantry Division	1	13	1	2		1	18
3rd Infantry Division	4	11		1		1	17
7th Infantry Division*	22	26	8	3			59
24th Infantry Division		6					6
25th Infantry Division	1	6	1	3			11
11th Airborne Division	1	15					16
5th RCT	1	14	1				16
Other Units (10)	11	10					21
Total 01/16–01/24/51	44	115	11	9		2	181

*Primarily 17th Infantry Regiment

Marine losses during the opening weeks of 1951 were minimal, with 13 fatalities in 24 days, including three marine pilots, one lost in a crash at sea and two lost in crashes over land. One sailor, most likely a corpsman with the marines, was also lost in ground action during the period. According to chronologies of the war, the marines were engaged at this time in neutralizing NKPA stragglers that had become guerrilla fighters in the South Korean hills in the vicinity of Masan, Pohang, Sondong and Andong.

In this period, the Navy lost 3 airmen in crashes over land and reported two fatalities at sea, one from small arms fire and one from an explosive device.

As 1951 began, the U.S. Air Force continued to experience losses that appeared to be unrelated to the intensity of the fighting on the ground. During the first 24 days of the year, the Air Force reported 30 fatalities in air crashes. These losses are summarized in Table 56.

Table 56 — Post-offensive, U.S. Air Force

Fixed Wing Crash Over Land	
Pilot, Killed in Action	6
Pilot, Died of Wounds	1
Pilot, Died while Missing	8
Pilot, Died in Captivity	1
Aircrew, Killed in Action	7
Aircrew, Died while Missing	5
Non-Aircrew, Killed in Action	1
Non-Aircrew, Died while Missing	1
Total 01/01–01/24/50	30

Operation Thunderbolt

On January 25, 1951, two months after the CCF mounted its counteroffensive to drive UN forces out of North Korea, the six U.S. Army divisions and two RCTs that had taken the brunt of the onslaught, began to strike back. Called Operation Thunderbolt, the UN offensive went on for four weeks with a cost of 6,861 in U.S. Army casualties. Figure 13 shows the distribution of these casualties over the period of the battle.

For the most part, the casualties represented in Figure 13 include significant contributions from every major unit in the offensive. Some units took major hits on certain days, but no unit emerged from the operation without substantial losses. Several specific battles have been identified as critical to success of the offensive. The costs of these battles will be summarized below. However, whether or not a specific battle made it into historical records, the fighting was just as intense, the wounds just as severe and the exploits of the fighting men just as noteworthy. This fact is exemplified by two Medals of Honor awarded for action in the early days of this campaign.

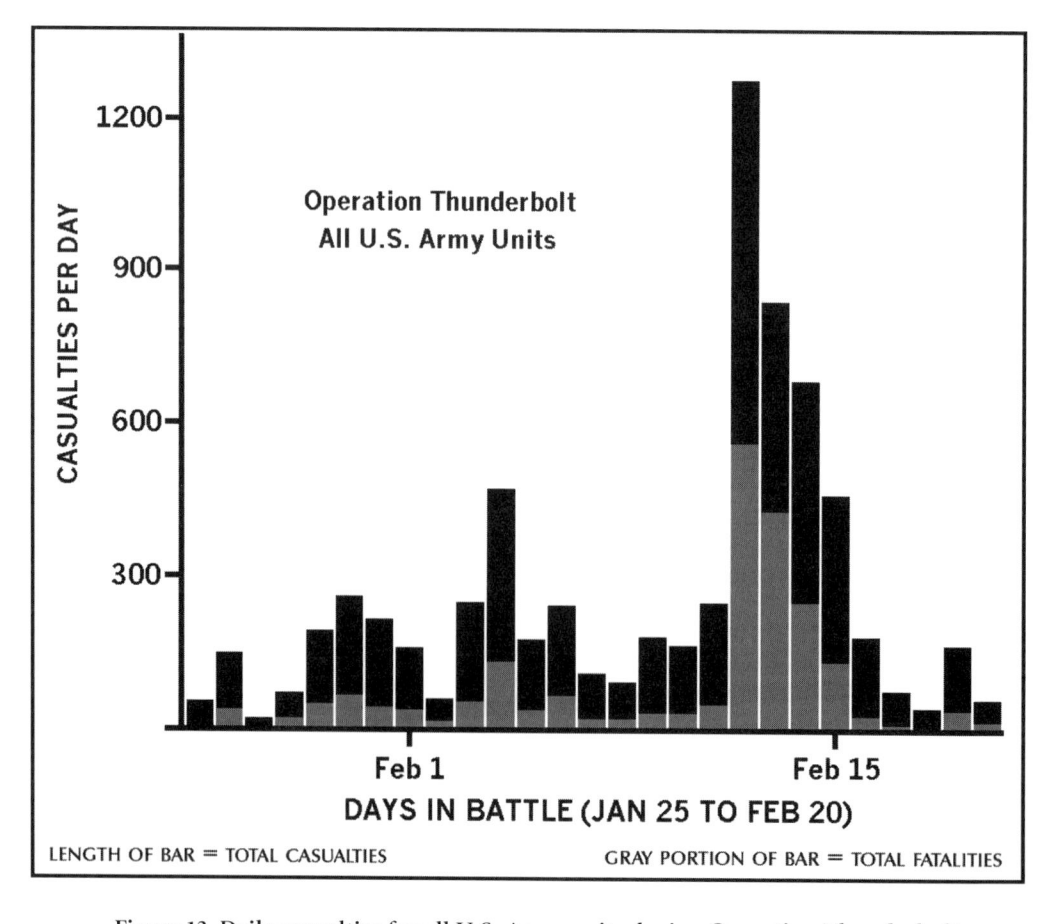

Figure 13. Daily casualties for all U.S. Army units during Operation Thunderbolt.

I. The Peninsular War

MEDAL OF HONOR: CARL H. DODD

Awarded to: First Lieutenant (then 2d Lt.) Carl H. Dodd, Kenvir, KY, U.S. Army, Company E, 5th Infantry Regiment, 24th Infantry Division. Near Subuk, Korea, 30 and 31 January 1951.

1st Lt. Dodd, Company E, distinguished himself by conspicuous gallantry and intrepidity above and beyond the call of duty in action against the enemy. First Lt. Dodd, given the responsibility of spearheading an attack to capture Hill 256, a key terrain feature defended by a well-armed, crafty foe who had withstood several previous assaults, led his platoon forward over hazardous terrain under hostile small-arms, mortar, and artillery fire from well-camouflaged enemy emplacements which reached such intensity that his men faltered. With utter disregard for his safety, 1st Lt. Dodd moved among his men, reorganized and encouraged them, and then single-handedly charged the first hostile machinegun nest, killing or wounding all its occupants. Inspired by his incredible courage, his platoon responded magnificently and, fixing bayonets and throwing grenades, closed on the enemy and wiped out every hostile position as it moved relentlessly onward to its initial objective. Securing the first series of enemy positions, 1st Lt. Dodd again reorganized his platoon and led them across a narrow ridge and onto Hill 256. Firing his rifle and throwing grenades, he advanced at the head of his platoon despite the intense concentrated hostile fire which was brought to bear on their narrow avenue of approach. When his platoon was still 200 yards from the objective he moved ahead and with his last grenade destroyed an enemy mortar killing the crew. Darkness then halted the advance but at daybreak 1st Lt. Dodd, again boldly advancing ahead of his unit, led the platoon through a dense fog against the remaining hostile positions. With bayonet and grenades he continued to set pace without regard for the danger to his life, until he and his troops had eliminated the last of the defenders and had secured the final objective. First Lt. Dodd's superb leadership and extraordinary heroism inspired his men to overcome this strong enemy defense reflecting the highest credit upon himself and upholding the esteemed traditions of the military service.

MEDAL OF HONOR: ROBERT M. McGOVERN

Awarded to: First Lieutenant Robert M. McGovern, Washington, DC, U.S. Army, Company A, 5th Cavalry Regiment, 1st Cavalry Division. Near Kamyangjan-ni, Korea, 30 January 1951.

1st Lt. McGovern, a member of Company A, distinguished himself by conspicuous gallantry and intrepidity at the risk of life above and beyond the call of duty in action against an armed enemy of the United Nations. As 1st Lt. McGovern led his platoon up a slope to engage hostile troops emplaced in bunker-type pillboxes with connecting trenches, the unit came under heavy machinegun and rifle fire from the crest of the hill, approximately 75 yards distant. Despite a wound sustained in this initial burst of withering fire, 1st Lt. McGovern, assured the men of his ability to continue on and urged them forward. Forging up the rocky incline, he fearlessly led the platoon to within several yards of its objective when the ruthless foe threw and rolled a vicious barrage of handgrenades on the group and halted the advance. Enemy fire increased in volume and intensity and 1st Lt. McGovern realizing that casualties were rapidly increasing and the morale of his men badly shaken, hurled back several grenades before they exploded. Then, disregarding his painful wound and weakened condition he charged a machinegun emplacement which was raking his position with flanking fire. When he was within 10 yards of the position a burst of fire ripped the carbine from his hands, but, undaunted, he continued his lone-man assault and, firing his pistol and throwing grenades, killed 7 hostile soldiers before falling mortally wounded in front of the gun he had silenced. 1st Lt. McGovern's incredible display of valor imbued his men with indomitable resolution to avenge his death. Fixing bayonets and throwing grenades, they charged with such ferocity that hostile positions were overrun and the enemy routed from the hill. The inspirational leadership, unflinching courage, and intrepid actions of 1st Lt. McGovern reflected utmost glory on himself and the honored tradition of the military services.

On February 1, the 23rd Infantry Regiment of the 2nd Division — plus the 37th FA Battalion and a contingent of French soldiers — engaged a substantial CCF force at what became know as "The Twin Tunnels," near the village of Sinchon. Reports suggest that the Chinese were soundly beaten in the battle, giving momentum to the offensive. If a measure of victory is the scarcity of one's own casualties in a battle compared to those of the adversary, then this was indeed a major victory. Total losses in the 23rd Infantry and the 37th FA Bn. that day were 22 killed and 55 wounded. One member of the 23rd Infantry was awarded the Medal of Honor for his part in making this operation a success.

Medal of Honor: Hubert L. Lee

Awarded to: Master Sergeant Hubert L. Lee, Leland, MS, U.S. Army, Company I, 23d Infantry Regiment, 2d Infantry Division. Near Ipori, Korea, 1 February 1951.

M/Sgt. Lee, a member of Company I, distinguished himself by conspicuous gallantry and intrepidity above and beyond the call of duty in action against the enemy. When his platoon was forced from its position by a numerically superior enemy force, and his platoon leader wounded, M/Sgt. Lee assumed command, regrouped the remnants of his unit, and led them in repeated assaults to regain the position. Within 25 yards of his objective he received a leg wound from grenade fragments, but refused assistance and continued the attack. Although forced to withdraw 5 times, each time he regrouped his remaining men and renewed the assault. Moving forward at the head of his small group in the fifth attempt, he was struck by an exploding grenade, knocked to the ground, and seriously wounded in both legs. Still refusing assistance, he advanced by crawling, rising to his knees to fire, and urging his men to follow. While thus directing the final assault he was wounded a third time, by small-arms fire. Persistently continuing to crawl forward, he directed his men in a final and successful attack which regained the vital objective. His intrepid leadership and determination led to the destruction of 83 of the enemy and withdrawal of the remainder, and was a vital factor in stopping the enemy attack. M/Sgt. Lee's indomitable courage, consummate valor, and outstanding leadership reflect the highest credit upon himself and are in keeping with the finest traditions of the infantry and the U.S. Army.

I. The Peninsular War

M/Sgt. Lee was returned to duty on March 26, 1951.

It is obvious from Figure 13 that the most costly battles in this early phase of the UN offensive occurred in the period between February 11 and 15. In these battles, the battle of Hoengsong (11–13) and the battle of Chipyong-ni (13–15), elements of the U.S. 2nd Infantry Division had to defend against major counterattacks by the CCF. Details of 2nd Division losses in these battle are summarized in Table 57.

Table 57 — Battles of Hoengsong and Chipyong-ni, 2nd Infantry Division

	KIA	WIA	POW Returned	POW Died	MIA Returned	MIA Died	Unit Total
02/11/51							
9th Inf, 2nd Div	12	41	6	6		4	69
38th Inf, 2nd Div		13	2				15
23rd Inf, 2nd Div		2					2
Other Units (5)		10	5				15
Day Total 02/11/51	12	66	13	6		4	101
02/12/51							
9th Inf, 2nd Div	37	21	27	41	1	20	147
38th Inf, 2nd Div	195	218	96	88	19	67	683
23rd Inf, 2nd Div		9					9
15th FA Bn, 2nd Inf Div	3	45	6	1			55
503rd FA Bn, 2nd Inf Div	21	17	25	25	1	10	99
82nd AAA Bn, 2nd Inf Div	3	13	3		1		20
Other Units (4)		4	2	2			8
Day Total 02/12/51	259	327	159	157	22	97	1021
02/13/51							
9th Inf, 2nd Div	4	4	3	3			14
23rd Inf, 2nd Div	8	20					28
38th Inf, 2nd Div	68	46	37	40		15	206
15th FA Bn, 2nd Inf Div	86	29	34	84	5	34	272
82nd AAA Bn, 2nd Inf Div	12	9	10	16		5	52
Other Units (5)	1	20	3	2			26
Day Total 02/13/51	179	128	87	145	5	54	598
02/14/50							
9th Inf, 2nd Div	66	64	15	17	1	12	175
23rd Inf, 2nd Div	23	45			1		69
38th Inf, 2nd Div	2	17	1	1			21
2nd Recon Co, 2nd Inf Div	30	20	4	4	1	6	65
Other Units (6)	3	11				1	15
Day Total 02/14/51	124	157	20	22		19	345
02/15/51							
9th Inf, 2nd Div		1					1
23rd Inf, 2nd Div	30	102	2	4		3	141
38th Inf, 2nd Div	7	17	1				25
Other Units (5)	2	20					22
Day Total 02/15/51	39	140	3	4		3	189
Total 2nd Div 02/11–02/15/51	613	818	282	334	30	177	2254

Two Medals of Honor were awarded to men from the 2nd Division for their heroism in these battles.

Medal of Honor: Charles R. Long

Awarded to: Sergeant Charles R. Long, Kansas City, MO, U.S. Army, Company M, 38th Infantry Regiment, 2d Infantry Division. Near Hoengsong, Korea, 12 February 1951.

> Sgt. Long, a member of Company M, distinguished himself by conspicuous gallantry and intrepidity above and beyond the call of duty in action against an armed enemy of the United Nations. When Company M, in a defensive perimeter on Hill 300, was viciously attacked by a numerically superior hostile force at approximately 0300 hours and ordered to withdraw, Sgt. Long, a forward observer for the mortar platoon, voluntarily remained at his post to provide cover by directing mortar fire on the enemy. Maintaining radio contact with his platoon, Sgt. Long coolly directed accurate mortar fire on the advancing foe. He continued firing his carbine and throwing handgrenades until his position was surrounded and he was mortally wounded. Sgt. Long's inspirational, valorous action halted the onslaught, exacted a heavy toll of enemy casualties, and enabled his company to withdraw, reorganize, counterattack, and regain the hill strongpoint. His unflinching courage and noble self-sacrifice reflect the highest credit on himself and are in keeping with the honored traditions of the military service.

Medal of Honor: William S. Sitman

Awarded to: Sergeant First Class, William S. Sitman, Bellwood, PA, U.S. Army, Company M, 23d Infantry Regiment, 2d Infantry Division. Near Chipyong-ni, Korea, 14 February 1951.

> Sfc. Sitman distinguished himself by conspicuous gallantry and intrepidity above and beyond the call of duty in action against an armed enemy of the United Nations. Sfc. Sitman, a machinegun section leader of Company M, was attached to Company I, under attack by a numerically superior hostile force. During the encounter when an enemy grenade knocked out his machinegun, a squad from Company I, immediately emplaced a light machinegun and Sfc. Sitman and his men remained to provide security for the crew. In the ensuing action, the enemy lobbed a grenade into the position and Sfc. Sitman, fully aware of the odds against him, selflessly threw himself on it, absorbing the full force of the explosion with his body. Although mortally wounded in this fearless display of valor, his intrepid act saved 5 men from death or serious injury, and enabled them to continue inflicting withering fire on the ruthless foe throughout the attack. Sfc. Sitman's noble self-sacrifice and consummate devotion to duty reflect lasting glory on himself and uphold the honored traditions of the military service.

One other unit should be identified in relation to the battle of Chipyong-ni. In that battle, the 5th Cavalry Regiment reprised the role it made famous in old cowboy movies—"saved by the cavalry." A small contingent from the 5th Cav., reinforced with tanks, arrived at Chipyong-ni just as the surrounded and badly outnumbered 23rd Infantry and its supporting units were running out of ammunition. For the 5th Cav., the rescue did not come without significant cost. Table 58 is a listing of casualties in the regiment that day.

I. The Peninsular War

Table 58 — Chipyong-ni, 5th Cavalry Regiment

	KIA	WIA	POW Returned	POW Died	MIA Returned	MIA Died	Unit Total
5th Cav, 1st Cav Division 02/15/51	25	45	1	6		5	82

The other major day of losses shown in Figure 13, February 4, is not identified with any specific battle, but on that day the 19th Infantry Regiment of the 24th Division took almost half of the total of 468 casualties — and virtually all of the captured and missing. A breakdown of those casualties is shown in Table 59.

Table 59 — Unnamed Battle, 19th Infantry Regiment

	KIA	WIA	POW Returned	POW Died	MIA Returned	MIA Died	Unit Total
19th Inf, 24th Inf Div	49	119	22	16	1	2	209
Other Units (30)	62	196	1				259
Total 02/04/51	111	315	23	16	1	2	468

No better description of the tenor of this day's fighting can be found than in the award of the Medal of Honor to one of its participants.

MEDAL OF HONOR: STANLEY T. ADAMS

Awarded to: Master Sergeant (then Sfc.) Stanley T. Adams, Olathe, KS, U.S. Army, Company A, 19th Infantry Regiment. Near Sesim-ni, Korea, 4 February 1951

> M/Sgt. Adams, Company A, distinguished himself by conspicuous gallantry and intrepidity above and beyond the call of duty in action against an enemy. At approximately 0100 hours, M/Sgt. Adams' platoon, holding an outpost some 200 yards ahead of his company, came under a determined attack by an estimated 250 enemy troops. Intense small-arms, machine-gun, and mortar fire from 3 sides pressed the platoon back against the main line of resistance. Observing approximately 150 hostile troops silhouetted against the skyline advancing against his platoon, M/Sgt. Adams leaped to his feet, urged his men to fix bayonets, and he, with 13 members of his platoon, charged this hostile force with indomitable courage. Within 50 yards of the enemy M/Sgt. Adams was knocked to the ground when pierced in the leg by an enemy bullet. He jumped to his feet and, ignoring his wound, continued on to close with the enemy when he was knocked down 4 times from the concussion of grenades which had bounced off his body. Shouting orders he charged the enemy positions and engaged them in hand-to-hand combat where man after man fell before his terrific onslaught with bayonet and rifle butt. After nearly an hour of vicious action M/Sgt. Adams and his comrades routed the fanatical foe, killing over 50 and forcing the remainder to withdraw. Upon receiving orders that his battalion was moving back he provided cover fire while his men withdrew. M/Sgt. Adams' superb leadership, incredible courage, and consummate devotion to duty so inspired his comrades that the enemy attack was completely thwarted, saving his battalion from possible disaster. His sustained personal bravery and indomitable fighting spirit against overwhelming odds reflect the

utmost glory upon himself and uphold the finest traditions of the infantry and the military service.

The following two awards of the Medal of Honor illustrate that the fighting remained intense, even for units that were not involved in major battles.

MEDAL OF HONOR: LEWIS L. MILLETT

Awarded to: Captain Lewis L. Millett, Mechanic Falls, ME, U.S. Army, Company E, 27th Infantry Regiment. Vicinity of Soam-Ni, Korea, 7 February 1951.

> Capt. Millett, Company E, distinguished himself by conspicuous gallantry and intrepidity above and beyond the call of duty in action. While personally leading his company in an attack against a strongly held position he noted that the 1st Platoon was pinned down by small-arms, automatic, and antitank fire. Capt. Millett ordered the 3d Platoon forward, placed himself at the head of the 2 platoons, and, with fixed bayonet, led the assault up the fire-swept hill. In the fierce charge Capt. Millett bayoneted 2 enemy soldiers and boldly continued on, throwing grenades, clubbing and bayoneting the enemy, while urging his men forward by shouting encouragement. Despite vicious opposing fire, the whirlwind hand-to-hand assault carried to the crest of the hill. His dauntless leadership and personal courage so inspired his men that they stormed into the hostile position and used their bayonets with such lethal effect that the enemy fled in wild disorder. During this fierce onslaught Capt. Millett was wounded by grenade fragments but refused evacuation until the objective was taken and firmly secured. The superb leadership, conspicuous courage, and consummate devotion to duty demonstrated by Capt. Millett were directly responsible for the successful accomplishment of a hazardous mission and reflect the highest credit on himself and the heroic traditions of the military service.

MEDAL OF HONOR: DARWIN W. KYLE

Awarded to: Second Lieutenant Darwin K. Kyle, Racine, WI, U.S. Army, Company K, 7th Infantry Regiment, 3d Infantry Division. Near Kamil-ni, Korea, 16 February 1951.

> 2d Lt. Kyle, distinguished himself by conspicuous gallantry and intrepidity above and beyond the call of duty in action against the enemy. When his platoon had been pinned down by intense fire, he completely exposed himself to move among and encourage his men to continue the advance against enemy forces strongly entrenched on Hill 185. Inspired by his courageous leadership, the platoon resumed the advance but was again pinned down when an enemy machinegun opened fire, wounding 6 of the men. 2d Lt. Kyle immediately charged the hostile emplacement alone, engaged the crew in hand-to-hand combat, killing all 3. Continuing on toward the objective, his platoon suddenly received an intense automatic-weapons fire from a well-concealed hostile position on its right flank. Again leading his men in a daring bayonet charge against this position, firing his carbine and throwing grenades, 2d Lt. Kyle personally destroyed 4 of the enemy before he was killed by a burst from an enemy submachinegun. The extraordi-

nary heroism and outstanding leadership of 2d Lt. Kyle, and his gallant self-sacrifice, reflect the highest credit upon himself and are in keeping with the esteemed traditions of the military service.

A summary of all U.S. Army casualties in Operation Thunderbolt is shown Table 60.

Table 60 — Operation Thunderbolt, All U.S. Army Units

	KIA	WIA	POW Returned	POW Died	MIA Returned	MIA Died	Unit Total
1st Cavalry Division	234	958	5	7		5	1209
2nd Infantry Division	696	1100	291	340	33	184	2644
3rd Infantry Division	165	553	4		1	1	724
7th Infantry Division	59	209	7	6		3	284
24th Infantry Division	140	512	30	29	1	4	716
25th Infantry Division	120	470	2	1	2		595
187th Airborne Regt/RCT	86	316			2	2	406
5th RCT	26	109	1		1		137
Other Units (36)*	24	113	1	8			146
Total 01/25–02/20/51	1550	4340	341	391	40	199	6861

*Of the nine men reported captured in non-divisional units, all but one were assigned to the 8202nd Military Missions Commission. So far in the war, this unit has reported a total of 28 casualties, 15 of them captured, 11 of whom died in captivity.

During the period of Operation Thunderbolt, U.S. Marine losses remained light, although slightly elevated compared to the opening weeks of the year. In the period, marine fatalities totaled 41, including one in an aircraft loss identified as a ground casualty. Two Navy corpsmen were also lost in the period.

Other Navy losses during the period are summarized in Table 61.

Table 61 — Operation Thunderbolt, U.S. Navy

Fixed Wing Crash Over Land	
Pilot, Died while Missing	3
Fixed Wing Crash At Sea	
Pilot, Killed in Action	1
Sea Casualty	
Explosive Device, Killed in Action	7
Explosive Device, Died while Missing	1
Total 01/25–02/20/50	12

Air Force fatalities continued at about the same levels as in past periods, except for considerably increased losses on February 11 and 12, during the battle of Hoengsong. On those days, 14 airmen were lost in plane crashes. A summary of Air Force losses in the period is shown in Table 62.

Table 62 — Operation Thunderbolt, U.S. Air Force

Fixed Wing Crash Over Land	
Pilot, Killed in Action	2
Pilot, Died of Wounds	1
Pilot, Died while Missing	15
Pilot, Died in Captivity	1
Aircrew, Killed in Action	1
Aircrew, Died of Wounds	1
Aircrew, Died while Missing	4
Non-Aircrew, Died while Missing	4
Fixed Wing Crash At Sea	
Pilot, Died while Missing	1
Ground Casualty	
Small-arms Fire, Died in Captivity	1
Unknown, Died in Captivity	2
Total 01/25–02/20/51	33

The UN Offensive Continues

On February 21, 1951, the major thrust of the continuing UN offensive became known as Operation Killer. For the next two weeks, four U.S. Army divisions plus the 1st Marine Division pushed to drive the CCF north of the Han River. No single unit experienced any extraordinary casualty count in this operation, but the pace of the losses was still significant, albeit reduced in comparison to some earlier operations. A summary of U.S. Army casualties in the operation is shown in Table 63.

Table 63 — Operation Killer, All U.S. Army Units

	KIA	WIA	POW Returned	POW Died	MIA Returned	MIA Died	Unit Total
1st Cavalry Division	51	214	1				266
2nd Infantry Division	65	341	5				411
7th Infantry Division	35	170	2	2	1	1	211
24th Infantry Division	10	32	1				43
Other Units (35)	20	127				1	148
Total 02/21–03/06/51	181	884	9	2	1	2	1079

The following Medal of Honor citation describes the intensity of the combat on one of the days of this operation, February 26. It is unquestionably due in large measure to the valiant exploits of Cpl. Ingman that only one death other than the corporal himself was reported in the 17th Infantry that day.

MEDAL OF HONOR: EINAR H. INGMAN, JR.

Awarded to: Sergeant (then Cpl.) Einar H. Ingman, Jr., Tomahawk, WI, U.S. Army, Company E, 17th Infantry Regiment, 7th Infantry Division. Near Maltari, Korea, 26 February 1951.

Sgt. Ingman, a member of Company E, distinguished himself by conspicuous gallantry and intrepidity above and beyond the call of duty in action against the enemy. The 2 leading squads of the assault platoon of his company, while attacking a strongly fortified ridge held by the enemy, were pinned down by withering fire and both squad leaders and several men were wounded. Cpl. Ingman assumed command, reorganized and combined the 2 squads, then moved from 1 position to another, designating fields of fire and giving advice and encouragement to the men. Locating an enemy machinegun position that was raking his men with devastating fire he charged it alone, threw a grenade into the position, and killed the remaining crew with rifle fire. Another enemy machinegun opened fire approximately 15 yards away and inflicted additional casualties to the group and stopped the attack. When Cpl. Ingman charged the second position he was hit by grenade fragments and a hail of fire which seriously wounded him about the face and neck and knocked him to the ground. With incredible courage and stamina, he arose instantly and, using only his rifle, killed the entire guncrew before falling unconscious from his wounds. As a result of the singular action by Cpl. Ingman the defense of the enemy was broken, his squad secured its objective, and more than 100 hostile troops abandoned their weapons and fled in disorganized retreat. Cpl. Ingman's indomitable courage, extraordinary heroism, and superb leadership reflect the highest credit on himself and are in keeping with the esteemed traditions of the infantry and the U.S. Army.

Cpl. Ingman was wounded in the fall of 1950 and spent two months in the hospital before returning to duty. The wounds from this action required his evacuation to the States, where he was separated from the service on April 28, 1951.

In addition to the losses recorded above, U.S. Marine losses totaled 76, including two airmen lost. One was a pilot killed in a crash over land and other listed simply as "aircraft lost, ground casualty." Most of the marine losses occurred on the first three days of March. Two Navy corpsmen were also lost in the action. They were the only Navy losses in the period.

Air Force losses totaled 18. They are summarized in Table 64.

Table 64 — Operation Killer, U.S. Air Force

Fixed Wing Crash Over Land	
Pilot, Killed in Action	1
Pilot, Died while Missing	6
Aircrew, Died while Missing	9
Non-Aircrew, Died while Missing	2
Total 02/21–03/06/51	18

Operation Ripper

Now, in an effort to drive all CCF and NKPA forces out of their entrenched positions below the 38th Parallel, seven U.S. Divisions and two RCTs participate in a massive offensive called Operation Ripper. The offensive began on March 7 and continued into early April. Considering the scope of the operation, the number of enemy to be encountered and the amount of territory to be taken, it is a credit to the strategic planners of this operation and the skill and determination of the fighting men involved that casualties were no greater than they were. During the operation, Seoul

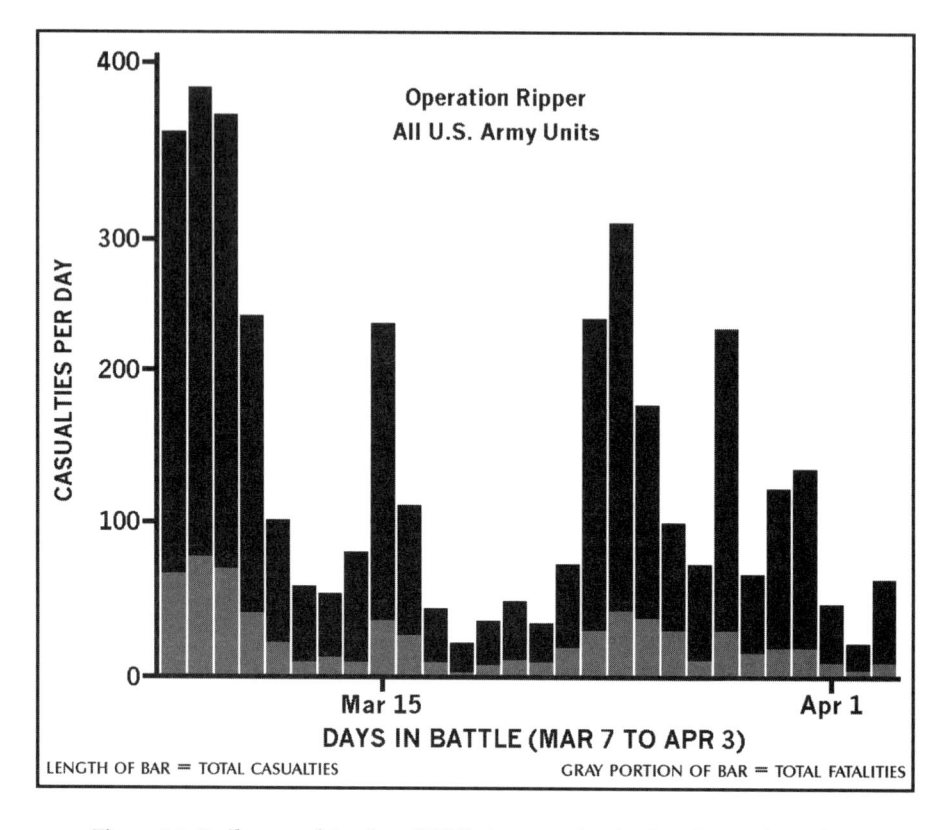

Figure 14. Daily casualties for all U.S. Army units during Operation Ripper.

was recaptured by UN forces. Figure 14 shows the distribution of casualties among U.S. Army units in the operation.

Perhaps the most notable feature of Figure 14 in comparison to graphs of battles earlier in the war is the significantly lower proportion of deaths among the casualties in this operation. And, as summary totals in Table 65 indicate, the number of Americans captured or missing was extremely low. Clearly, the initiative was with UN in this battle.

From the casualty count for the first few days, this operation clearly started off with a bang. Although certain units tended to have more casualties on certain days, no single unit experienced extraordinary casualties on any day, except for the 187th RCT, which accounted for almost half of the 232 casualties reported on March 23. On that day, the 187th (along with the attached 2nd and 4th Ranger Companies) conducted the last airborne assault of the war. Called Operation Tomahawk, this engagement dropped the paratroopers on Munsan-ni, 20 miles northwest of Seoul.

Of the 106 battle casualties reported in the assaulting units that day, 75 were marked with casualty type "injured in action other than wounds" and were presumably jump injuries. Nine of these injuries were serious enough for the individuals to be evacuated to the U.S. and 13 others were injured so severely that the individuals had to be separated from the service as a result of their trauma. With this high a proportion of severe jump injuries, it is quite possible that some or all of the five KIAs

I. The Peninsular War

reported in those units that day could have died in the jump. The 187th RCT went on to sustain the highest casualty count of any regimental-sized unit in the battle.

Table 65 summarizes all U.S. Army casualties in Operation Ripper.

Table 65 — Operation Ripper, All U.S. Army Units

	KIA	WIA	POW Returned	POW Died	MIA Returned	MIA Died	Unit Total
1st Cavalry Division							
5th Cav, 1st Cav Div	35	110	6	1			152
7th Cav, 1st Cav Div	27	129			2		158
8th Cav, 1st Cav Div	18	107					125
Other 1st Cav Units (5)	4	27					31
Total 03/07–04/03/51	84	373	6	1	2		466
2nd Infantry Division							
9th Inf, 2nd Div	34	133					167
23rd Inf, 2nd Div	41	183					224
38th Inf, 2nd Div	52	253	4		3	1	313
Other 2nd Div Units (8)	8	35					43
Total 03/07–04/03/51	135	604	4		3	1	747
3rd Infantry Division							
7th Inf 3rd Inf Div	15	100					115
65th Inf, 3rd Inf Div	18	77					95
15th Inf, 3rd Inf Div	20	121					141
Other 3rd Div Units (9)	13	25					38
Total 03/07–04/03/51	66	323					389
7th Infantry Division							
17th Inf, 7th Inf Div	26	86	2		1		115
32nd Inf, 7th Inf Div	16	61					77
31st Inf, 7th Inf Div	1	4					5
Other 7th Div Units (8)	4	16					20
Total 03/07–04/03/51	47	167	2		1		217
24th Infantry Division							
19th Inf, 24th Inf Div	57	255	4				316
21st Inf, 24th Inf Div	18	94	3		1		116
Other 24th Div Units (6)	3	27					30
Total 03/07–04/03/51	78	376	7		1		462
25th Infantry Division							
24th Inf, 25th Inf Div	78	319	2				399
27th Inf, 25th Inf Div	30	163					193
35th Inf, 25th Inf Div	27	115					142
Other 25th Div Units (10)	8	45					53
Total 03/07–04/03/51	143	642	2				787
187th RCT							
187th RCT	83	374	1				458
4th Ranger Company	1	15	1				17
2nd Ranger Company	1	3					4
Total 03/07–04/03/51	85	392	2				479
5th RCT							
5th RCT	20	115	1		1		137
Supporting Units (2)	1	3					4
Total 03/07–04/03/51	21	118	1		1		141
Non Divisional Units (32)	13	78	5				96
Total All Units 03/07–04/03/51	672	3073	29	1	8	1	3784

In the early days of this operation, when the high casualty count suggests that the intensity of the combat was the greatest, two Medals of Honor were awarded.

Medal of Honor: Nelson V. Brittin

Sergeant First Class Nelson V. Brittin, Audubon, NJ, U.S. Army, Company I, 19th Infantry Regiment. Vicinity of Yonggong-ni, Korea, 7 March 1951.

> Sfc. Brittin, a member of Company I, distinguished himself by conspicuous gallantry and intrepidity above and beyond the call of duty in action. Volunteering to lead his squad up a hill, with meager cover against murderous fire from the enemy, he ordered his squad to give him support and, in the face of withering fire and bursting shells, he tossed a grenade at the nearest enemy position. On returning to his squad, he was knocked down and wounded by an enemy grenade. Refusing medical attention, he replenished his supply of grenades and returned, hurling grenades into hostile positions and shooting the enemy as they fled. When his weapon jammed, he leaped without hesitation into a foxhole and killed the occupants with his bayonet and the butt of his rifle. He continued to wipe out foxholes and, noting that his squad had been pinned down, he rushed to the rear of a machinegun position, threw a grenade into the nest, and ran around to its front, where he killed all 3 occupants with his rifle. Less than 100 yards up the hill, his squad again came under vicious fire from another camouflaged, sandbagged, machinegun nest well-flanked by supporting riflemen. Sfc. Brittin again charged this new position in an aggressive endeavor to silence this remaining obstacle and ran direct into a burst of automatic fire which killed him instantly. In his sustained and driving action, he had killed 20 enemy soldiers and destroyed 4 automatic weapons. The conspicuous courage, consummate valor, and noble self-sacrifice displayed by Sfc. Brittin enabled his inspired company to attain its objective and reflect the highest glory on himself and the heroic traditions of the military service.

Medal of Honor: Raymond Harvey

Awarded to: Captain Raymond Harvey, Pasadena, CA, U.S. Army, Company C, 17th Infantry Regiment. Vicinity of Taemi-Dong, Korea, 9 March 1951.

> Capt. Harvey Company C, distinguished himself by conspicuous gallantry and intrepidity above and beyond the call of duty in action. When his company was pinned down by a barrage of automatic weapons fire from numerous well-entrenched emplacements, imperiling accomplishment of its mission, Capt. Harvey braved a hail of fire and exploding grenades to advance to the first enemy machinegun nest, killing its crew with grenades. Rushing to the edge of the next emplacement, he killed its crew with carbine fire. He then moved the 1st Platoon forward until it was again halted by a curtain of automatic fire from well fortified hostile positions. Disregarding the hail of fire, he personally charged and neutralized a third emplacement. Miraculously escaping death from intense crossfire, Capt. Harvey continued to lead the assault. Spotting an enemy pillbox well camouflaged by logs, he moved close enough to sweep the emplacement with carbine fire and throw grenades through the openings, annihilating its 5 occupants. Though wounded he then turned to order the company for-

ward, and, suffering agonizing pain, he continued to direct the reduction of the remaining hostile positions, refusing evacuation until assured that the mission would be accomplished. Capt. Harvey's valorous and intrepid actions served as an inspiration to his company, reflecting the utmost glory upon himself and upholding the heroic traditions of the military service.

Capt. Harvey was returned to duty on May 22, 1951.

Casualties in the 1st Marine Division were sporadic throughout the operation, reaching a maximum of 15 fatalities on March 15 and falling to less than one per day for the last 11 days of the battle. The total of Marine fatalities for the operation was 71, including two pilots lost in fixed-wing crashes over land and two simply listed as "aircraft loss, ground action." Two sailors, presumably corpsmen, were also lost in ground action during the operation.

The five other U.S. Navy fatalities in the operation were all pilots lost in fixed-wing plane crashes, four over land and one at sea. Three of them were reported missing and declared dead.

The Air Force continued to report consistent losses through this operation. On one day, March 29, 12 airmen were lost, 10 of them at sea—two pilots, five aircrew and three non-aircrew, all reported missing and never recovered. Table 66 shows a summary of the 41 Air Force losses during the period of the operation.

Table 66 — Operation Ripper, U.S. Air Force

Fixed Wing Crash Over Land	
Pilot, Killed in Action	5
Pilot, Died while Missing	21
Aircrew, Died while Missing	3
Non-Aircrew, Died while Missing	1
Fixed Wing Crash At Sea	
Pilot, Died while Missing	2
Aircrew, Died while Missing	5
Non-Aircrew, Died while Missing	4
Total 03/07–04/03/51	41

UN April Offensives

The month of April 1951 gave some of the fiercest fighting of the Korean War. Punctuated by two major UN offensives and a massive CCF counteroffensive, U.S. casualty figures were substantial. Figure 15 shows the distribution of those casualties over the four-week period of the conflict.

Early in April, to secure the 38th Parallel (Phase Line Kansas) as the defense line in the vicinity of "The Iron Triangle" (the sector outlined by the North Korean cities of Kumhwa, Chorwon and Pyonggang), UN forces launched Operation Rugged. Six U.S. Army Divisions were involved in the operation. Overlapping in time, and with several of the same units involved, Operation Dauntless was launched to secure Phase Line Utah in a different part of the front. Because of the overlapping times of these operations (spanning the period from April 4 to April 21), and the commitment of many of the same units to the two operations, no attempt will be made here to deal

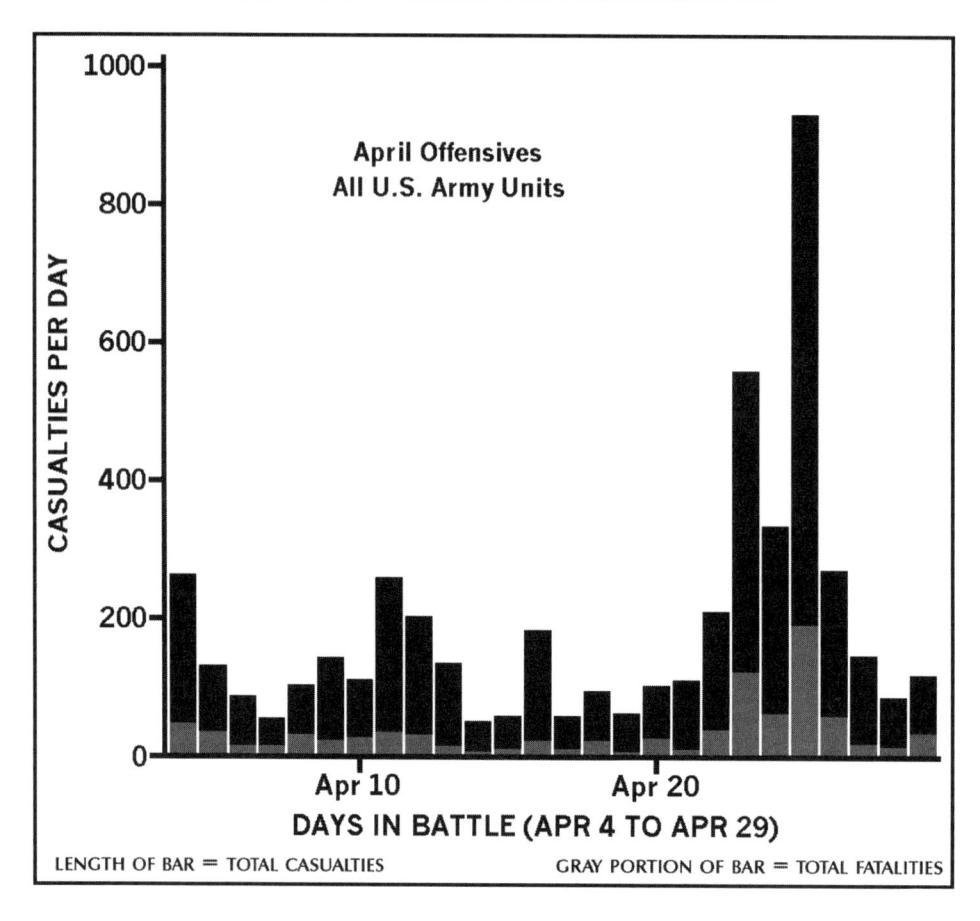

Figure 15. Daily casualties for all U.S. Army units during the April Offensives.

with them as separate campaigns. In Table 67 is a summary of the U.S. Army casualties in these two operations. Again, in these offensives, the low proportion of KIA, missing and captured confirms that UN forces maintained control of the combat.

Table 67 — April 1951 Offensives, All U.S. Army Units

	KIA	WIA	POW Returned	POW Died	MIA Returned	MIA Died	Unit Total
1st Cavalry Division							
5th Cav, 1st Cav Div		2					2
7th Cav, 1st Cav Div	26	80					106
8th Cav, 1st Cav Div	4	19					23
Other 1st Cav Units (8)	8	20					28
Total	38	121					159
2nd Infantry Division							
23rd Inf, 2nd Div	28	118					146
38th Inf, 2nd Div		1					1
Other 2nd Div Units (6)	3	27					30
Total	31	146					177

(continued on next page)

I. The Peninsular War

Table 67 (*cont.*)

	KIA	WIA	POW Returned	POW Died	MIA Returned	MIA Died	Unit Total
3rd Infantry Division							
7th Inf 3rd Inf Div	3	23					26
65th Inf, 3rd Inf Div	5	98					103
15th Inf, 3rd Inf Div		1					1
Other 3rd Div Units (7)	5	29					34
Total	13	151					164
7th Infantry Division							
17th Inf, 7th Inf Div	40	161	1				202
32nd Inf, 7th Inf Div	4	27	1			1	33
Other 7th Div Units (7)	8	25	1				34
Total	52	213	3			1	269
24th Infantry Division							
21st Inf, 24th Inf Div	38	158	1				197
19th Inf, 24th Inf Div	49	303					352
34th Inf, 24th Inf Div		1					1
Other 24th Div Units (6)	8	28					36
Total	95	490	1				586
25th Infantry Division							
24th Inf, 25th Inf Div	29	294	2			2	327
27th Inf, 25th Inf Div	32	98					130
35th Inf, 25th Inf Div	9	46					55
Other 25th Div Units (9)	3	20					23
Total	73	458	2			2	535
5th RCT	25	113					138
3rd Ranger Company	4	24					28
4th Ranger Company	3	13					16
5th Ranger Company	3	12					15
8th Ranger Company	2	7					9
Total Ranger Companies	12	56					68
Total Other Units (26)	15	64					79
Total All Units 04/04–04/21/51	354	1812	6			3	2175

Marine losses in these operations were moderate, with maximums of six KIA on the first day of the operation and five on the following day. These losses included a pilot lost in an air crash over land each of these days. In addition, one Navy corpsman was killed on April 5. He was awarded the Medal of Honor for his valor in the action.

Medal of Honor: Richard D. Dewert

Awarded to: Richard D. Dewert, Taunton, MA, Hospital Corpsman, U.S. Navy. Hospital Corpsman attached to Marine infantry company, 1st Marine Division. Korea, 5 April 1951.

> For conspicuous gallantry and intrepidity at the risk of his life above and beyond the call of duty while serving as a HC, in action against enemy aggressor forces. When a fire team from the point platoon of his company was pinned down by a deadly barrage of hostile automatic weapons fired

and suffered many casualties, HC Dewert rushed to the assistance of one of the more seriously wounded and, despite a painful leg wound sustained while dragging the stricken marine to safety, steadfastly refused medical treatment for himself and immediately dashed back through the fireswept area to carry a second wounded man out of the line of fire. Undaunted by the mounting hail of devastating enemy fire, he bravely moved forward a third time and received another serious wound in the shoulder after discovering that a wounded marine had already died. Still persistent in his refusal to submit to first aid, he resolutely answered the call of a fourth stricken comrade and, while rendering medical assistance, was himself mortally wounded by a burst of enemy fire. His courageous initiative, great personal valor, and heroic spirit of self-sacrifice in the face of overwhelming odds reflect the highest credit upon HC Dewert and enhance the finest traditions of the U.S. Naval Service. He gallantly gave his life for his country.

Total Marine fatalities in the period were 25, including four pilots lost in plane crashes—three over land and one at sea—and two in aircraft losses on the ground.

All Navy losses in the period, except for the corpsman listed above and one officer also killed in ground action, were six pilots lost in crashes over land. Three of the pilots were killed in action and three were reported missing and never found.

Air Force losses in the period were substantial, almost half of them the result of the war's first major air combat. On April 12, a B-29 formation was attacked by an estimated 40 MIG fighters. Nine MIGs were shot down, but three B-29s were also lost. A total of 22 airmen were lost that day, four killed in action and 18 reported as missing and declared dead. Total U.S. Air Force losses in the period are indicated in Table 68.

Table 68 — April 1951 Offensives, U.S. Air Force

Fixed Wing Crash Over Land	
Pilot, Killed in Action	4
Pilot, Died while Missing	17
Aircrew, Killed in Action	5
Aircrew, Died of Wounds	1
Aircrew, Died while Missing	23
Non-Aircrew, Died while Missing	4
Total 04/04–04/21/51	54

First CCF Spring Counteroffensive

On April 22, 1951, the CCF struck back with an estimated 250 thousand men. As Figure 15 indicates, U.S. Army losses for the next week increased substantially, as units grudgingly gave up ground to fanatical attackers. Along with the U.S. Marines, the ROK army and French and British units, they held the line north of Seoul and prevented its recapture by the communists. The effort was not without significant cost.

The worst day was April 25, when several U.S. Army units were overrun. Table 69 shows total Army casualties on that day, with those units specifically identified that suffered the greatest losses.

I. The Peninsular War

Table 69 — Bad Day in April, All U. S. Army Units

	KIA	WIA	POW Returned	POW Died	MIA Returned	MIA Died	Unit Total
5th RCT	26	104	20	4	4	2	160
555th FA Bn, 5th RCT	12	61	27	2	1	1	104
8th Ranger Company	2	21					23
7th Inf 3rd Inf Div	30	105	27	7	1	15	185
Other 3rd Div Units (6)	3	25	4	1			33
35th Inf, 25th Inf Div	28	73	39	3	1	3	147
Other 25th Div Units (6)	7	20	4				31
1st Cavalry Division	11	51	16*	2		1	81
2nd Infantry Division	1	3	1				5
7th Infantry Division	4	16					20
24th Infantry Division	15	90	13	2		5	125
Other Units (5)	3	10		1			14
Total 04/25/51	142	579	151	22	7	27	928

*All 16 of these POWs were in the 6th Tank Battalion.

The 8th Ranger Company, which was attached to the 5th RCT, is identified here because reports have suggested that only 65 Rangers survived being entrapped by CCF forces that day. It appears that those reports may have been exaggerated. However, the "Triple Nickel," the 555th FA Battalion of the 5th RCT, did not fare as well. Its losses were substantial, adding to its history from the Pusan Perimeter as an ill-fated unit.

In this action, five Medals of Honor were awarded, four to members of the 3rd Division's 7th Infantry Regiment and one to a member of the 24th Divisions 21st Infantry Regiment.

Medal of Honor: Clair Goodblood

Awarded to: Corporal Clair Goodblood, Burnham, ME, U.S. Army, Company D, 7th Infantry Regiment, 3rd Infantry Division. Near Popsu-dong, Korea, 24 and 25 April 1951.

> Cpl. Goodblood, a member of Company D, distinguished himself by conspicuous gallantry and intrepidity at the risk of his life above and beyond the call of duty in action against an armed enemy of the United Nations. Cpl. Goodblood, a machine gunner, was attached to Company B in defensive positions on thickly wooded key terrain under attack by a ruthless foe. In bitter fighting which ensued, the numerically superior enemy infiltrated the perimeter, rendering the friendly positions untenable. Upon order to move back, Cpl. Goodblood voluntarily remained to cover the withdrawal and, constantly vulnerable to heavy fire, inflicted withering destruction on the assaulting force. Seeing a grenade lobbed at his position, he shoved his assistant to the ground and flinging himself upon the soldier attempted to shield him. Despite his valorous act both men were wounded. Rejecting aid for himself, he ordered the ammunition bearer to evacuate the injured man for medical treatment. He fearlessly maintained his l-man defense, sweeping the onrushing assailants with fire until an enemy banzai charge carried the hill and silenced his gun. When friendly elements regained the commanding ground, Cpl. Goodblood's body was found lying beside his gun

and approximately 100 hostile dead lay in the wake of his field of fire. Through his unflinching courage and willing self-sacrifice the onslaught was retarded, enabling his unit to withdraw, regroup, and resecure the strongpoint. Cpl. Goodblood's inspirational conduct and devotion to duty reflect lasting glory on himself and are in keeping with the noble traditions of the military service.

Medal of Honor: Hiroshi H. Miyamura

Awarded to: Corporal Hiroshi H. Miyamura, Gallup, NM, U.S. Army, Company H, 7th Infantry Regiment, 3rd Infantry Division. Near Taejon-ni, Korea, 24 and 25 April 1951

> Cpl. Miyamura, a member of Company H, distinguished himself by conspicuous gallantry and intrepidity above and beyond the call of duty in action against the enemy. On the night of 24 April, Company H was occupying a defensive position when the enemy fanatically attacked threatening to overrun the position. Cpl. Miyamura, a machinegun squad leader, aware of the imminent danger to his men unhesitatingly jumped from his shelter wielding his bayonet in close hand-to-hand combat killing approximately 10 of the enemy. Returning to his position, he administered first aid to the wounded and directed their evacuation. As another savage assault hit the line, he manned his machinegun and delivered withering fire until his ammunition was expended. He ordered the squad to withdraw while he stayed behind to render the gun inoperative. He then bayoneted his way through infiltrated enemy soldiers to a second gun emplacement and assisted in its operation. When the intensity of the attack necessitated the withdrawal of the company Cpl. Miyamura ordered his men to fall back while he remained to cover their movement. He killed more than 50 of the enemy before his ammunition was depleted and he was severely wounded. He maintained his magnificent stand despite his painful wounds, continuing to repel the attack until his position was overrun. When last seen he was fighting ferociously against an overwhelming number of enemy soldiers. Cpl. Miyamura's indomitable heroism and consummate devotion to duty reflect the utmost glory on himself and uphold the illustrious traditions on the military service.

Cpl. Miyamura was captured in this action and remained a POW until he was released in operation Big Switch on August 20, 1953.

Medal of Honor: John Essebagger, Jr.

Awarded to: Corporal John Essebagger, Jr., Holland, MI, U.S. Army, Company A, 7th Infantry Regiment, 3d Infantry Division. Near Popsudong, Korea, 25 April 1951.

> Cpl. Essebagger, a member of Company A, distinguished himself by conspicuous gallantry and outstanding courage above and beyond the call of duty in action against the enemy. Committed to effect a delaying action to cover the 3d Battalion's withdrawal through Company A, Cpl. Essebagger, a member of 1 of 2 squads maintaining defensive positions in key terrain and defending the company's right flank, had participated in repulsing

numerous attacks. In a frenzied banzai charge the numerically superior enemy seriously threatened the security of the planned route of withdrawal and isolation of the small force. Badly shaken, the grossly outnumbered detachment started to fall back and Cpl. Essebagger, realizing the impending danger, voluntarily remained to provide security for the withdrawal. Gallantly maintaining a l-man stand, Cpl. Essebagger raked the menacing hordes with crippling fire and, with the foe closing on the position, left the comparative safety of his shelter and advanced in the face of overwhelming odds, firing his weapon and hurling grenades to disconcert the enemy and afford time for displacement of friendly elements to more tenable positions. Scorning the withering fire and bursting shells, Cpl. Essebagger continued to move forward, inflicting destruction upon the fanatical foe until he was mortally wounded. Cpl. Essebagger's intrepid action and supreme sacrifice exacted a heavy toll in enemy dead and wounded, stemmed the onslaught, and enabled the retiring squads to reach safety. His valorous conduct and devotion to duty reflected lasting glory upon himself and was in keeping with the noblest traditions of the infantry and the U.S. Army.

MEDAL OF HONOR: CHARLES L. GILLILAND

Awarded to: Corporal (then Pfc.) Charles L. Gilliland, Yellville (Marion County), AR, U.S. Army, Company I, 7th Infantry Regiment, 3d Infantry Division. Near Tongmang-ni, Korea, 25 April 1951.

Cpl. Gilliland, a member of Company I, distinguished himself by conspicuous gallantry and outstanding courage above and beyond the call of duty in action against the enemy. A numerically superior hostile force launched a coordinated assault against his company perimeter, the brunt of which was directed up a defile covered by his automatic rifle. His assistant was killed by enemy fire but Cpl. Gilliland, facing the full force of the assault, poured a steady fire into the foe which stemmed the onslaught. When 2 enemy soldiers escaped his raking fire and infiltrated the sector, he leaped from his foxhole, overtook and killed them both with his pistol. Sustaining a serious head wound in this daring exploit, he refused medical attention and returned to his emplacement to continue his defense of the vital defile. His unit was ordered back to new defensive positions but Cpl. Gilliland volunteered to remain to cover the withdrawal and hold the enemy at bay. His heroic actions and indomitable devotion to duty prevented the enemy from completely overrunning his company positions. Cpl. Gilliland's incredible valor and supreme sacrifice reflect lasting glory upon himself and are in keeping with the honored traditions of the military service.

MEDAL OF HONOR: RAY E. DUKE

Awarded to: Sergeant First Class Ray E. Duke, Whitwell (Marion County) TN, U.S. Army, Company C, 21st Infantry Regiment, 24th Infantry Division. Near Mugok, Korea, 26 April 1951.

Sfc. Duke, a member of Company C, distinguished himself by conspicuous gallantry and outstanding courage above and beyond the call of duty in action against the enemy. Upon learning that several of his men were isolated and heavily engaged in an area yielded by his platoon when ordered to withdraw, he led a small force in a daring assault which recovered the position and the beleaguered men. Another enemy attack in strength resulted in numerous casualties but Sfc. Duke, although wounded by mortar fragments, calmly moved along his platoon line to coordinate fields of fire and to urge his men to hold firm in the bitter encounter. Wounded a second time he received first aid and returned to his position. When the enemy again attacked shortly after dawn, despite his wounds, Sfc. Duke repeatedly braved withering fire to insure maximum defense of each position. Threatened with annihilation and with mounting casualties, the platoon was again ordered to withdraw when Sfc. Duke was wounded a third time in both legs and was unable to walk. Realizing that he was impeding the progress of 2 comrades who were carrying him from the hill, he urged them to leave him and seek safety. He was last seen pouring devastating fire into the ranks of the onrushing assailants. The consummate courage, superb leadership, and heroic actions of Sfc. Duke, displayed during intensive action against overwhelming odds, reflect the highest credit upon himself, the infantry, and the U.S. Army.

Total U.S. Army casualties in the eight days of the counteroffensive are summarized in Table 70.

Table 70 — First CCF Spring Counteroffensive, All U.S. Army Units

	KIA	WIA	POW Returned	POW Died	MIA Returned	MIA Died	Unit Total
1st Cavalry Division	45	153	33	3		1	235
2nd Infantry Division	12	75	1				88
3rd Infantry Division	79	334	40	9	3	16	481
7th Infantry Division	40	151				5	196
24th Infantry Division	75	298	85	14		20	492
25th Infantry Division	78	326	62	5	2	6	479
5th RCT	60	285	160	25	6	16	552
Other Units (24)	24	110	9	2			122
Total 04/22–04/29/51	413	1709	390	58	11	64	2645

Casualties in the 1st Marine Division during the CCF counteroffensive were concentrated mostly on April 23 and 24, when they suffered 81 of their total of 96 fatalities. Of the total fatalities, four were pilots killed in fixed wing crashes over land and one was a ground casualty in an aircraft loss. Two Navy men, assumed to be corpsmen, were also killed in ground action.

Two marines were awarded the Medal of Honor for their valor during this operation.

Medal of Honor: Herbert A. Littleton

Awarded to: Private First Class Herbert A. Littleton, Blackhawk, SD, U.S. Marine Corps Reserve, Company C, 1st Battalion, 7th Marines, 1st Marine Division (Rein.). Chungchon, Korea, 22 April 1951.

> For conspicuous gallantry and intrepidity at the risk of his life above and beyond the call of duty while serving as a radio operator with an artillery forward observation team of Company C, in action against enemy aggres-

sor forces. Standing watch when a well-concealed and numerically superior enemy force launched a violent night attack from nearby positions against his company, Pfc. Littleton quickly alerted the forward observation team and immediately moved into an advantageous position to assist in calling down artillery fire on the hostile force. When an enemy handgrenade was thrown into his vantage point shortly after the arrival of the remainder of the team, he unhesitatingly hurled himself on the deadly missile, absorbing its full, shattering impact in his body. By his prompt action and heroic spirit of self-sacrifice, he saved the other members of his team from serious injury or death and enabled them to carry on the vital mission which culminated in the repulse of the hostile attack. His indomitable valor in the face of almost certain death reflects the highest credit upon Pfc. Littleton and the U.S. Naval Service. He gallantly gave his life for his country.

MEDAL OF HONOR: HAROLD E. WILSON

Awarded to: Technical Sergeant Harold E. Wilson, Birmingham, AL, U.S. Marine Corps Reserve, Company G, 3d Battalion, 1st Marines, 1st Marine Division (Rein.). Korea, 23–24 April 1951.

For gallantry and intrepidity at the risk of his life above and beyond the call of duty while serving as platoon sergeant of a rifle platoon attached to Company G, in action against enemy aggressor forces on the night of 23–24 April 1951. When the company outpost was overrun by the enemy while his platoon, firing from hastily constructed foxholes, was engaged in resisting the brunt of a fierce mortar, machinegun, grenade, and small-arms attack launched by hostile forces from high ground under cover of darkness, T/Sgt. Wilson braved intense fire to assist the survivors back into the line and to direct the treatment of casualties. Although twice wounded by gunfire, in the right arm and the left leg, he refused medical aid for himself and continued to move about among his men, shouting words of encouragement. After receiving further wounds in the head and shoulder as the attack increased in intensity, he again insisted upon remaining with his unit. Unable to use either arm to fire, and with mounting casualties among our forces, he resupplied his men with rifles and ammunition taken from the wounded. Personally reporting to his company commander on several occasions, he requested and received additional assistance when the enemy attack became even more fierce and, after placing the reinforcements in strategic positions in the line, directed effective fire until blown off his feet by the bursting of a hostile mortar round in his face. Dazed and suffering from concussion, he still refused medical aid and, despite weakness from loss of blood, moved from foxhole to foxhole, directing fire, resupplying ammunition, rendering first aid, and encouraging his men. By his heroic actions in the face of almost certain death, when the unit's ability to hold the disadvantageous position was doubtful, he instilled confidence in his troops, inspiring them to rally repeatedly and turn back the furious assaults. At dawn, after the final attack had been repulsed, he personally accounted for each man in his platoon before walking unassisted 1/2 mile to the aid station where he submitted to treatment. His outstanding courage, initiative, and skilled leadership in the face of overwhelming odds were contributing factors in the success of his company's mission and reflect the highest credit upon T/Sgt. Wilson and the U.S. Naval Service.

Two Navy pilots were lost in the operation, one KIA and the other reported missing and declared dead, both from fixed-wing crashes over land.

Table 71 is a summary of U.S. Air Force losses during the counteroffensive.

Table 71—First CCF Spring Counteroffensive, U.S. Air Force

Fixed Wing Crash Over Land	
Pilot, Died of Wounds	1
Pilot, Died while Missing	6
Aircrew, Died while Missing	4
Total 04/22–04/29/51	11

Spring Interlude

After UN forces held against the first Spring CCF offensive, the level of combat subsided for a time as each side regrouped and prepared for further action. U.S. Army casualties were relatively light for the next 17 days, as indicated in the following table.

Table 72 — Post-Offensive (Spring 1951), All U.S. Army Units

	KIA	WIA	POW Returned	POW Died	MIA Returned	MIA Died	Unit Total
1st Cavalry Division	19	89	1	1			110
2nd Infantry Division	15	87	2	1		1	106
3rd Infantry Division	2	41					43
7th Infantry Division	3	17					20
24th Infantry Division	6	38					44
25th Infantry Division	5	34					39
5th RCT	1	15					16
Other Units (17)*	3	48				2	53
Total 04/30–05/16/51	54	369	3	2		3	431

*21 of these casualties were in the 5th Ranger Company on 05/14/51.

Casualties were similarly light for the U.S. Marines, who reported only 12 fatalities in the period, including two pilots KIA in fixed-wing crashes over land.

The Navy reported only two fatalities, both pilots, one KIA in a fixed-wing crash over land and the other lost in a fixed-wing crash at sea and never found.

U.S. Air Force losses in the period remained relatively unrelated to the level of fighting on the ground. Table 73 gives a summary of Air Force fatalities.

Table 73 — Post-Offensive (Spring 1951), U.S. Air Force

Fixed Wing Crash Over Land	
Pilot, Died while Missing	21
Pilot, Died in Captivity	1
Aircrew, Died while Missing	11
Non-Aircrew, Died while Missing	3
Total 04/30–/5/16/51	36

The Second CCF Spring Offensive and the UN Response

The CCF launched its second offensive on May 17, 1951. For the next month, battles raged all across central Korea, as opposing forces attempted to gain tactical advantage. Figure 16 shows the distribution of U.S. Army casualties in these battles.

The apparent goal of the initial CCF thrust was to break through UN defenses and push south to envelop the 8th Army. The communist planners directed their push in the eastern sector of the 120-mile front, currently held by the U.S. 2nd Infantry Division, the 1st Marine Division and two ROK divisions. UN lines held briefly but then gave way in the ROK sector, leaving the flank of 2nd Division exposed. The level of casualties early in the offensive tells the story of what happened in the 2nd Division as a result. Details of those losses are summarized in Table 74.

The 1st Ranger Company was included in this summary because total casualties, and particularly the numbers of killed, captured and missing was so high for so small a unit. The 8282nd Military Missions Commissions was included because a pattern is beginning to emerge in which personnel in these units (whose "missions" appear to be especially hazardous) seem to have an unusual facility for getting themselves captured (see also Tables 47 and 60).

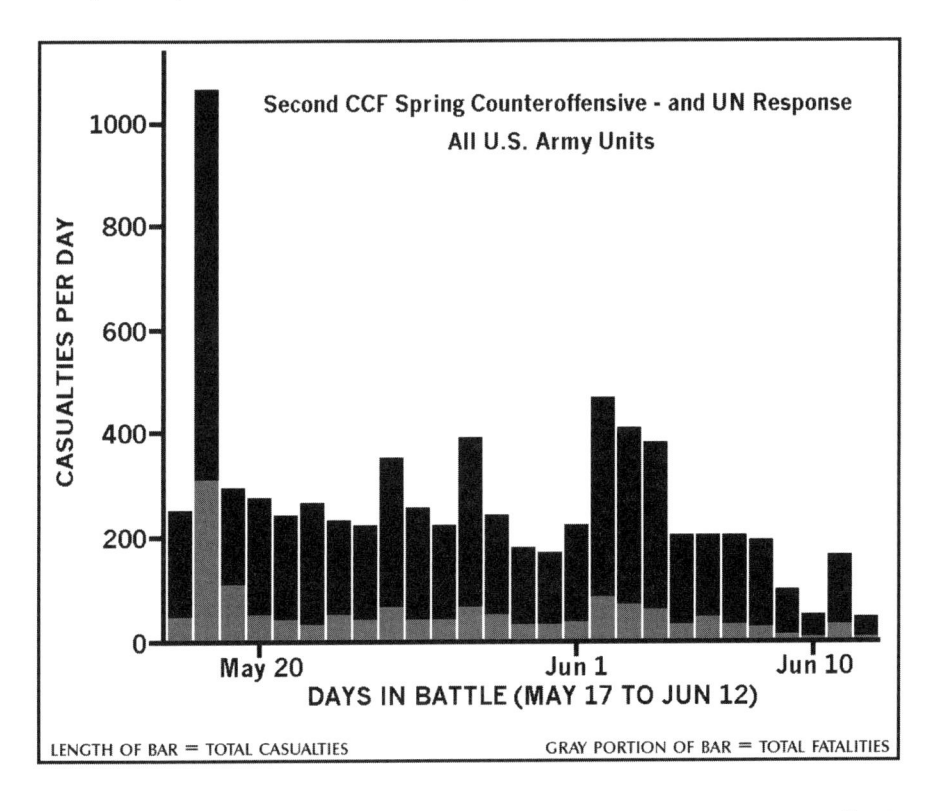

Figure 16. Daily casualties for all U.S. Army units during the Second CCF Spring Offensive and the UN Response.

Table 74 — Second CCF Spring Counteroffensive, 2nd Infantry Division

	KIA	WIA	POW Returned	POW Died	MIA Returned	MIA Died	Unit Total
2nd Division Units							
05/17/51							
23rd Inf, 2nd Div	5	24					29
38th Inf, 2nd Div	11	86	14	5	2	11	129
9th Inf, 2nd Div		2					2
Other 2nd Div Units (6)		10	3			1	14
Total 05/17/51	16	122	17	5	2	12	174
05/18/51							
23rd Inf, 2nd Div	87	104	142	26	27	8	394
38th Inf, 2nd Div	99	199	138	31	9	15	491
9th Inf, 2nd Div	4	18					22
Other 2nd Div Units (6)	12	19	2	1	1		35
Total 05/18/51	202	340	282	58	37	23	942
05/19/51							
23rd Inf, 2nd Div	4	27					31
38th Inf, 2nd Div	44	33	12	9		3	101
9th Inf, 2nd Div	14	30	3			4	51
Other 2nd Div Units (5)	2	3	2				7
Total 05/19/51	64	93	17	9		7	190
Total 2nd Div 05/17–05/19/51	282	555	316	72	39	42	1306
1st Ranger Company	23	22	6	2	2	1	56
8282nd Mil Missions Comm			9	3	1	3	16
Other Units (38)	32	189	9	1	4		235
Total 05/17–05/19/51	337	766	340	78	46	46	1613

Following these three days of combat, in which the 2nd Division, at obviously substantial cost, kept the attacking forces from penetrating UN lines, casualties in the division diminished to levels comparable to those of other units defending the front. However, the defensive battle continued for the next three days, and casualties were by no means trivial. Table 75 provides a summary of those casualties.

Table 75 — Second CCF Spring Counteroffensive, All U.S. Army Units

	KIA	WIA	POW Returned	POW Died	MIA Returned	MIA Died	Unit Total
1st Cavalry Division	15	86					101
2nd Infantry Division	17	74					91
3rd Infantry Division	32	146	1				179
7th Infantry Division	16	95					111
24th Infantry Division	15	54					69
25th Infantry Division	15	129					144
5th RCT	7	42					49
Other Units (11)*	2	36	1	2			41
Total 05/20–05/22/51	119	662	2	2			785

*The three captured individuals indicated here were all from the 20th Sig. Co, A-Gnd Liaisn

Clearly, although the CCF had its way briefly with the 2nd Division in its initial offensive thrust, casualty figures thereafter show no indication that their attack succeeded in any way.

During these three days of continuing defense, Medals of Honor were awarded for the heroic actions of two participants.

MEDAL OF HONOR: DONALD R. MOYER

Awarded to: Sergeant First Class Donald R. Moyer, Oakland, MI, U.S. Army, Company E, 35th Infantry Regiment, 25th Infantry Division. Near Seoul, Korea, 20 May 1951.

> Sfc. Moyer assistant platoon leader, Company E, distinguished himself by conspicuous gallantry and intrepidity at the risk of his life above and beyond the call of duty in action against an armed enemy of the United Nations. Sfc. Moyer's platoon was committed to attack and secure commanding terrain stubbornly defended by a numerically superior hostile force emplaced in well-fortified positions. Advancing up the rocky hill, the leading elements came under intense automatic weapons, small-arms, and grenade fire, wounding the platoon leader and platoon sergeant. Sfc. Moyer, realizing the success of the mission was imperiled, rushed to the head of the faltering column, assumed command and urged the men forward. Inspired by Sfc. Moyer's unflinching courage, the troops responded magnificently, but as they reached the final approaches to the rugged crest of the hill, enemy fire increased in volume and intensity and the fanatical foe showered the platoon with grenades. Undaunted, the valiant group forged ahead, and as they neared the top of the hill, the enemy hurled a grenade into their midst. Sfc. Moyer, fully aware of the odds against him, unhesitatingly threw himself on the grenade, absorbing the full blast of the explosion with his body. Although mortally wounded in this fearless display of valor, Sfc. Moyer's intrepid act saved several of his comrades from death or serious injury, and his inspirational leadership and consummate devotion to duty contributed significantly to the subsequent seizure of the enemy stronghold and reflect lasting glory on himself and the noble traditions of the military service.

Database records indicate that Sfc. Moyer had been wounded earlier in the year and had returned to duty in March, after 10 weeks of hospitalization

MEDAL OF HONOR: JOSEPH C. RODRIGUEZ

Awarded to: Sergeant (then Pfc.) Joseph C. Rodriguez, San Bernardino, CA, U.S. Army, Company F, 17th Infantry Regiment, 7th Infantry Division. Near Munye-ri, Korea, 21 May 1951.

> Sgt. Rodriguez, distinguished himself by conspicuous gallantry and intrepidity at the risk of his life above and beyond the call of duty in action against an armed enemy of the United Nations. Sgt. Rodriguez, an assistant squad leader of the 2d Platoon, was participating in an attack against a fanatical hostile force occupying well-fortified positions on rugged commanding terrain, when his squad's advance was halted within approxi-

mately 60 yards by a withering barrage of automatic weapons and small-arms fire from 5 emplacements directly to the front and right and left flanks, together with grenades which the enemy rolled down the hill toward the advancing troops. Fully aware of the odds against him, Sgt. Rodriguez leaped to his feet, dashed 60 yards up the fire-swept slope, and, after lobbing grenades into the first foxhole with deadly accuracy, ran around the left flank, silenced an automatic weapon with 2 grenades and continued his whirlwind assault to the top of the peak, wiping out 2 more foxholes and then, reaching the right flank, he tossed grenades into the remaining emplacement, destroying the gun and annihilating its crew. Sgt. Rodriguez' intrepid actions exacted a toll of 15 enemy dead and, as a result of his incredible display of valor, the defense of the opposition was broken, and the enemy routed, and the strategic strongpoint secured. His unflinching courage under fire and inspirational devotion to duty reflect highest credit on himself and uphold the honored traditions of the military service.

Database records indicate that Sgt. Rodriguez was not wounded in this action, but *was* wounded six days later and returned to duty in early July after six weeks of rehabilitation.

Losses among U.S. Marines in the CCF offensive and the subsequent UN response exhibited a somewhat different pattern than did the casualties in Army units. The marines had elevated fatalities over the first four days of the operation, and then much reduced losses for the following six days. From casualty counts, it appears that U.S. Marine participation in the UN counterattack began later than the Army effort and lasted longer. Thus, marine casualties in the first 10 days of the operation will be summarized here, and then their losses in the counterattack will be shown later in a specific graph.

The 1st Marine Division lost a total of 24 men in the first four days of the second CCF spring offensive (a maximum of nine on May 20). Two of these were pilots lost in plane crashes over land. Three presumed Navy corpsmen were killed in the same period. In the following six days, eight marines and two corpsmen died. Other Navy losses and all Air Force losses in these first ten days will be included in single summaries at the end of this section.

UN Counterattack

Beginning about May 23, the 8th Army surprised the badly battered communist army by mounting a major offensive. First called Operation Detonate and later Operation Piledriver, these operations were intended to recover the territory lost in the two CCF offensives. As Figure 16 suggests, these operations continued — and continued to produce significant U.S. Army casualties — through about June 12. Table 76 is an accounting of those casualties by major unit.

Although some units obviously had higher numbers of casualties on some days, there were no days during this period when any single unit took casualties in extraordinary numbers. On each of four of the days during the battle, one American soldier earned the Medal of Honor for his heroic actions.

Table 76 — Operations Detonate and Piledriver, All U.S. Army Units

	KIA	WIA	POW Returned	POW Died	MIA Returned	MIA Died	Unit Total
1st Cavalry Division	76	623	5				704
2nd Infantry Division	126	682	2	2	2	4	818
3rd Infantry Division	120	543				7	670
7th Infantry Division	195	814	2				1011
24th Infantry Division	50	178	1	1			230
25th Infantry Division	132	606	2				740
187 Airborne Regt/RCT	110	443	6	3	2	4	568
5th RCT	4	11					15
Other Units (43)	25	144	3	1		1	174
Total 05/23–06/12/51	838	4044	21	7	4	16	4756

MEDAL OF HONOR: RODOLFO P. HERNANDEZ

Awarded to: Corporal Rodolfo P. Hernandez, Fowler, CA, U.S. Army, Company G, 187th Airborne Regimental Combat Team. Near Wontong-ni, Korea, 31 May 1951

> Cpl. Hernandez, a member of Company G, distinguished himself by conspicuous gallantry and intrepidity above and beyond the call of duty in action against the enemy. His platoon, in defensive positions on Hill 420, came under ruthless attack by a numerically superior and fanatical hostile force, accompanied by heavy artillery, mortar, and machinegun fire which inflicted numerous casualties on the platoon. His comrades were forced to withdraw due to lack of ammunition but Cpl. Hernandez, although wounded in an exchange of grenades, continued to deliver deadly fire into the ranks of the onrushing assailants until a ruptured cartridge rendered his rifle inoperative. Immediately leaving his position, Cpl. Hernandez rushed the enemy armed only with rifle and bayonet. Fearlessly engaging the foe, he killed 6 of the enemy before falling unconscious from grenade, bayonet, and bullet wounds but his heroic action momentarily halted the enemy advance and enabled his unit to counterattack and retake the lost ground. The indomitable fighting spirit, outstanding courage, and tenacious devotion to duty clearly demonstrated by Cpl. Hernandez reflect the highest credit upon himself, the infantry, and the U.S. Army.

Cpl. Hernandez was wounded seriously enough in this action that he had to be evacuated to States and was separated from the service. The disposition date was July 6, 1951.

MEDAL OF HONOR: CORNELIUS H. CHARLTON

Awarded to: Sergeant Cornelius H. Charlton, Bronx, NY, U.S. Army, Company C, 24th Infantry Regiment, 25th Infantry Division. Near Chipo-ri, Korea, 2 June 1951.

> Sgt. Charlton, a member of Company C, distinguished himself by conspicuous gallantry and intrepidity above and beyond the call of duty in

action against the enemy. His platoon was attacking heavily defended hostile positions on commanding ground when the leader was wounded and evacuated. Sgt. Charlton assumed command, rallied the men, and spearheaded the assault against the hill. Personally eliminating 2 hostile positions and killing 6 of the enemy with his rifle fire and grenades, he continued up the slope until the unit suffered heavy casualties and became pinned down. Regrouping the men he led them forward only to be again hurled back by a shower of grenades. Despite a severe chest wound, Sgt. Charlton refused medical attention and led a third daring charge which carried to the crest of the ridge. Observing that the remaining emplacement which had retarded the advance was situated on the reverse slope, he charged it alone, was again hit by a grenade but raked the position with a devastating fire which eliminated it and routed the defenders. The wounds received during his daring exploits resulted in his death but his indomitable courage, superb leadership, and gallant self-sacrifice reflect the highest credit upon himself the infantry, and the military service.

MEDAL OF HONOR: BENJAMIN F. WILSON

Awarded to: First Lieutenant (then M/Sgt.) Benjamin F. Wilson, Vashon, WA, U.S. Army Company I, 31st Infantry Regiment, 7th Infantry Division. Near Hwach'on-Myon, Korea, 5 June 1951.

1st Lt. Wilson distinguished himself by conspicuous gallantry and indomitable courage above and beyond the call of duty in action against the enemy. Company I was committed to attack and secure commanding terrain stubbornly defended by a numerically superior hostile force emplaced in well-fortified positions. When the spearheading element was pinned down by withering hostile fire, he dashed forward and, firing his rifle and throwing grenades, neutralized the position denying the advance and killed 4 enemy soldiers manning submachineguns. After the assault platoon moved up, occupied the position, and a base of fire was established, he led a bayonet attack which reduced the objective and killed approximately 27 hostile soldiers. While friendly forces were consolidating the newly won gain, the enemy launched a counterattack and 1st Lt. Wilson, realizing the imminent threat of being overrun, made a determined loneman charge, killing 7 and wounding 2 of the enemy, and routing the remainder in disorder. After the position was organized, he led an assault carrying to approximately 15 yards of the final objective, when enemy fire halted the advance. He ordered the platoon to withdraw and, although painfully wounded in this action, remained to provide covering fire. During an ensuing counterattack, the commanding officer and 1st Platoon leader became casualties. Unhesitatingly, 1st Lt. Wilson charged the enemy ranks and fought valiantly, killing 3 enemy soldiers with his rifle before it was wrested from his hands, and annihilating 4 others with his entrenching tool. His courageous delaying action enabled his comrades to reorganize and effect an orderly withdrawal. While directing evacuation of the wounded, he suffered a second wound, but elected to remain on the position until assured that all of the men had reached safety. 1st Lt. Wilson's sustained valor and intrepid actions reflect utmost credit upon himself and uphold the honored traditions of the military service.

The database has no record of Lt. (Msgt.) Wilson's wounds.

Medal of Honor: Jack G. Hanson

Awarded to: Private First Class Jack G. Hanson, Escaptawpa, MS, U.S. Army, Company F, 31st Infantry Regiment, 7th Infantry Division. Near Pachi-dong, Korea, 7 June 1951.

> Pfc. Hanson, a machine gunner with the 1st Platoon, Company F, distinguished himself by conspicuous gallantry and intrepidity at the risk of his life above and beyond the call of duty in action against an armed enemy of the United Nations. The company, in defensive positions on two strategic hills separated by a wide saddle, was ruthlessly attacked at approximately 0300 hours, the brunt of which centered on the approach to the divide within range of Pfc. Hanson's machinegun. In the initial phase of the action, 4 riflemen were wounded and evacuated and the numerically superior enemy, advancing under cover of darkness, infiltrated and posed an imminent threat to the security of the command post and weapons platoon. Upon orders to move to key terrain above and to the right of Pfc. Hanson's position, he voluntarily remained to provide protective fire for the withdrawal. Subsequent to the retiring elements fighting a rearguard action to the new location, it was learned that Pfc. Hanson's assistant gunner and 3 riflemen had been wounded and had crawled to safety, and that he was maintaining a lone-man defense. After the 1st Platoon reorganized, counterattacked, and resecured its original positions at approximately 0530 hours, Pfc. Hanson's body was found lying in front of his emplacement, his machinegun ammunition expended, his empty pistol in his right hand, and a machete with blood on the blade in his left hand, and approximately 22 enemy dead lay in the wake of his action. Pfc. Hanson's consummate valor, inspirational conduct, and willing self-sacrifice enabled the company to contain the enemy and regain the commanding ground, and reflect lasting glory on himself and the noble traditions of the military service.

As was pointed out earlier, the participation in the May 1951 UN counterattack by the 1st Marine Division started and ended a few days later than that of U.S. Army units—at least in terms of their respective casualty patterns. Marine losses by day in this battle are shown in Figure 17.*

Included in the data presented in Figure 17 are marine losses in an operation called the Battle for the Punchbowl, which is reported to have taken place between June 10 and 16. Because the casualty figures for those dates cannot be distinguished in number from other dates before and after, no effort will be made here to identify specifically the losses in that battle.

Total marine fatalities in the period shown in Figure 17 were 230, including five pilots lost in fixed-wing crashes over land and two men killed in aircraft loss on the

---

The dates in the figure on which no fatalities are indicated require some further discussion. It seems unlikely that, in a battle in which losses occurred consistently over an extended period of days, there would be days with no losses at all. Of course, anything is possible, but given the problems inherent in the database used to generate the data, that is probably not the case—although a better explanation remains elusive at present. The initial introduction to the database pointed out that about two percent of the records used to compile losses for U.S. Marine units have occurrence dates that cannot be used because they refer to dates after the end of the war. In addition, many of these records are also missing data about the cause of the casualty. Thus, there is no way at present to reconcile any of these records with the apparently missing data in Figure 17, or any other anomaly that may come up in the presentation of casualty figures for the Marine Corps.

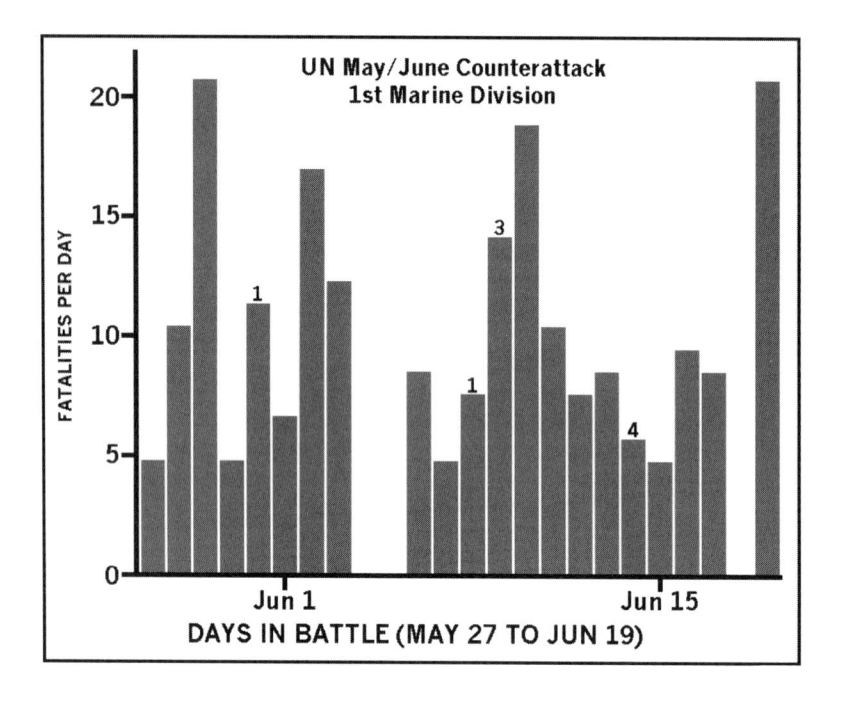

Figure 17. Daily fatalities for U.S. Marine units during the UN May/June 1951 counterattack. The numbers over the bars on some dates indicate the number of presumed Navy corpsmen killed in ground action on those days.

ground. As the figure indicates, nine presumed navy corpsmen were also lost in this action. On each of the two days recording the highest level of casualties in this operation, Medals of Honor were awarded to marines for their bravery in the fighting.

MEDAL OF HONOR: WHITT L. MORELAND

Awarded to: Private First Class Whitt L. Moreland, Austin, TX, U.S. Marine Corps Reserve, Company C, 1st Battalion, 5th Marines, 1st Marine Division (Rein.). Kwagch'i-Dong, Korea, 29 May 1951.

> For conspicuous gallantry and intrepidity at the risk of his life above and beyond the call of duty while serving as an intelligence scout attached to Company C, in action against enemy aggressor forces. Voluntarily accompanying a rifle platoon in a daring assault against a strongly defended enemy hill position, Pfc. Moreland delivered accurate rifle fire on the hostile emplacement and thereby aided materially in seizing the objective. After the position had been secured, he unhesitatingly led a party forward to neutralize an enemy bunker which he had observed some 400 meters beyond, and moving boldly through a fire-swept area, Almost reached the hostile emplacement when the enemy launched a volley of handgrenades on his group. Quick to act despite the personal danger involved, he kicked several of the grenades off the ridge line where they exploded harmlessly and, while attempting to kick away another, slipped and fell near the deadly missile. Aware that the sputtering grenade would explode before he could

regain his feet and dispose of it, he shouted a warning to his comrades, covered the missile with his body and absorbed the full blast of the explosion, but in saving his companions from possible injury or death, was mortally wounded. His heroic initiative and valiant spirit of self-sacrifice in the face of certain death reflect the highest credit upon Pfc. Moreland and the U.S. Naval Service. He gallantly gave his life for his country.

MEDAL OF HONOR: CHARLES G. ABRELL

Awarded to: Corporal Charles G. Abrell, Terre Haute, IN, U.S. Marine Corps, Company E, 2d Battalion, 1st Marines, 1st Marine Division (Rein.). Hangnyong, Korea, 10 June 1951

> For conspicuous gallantry and intrepidity at the risk of his life above and beyond the call of duty while serving as a fire team leader in Company E, in action against enemy aggressor forces. While advancing with his platoon in an attack against well-concealed and heavily fortified enemy hill positions, Cpl. Abrell voluntarily rushed forward through the assaulting squad which was pinned down by a hail of intense and accurate automatic-weapons fire from a hostile bunker situated on commanding ground. Although previously wounded by enemy handgrenade fragments, he proceeded to carry out a bold, single-handed attack against the bunker, exhorting his comrades to follow him. Sustaining 2 additional wounds as he stormed toward the emplacement, he resolutely pulled the pin from a grenade clutched in his hand and hurled himself bodily into the bunker with the live missile still in his grasp. Fatally wounded in the resulting explosion which killed the entire enemy guncrew within the stronghold, Cpl. Abrell, by his valiant spirit of self-sacrifice in the face of certain death, served to inspire all his comrades and contributed directly to the success of his platoon in attaining its objective. His superb courage and heroic initiative sustain and enhance the highest traditions of the U.S. Naval Service. He gallantly gave his life for his country.

On June 12, the U.S. Navy destroyer *Walke* hit a mine off Hungnam harbor, with the loss of 26 sailors killed in action. Other U.S. Navy losses in the period between May 17 and June 19 include six pilots lost in fixed wing air crashes over land, two of whom were never found and declared dead, and one sea casualty reported on May 18, who later died in captivity.

Air Force losses in the period May 17 to June 19 are summarized in Table 77.

Table 77 — May/June Actions, U.S. Air Force

Fixed Wing Crash Over Land	
Pilot, Killed in Action	3
Pilot, Died while Missing	27
Pilot, Died in Captivity	1
Aircrew, Died while Missing	16
Aircrew, Died in Captivity	2
Non-Aircrew, Died while Missing	6
Ground Casualty	
Small-arms Fire, Died of Wounds	1
Total 05/17–06/19/51	56

Dueling

For the next two and a half months, U.S. Army casualties remained at a relatively low level, averaging perhaps 40 per day. Clearly, the fighting continued, but there were no major offensives on either side. Except for one identified battle in late July, no single unit was engaged in sustained combat for more than a day or two and all units shared fairly equally in the fighting. Army losses in this period will be shown in three periods; the period before the Battle of Taeusan, the five days of that battle and the three and a half weeks following the battle. Table 78 is a summary of U.S. Army casualties in the first of those periods, from June 16 to July 25, 1951.

Table 78 — June/July 1951 Combat, All U.S. Army Units

	KIA	WIA	POW Returned	POW Died	MIA Returned	MIA Died	Unit Total
1st Cavalry Division	70	206				2	278
2nd Infantry Division	24	105	3	2			134
3rd Infantry Division	45	268	3			3	319
7th Infantry Division	19	75					94
24th Infantry Division	95	496	2			2	595
25th Infantry Division	26	93	5			5	129
5th RCT	14	49					63
Other Units (37)	14	88	2			3	107
Total 06/13–07/25/51	307	1380	15	2		15	1719

The combat that took place during these weeks tended to be more periodic, but it remained intense, as evidenced by the two Medals of Honor that were awarded during the fighting.

MEDAL OF HONOR: EMORY L. BENNETT

Awarded to: Private First Class Emory L. Bennett, Cocoa, FL, U.S. Army, Company B, 15th Infantry Regiment, 3d Infantry Division. Near Sobangsan, Korea, 24 June 1951.

> Pfc. Bennett a member of Company B, distinguished himself by conspicuous gallantry and intrepidity at the risk of his life above and beyond the call of duty in action against an armed enemy of the United Nations. At approximately 0200 hours, 2 enemy battalions swarmed up the ridge line in a ferocious banzai charge in an attempt to dislodge Pfc. Bennett's company from its defensive positions. Meeting the challenge, the gallant defenders delivered destructive retaliation, but the enemy pressed the assault with fanatical determination and the integrity of the perimeter was imperiled. Fully aware of the odds against him, Pfc. Bennett unhesitatingly left his foxhole, moved through withering fire, stood within full view of the enemy, and, employing his automatic rifle, poured crippling fire into the ranks of the onrushing assailants, inflicting numerous casualties. Although wounded, Pfc. Bennett gallantly maintained his l-man defense and the attack was momentarily halted. During this lull in battle, the company regrouped for counterattack, but the numerically superior foe soon infiltrated into the position. Upon orders to move back, Pfc. Bennett vol-

untarily remained to provide covering fire for the withdrawing elements, and, defying the enemy, continued to sweep the charging foe with devastating fire until mortally wounded. His willing self-sacrifice and intrepid actions saved the position from being overrun and enabled the company to effect an orderly withdrawal. Pfc. Bennett's unflinching courage and consummate devotion to duty reflect lasting glory on himself and the military service.

Medal of Honor: Leroy A. Mendonca

Awarded to: Sergeant Leroy A. Mendonca, Honolulu, T.H., U.S. Army, Company B, 7th Infantry Regiment, 3d Infantry Division. Near Chich-on, Korea, 4 July 1951.

Sgt. LeRoy A. Mendonca, distinguished himself by conspicuous gallantry above and beyond the call of duty in action against the enemy. After his platoon, in an exhaustive fight, had captured Hill 586, the newly won positions were assaulted during the night by a numerically superior enemy force. When the 1st Platoon positions were outflanked and under great pressure and the platoon was ordered to withdraw to a secondary line of defense, Sgt. Mendonca voluntarily remained in an exposed position and covered the platoon's withdrawal. Although under murderous enemy fire, he fired his weapon and hurled grenades at the onrushing enemy until his supply of ammunition was exhausted. He fought on, clubbing with his rifle and using his bayonet until he was mortally wounded. After the action it was estimated that Sgt. Mendonca had accounted for 37 enemy casualties. His daring actions stalled the crushing assault, protecting the platoon's withdrawal to secondary positions, and enabling the entire unit to repel the enemy attack and retain possession of the vital hilltop position. Sgt. Mendonca's extraordinary gallantry and exemplary valor are in keeping with the highest traditions of the U.S. Army.

Beginning on July 26, the 38th Infantry Regiment of the U.S. 2nd Infantry Division engaged the enemy in the Battle of Taeusan (Hill 1179) on the western edge of the Punchbowl. The battle continued through July 30, when the 38th succeeded in securing the hill. Table 79 shows the distribution of U.S. Army casualties during the five days of the battle.

Table 79 — Battle of Taeusan, 38th Infantry Regiment

	KIA	WIA	POW Returned	POW Died	MIA Returned	MIA Died	Unit Total
2nd Infantry Division							
38th Inf, 2nd Div	41	281				1	1	324
Other 2nd Div Units (5)	9	27					36
Total 2nd Division	50	308			1	1	360
All Other Units (15)	10	53				1	64
Total 07/26–07/30/51	60	361			1	2	424

Following this battle, combat for U.S. Army units continued for the next 26 days at roughly the same pace as it had during the preceding month. The fighting was periodically intense and most all major units contributed to the effort. Table 80 summarizes the casualties as a result of that effort.

Table 80 — August 1951 Combat, All U.S. Army Units

	KIA	WIA	POW Returned	POW Died	MIA Returned	MIA Died	Unit Total
1st Cavalry Division	56	192	4			4	256
2nd Infantry Division	32	232				2	266
3rd Infantry Division	22	52	10			2	86
7th Infantry Division	8	49					57
24th Infantry Division	6	19					25
25th Infantry Division	38	115				3	156
5th RCT	8	53					61
Total Other Units (12)	2	29					31
Total 07/31–08/25/51	**172**	**741**	**14**			**11**	**938**

Casualties in the 1st Marine Division, for the two months since fighting subsided in mid June, were minimal. Marine fatalities between June 20 and August 25 totaled 55, including five pilots lost in fixed wing crashes over land, three of them KIA and two missing, never found and declared dead. One Navy corpsman also died in ground action with the marines in this period.

Other naval personnel lost in the period were all airmen killed in fixed-wing air crashes over land, nine pilots and one aircrew member. Five of the pilots were reported missing, never found and declared dead. During the period, one naval helicopter pilot was awarded the Medal of Honor for his valiant actions.

Medal of Honor: John Kelvin Koelsch

Awarded to: Lieutenant (j.g.) John Kelvin Koelsch, Los Angeles, CA, U.S. Navy, Navy helicopter rescue unit. North Korea, 3 July 1951.

> For conspicuous gallantry and intrepidity at the risk of his life above and beyond the call of duty while serving with a Navy helicopter rescue unit. Although darkness was rapidly approaching when information was received that a marine aviator had been shot down and was trapped by the enemy in mountainous terrain deep in hostile territory, Lt. (j.g.) Koelsch voluntarily flew a helicopter to the reported position of the downed airman in an attempt to effect a rescue. With an almost solid overcast concealing everything below the mountain peaks, he descended in his unarmed and vulnerable aircraft without the accompanying fighter escort to an extremely low altitude beneath the cloud level and began a systematic search. Despite the increasingly intense enemy fire, which struck his helicopter on 1 occasion, he persisted in his mission until he succeeded in locating the downed pilot, who was suffering from serious burns on the arms and legs. While the victim was being hoisted into the aircraft, it was struck again by an accurate burst of hostile fire and crashed on the side of the mountain. Quickly extricating his crewmen and the aviator from the wreckage, Lt. (j.g.) Koelsch led them from the vicinity in an effort to escape from hostile troops, evading the enemy forces for 9 days and rendering such medical attention as possible to his severely burned companion until all were captured. Up to the time of his death while still a captive of the enemy, Lt. (j.g.) Koelsch steadfastly refused to aid his captors in any manner and served to inspire his fellow prisoners by his fortitude and consideration for others. His great personal valor and heroic spirit of self-sacrifice throughout sustain and enhance the finest traditions of the U.S. Naval Service.

I. The Peninsular War

Lt. (jg) Koelsch cannot be found in the database, nor can any records be found documenting marine fliers downed on or near the date indicated in the award.

Air Forces losses in this period continued to be significant. They are summarized in table 81.

Table 81—Summer 1951, U.S. Air Force

Fixed Wing Crash Over Land	
Pilot, Killed in Action	7
Pilot, Died of Wounds	1
Pilot, Died while Missing	38
Pilot, Died in Captivity	2
Aircrew, Killed in Action	1
Aircrew, Died while Missing	7
Non-Aircrew, Died while Missing	3
Total 06/20–08/25/51	59

Consolidation

The 8th Army spent September and October of 1951 defending territories it had captured in earlier offensives, and securing and consolidating positions that would facilitate their defense. From the battle losses, which were substantial, it is apparent that this undertaking involved every unit available to UN planners. Figure 18 shows the distribution of those losses in all U.S. Army units during the first half of this engagement.

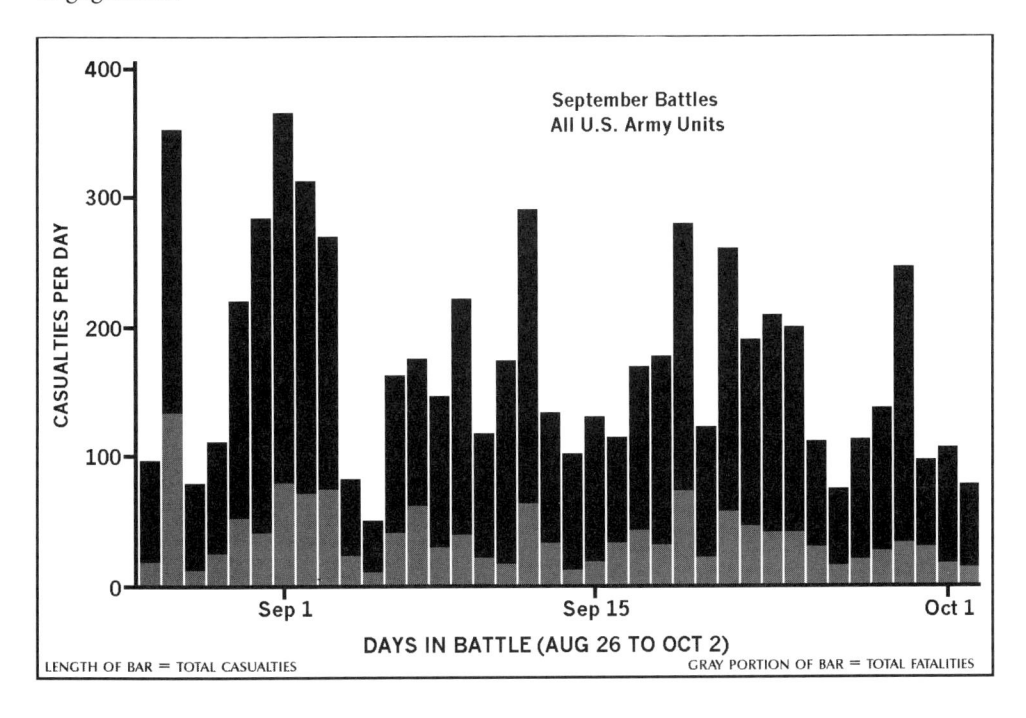

Figure 18. Daily casualties for all U.S. Army units during September Battles.

Table 82 shows how these casualties were distributed among the several U.S. Army units involved in the battles.

Table 82 — September 1951 Battles, All U.S. Army Units

	KIA	WIA	POW Returned	POW Died	MIA Returned	MIA Died	Unit Total
1st Cavalry Division	101	325	16			2	444
2nd Infantry Division	737	2360	35	4	1	18	3155
3rd Infantry Division	104	595	7			2	708
7th Infantry Division	231	890	9			2	1132
24th Infantry Division	19	61				1	81
25th Infantry Division	182	720	18		1	17	938
5th RCT	2	5					7
Other Units (36)	13	81	1			1	96
Total 08/26–10/03/51	1389	5037	86	4	2	43	6561

Several specific battles have been identified as having taken place during the period. The 2nd Division, as the table above suggests, was the primary participant in these battles. The first was the Battle of Bloody Ridge, which was reported in the chronology of the war to have taken place between August 18 and September 5. The second was the Battle of Heartbreak Ridge, which was reported to have occurred between September 13 and October 15. An inspection of 2nd Division casualties, however, indicates that the division was not engaged in intense and continuous fighting in either battle over either of the periods suggested in the reports. For example, the 2nd Division reported relatively few casualties in August until the 27th, when it becomes obvious that the Battle of Bloody Ridge began in earnest. Figure 19 shows the distribution of 2nd Division casualties during the period represented in Fig 18 and Table 82.

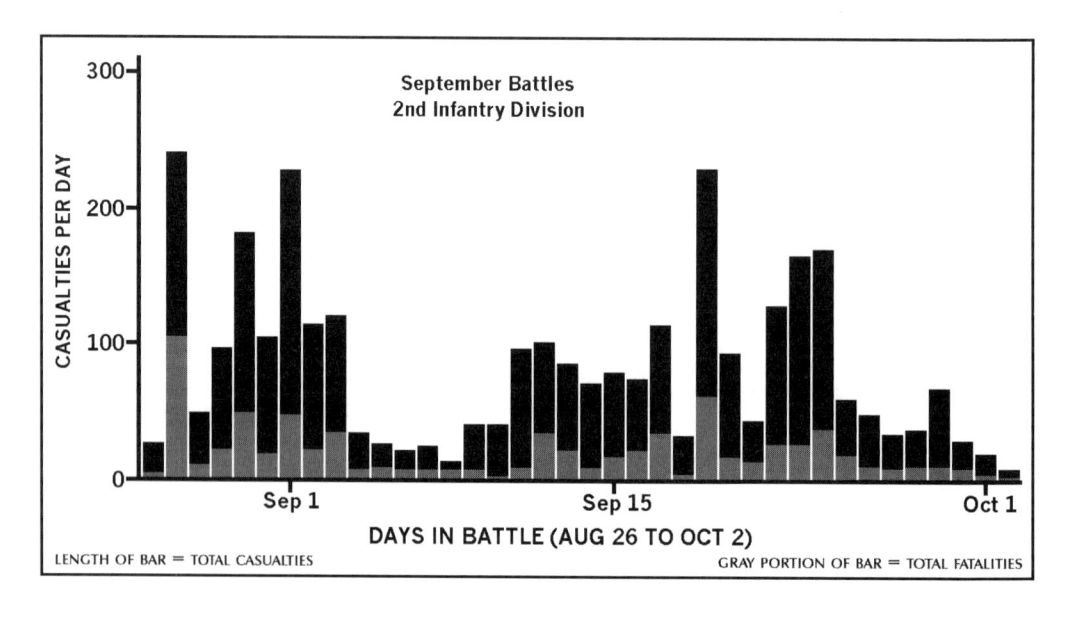

Figure 19. Daily casualties in the U.S. 2nd Infantry Division during September Battles.

Distribution of casualties among 2nd Division units during the Battle of Bloody Ridge (August 27 to September 3)* is shown in Table 83.

Table 83 — Bloody Ridge, 2nd Infantry Division

	KIA	WIA	POW Returned	POW Died	MIA Returned	MIA Died	Unit Total
2nd Infantry Division							
9th Inf, 2nd Div	144	472	4			5	625
38th Inf, 2nd Div	134	288	21	4		7	454
23rd Inf, 2nd Div	7	24					31
Other 2nd Div Units (8)	3	23					26
Total 2nd Div 08/27–09/03/51	288	807	25	4		12	1136

Two members of the 2nd Infantry Division earned Medal of Honor awards in this action.

MEDAL OF HONOR: LEE R. HARTELL

Awarded to: First Lieutenant Lee R. Hartell, Danbury CT, U.S. Army, Battery A, 15th Field Artillery Battalion, 2d Infantry Division. Near Kobangsan-ni, Korea, 27 August 1951.

> 1st. Lt. Hartell, a member of Battery A, distinguished himself by conspicuous gallantry and intrepidity at the risk of his life above and beyond the call of duty in action against an armed enemy of the United Nations. During the darkness of early morning, the enemy launched a ruthless attack against friendly positions on a rugged mountainous ridge. 1st Lt. Hartell, attached to Company B, 9th Infantry Regiment, as forward observer, quickly moved his radio to an exposed vantage on the ridge line to adjust defensive fires. Realizing the tactical advantage of illuminating the area of approach, he called for flares and then directed crippling fire into the onrushing assailants. At this juncture a large force of hostile troops swarmed up the slope in banzai charge and came within 10 yards of 1st Lt. Hartell's position. 1st Lt. Hartell sustained a severe hand wound in the ensuing encounter but grasped the microphone with his other hand and maintained his magnificent stand until the front and left flank of the company were protected by a close-in wall of withering fire, causing the fanatical foe to disperse and fall back momentarily. After the numerically superior enemy overran an outpost and was closing on his position, 1st Lt. Hartell, in a final radio call, urged the friendly elements to fire both batteries continuously. Although mortally wounded, 1st Lt. Hartell's intrepid actions contributed significantly to stemming the onslaught and enabled his company to maintain the strategic strongpoint. His consummate valor and unwavering devotion to duty reflect lasting glory on himself and uphold the noble traditions of the military service.

---

*When the chronology identifies a very lengthy battle, and the numbers of casualties don't indicate intense fighting over the entire period, the length of the battle will be considered to include only those days in which numbers of casualties occur that exceed significantly the numbers that are reported in the day-to-day combat taking place before and after the battle.

Medal of Honor: Edward C. Krzyzowski

Awarded to: Captain Edward C. Krzyzowski, Cicero, IL, U.S. Army, Company B, 9th Infantry Regiment, 2d Infantry Division. Near Tondul, Korea, from 31 August to 3 September 1951.

>Capt. Krzyzowski, distinguished himself by conspicuous gallantry and indomitable courage above and beyond the call of duty in action against the enemy as commanding officer of Company B. Spearheading an assault against strongly defended Hill 700, his company came under vicious crossfire and grenade attack from enemy bunkers. Creeping up the fire-swept hill, he personally eliminated 1 bunker with his grenades and wiped out a second with carbine fire. Forced to retire to more tenable positions for the night, the company, led by Capt. Krzyzowski, resumed the attack the following day, gaining several hundred yards and inflicting numerous casualties. Overwhelmed by the numerically superior hostile force, he ordered his men to evacuate the wounded and move back. Providing protective fire for their safe withdrawal, he was wounded again by grenade fragments, but refused evacuation and continued to direct the defense. On 3 September, he led his valiant unit in another assault which overran several hostile positions, but again the company was pinned down by murderous fire. Courageously advancing alone to an open knoll to plot mortar concentrations against the hill, he was killed instantly by an enemy sniper's fire. Capt. Krzyzowski's consummate fortitude, heroic leadership, and gallant self-sacrifice, so clearly demonstrated throughout 3 days of bitter combat, reflect the highest credit and lasting glory on himself, the infantry, and the U.S. Army.

From the distribution of 2nd Division casualties in the Battle of Heartbreak Ridge, it becomes apparent that the battle occurred in two phases. The first phase can be seen in Figure 19, beginning on about September 11, persisting for the next two weeks and then winding down toward the end of the month. The second phase will be considered later. Table 84 below shows the distribution of casualties in the 2nd Division during the first phase of this battle.

Table 84 — Heartbreak Ridge, 2nd Infantry Division

	KIA	WIA	POW Returned	POW Died	MIA Returned	MIA Died	Unit Total
2nd Infantry Division							
9th Inf, 2nd Div	104	330	1			1	436
23rd Inf, 2nd Div	228	798	5			4	1035
38th Inf, 2nd Div	37	131	3		1		172
37th FA Bn, 2nd Inf Div	11	35					46
Other 2nd Div Units (8)	6	38					44
Total 09/11–09/29/51	386	1332	9		1	5	1733

Another member of the 2nd Division was awarded the Medal of Honor for his valorous actions in this battle.

MEDAL OF HONOR: HERBERT K. PILILAAU

Awarded to: Private First Class Herbert K. Pililaau, Oahu, T.H., U.S. Army, Company C, 23d Infantry Regiment, 2nd Infantry Division. Near Pia-ri, Korea, 17 September 1951.

> Pfc. Pililaau, a member of Company C, distinguished himself by conspicuous gallantry and outstanding courage above and beyond the call of duty in action against the enemy. The enemy sent wave after wave of fanatical troops against his platoon which held a key terrain feature on "Heartbreak Ridge." Valiantly defending its position, the unit repulsed each attack until ammunition became practically exhausted and it was ordered to withdraw to a new position. Voluntarily remaining behind to cover the withdrawal, Pfc. Pililaau fired his automatic weapon into the ranks of the assailants, threw all his grenades and, with ammunition exhausted, closed with the foe in hand-to-hand combat, courageously fighting with his trench knife and bare fists until finally overcome and mortally wounded. When the position was subsequently retaken, more than 40 enemy dead were counted in the area he had so valiantly defended. His heroic devotion to duty, indomitable fighting spirit, and gallant self-sacrifice reflect the highest credit upon himself, the infantry, and the U.S. Army.

Although the 2nd Infantry Division accounted for almost half of all casualties lost in the September Battles, losses in some other units were significant. In most of these units, the losses did not show any identifiable pattern. They simply continued, more or less consistently, over the period. In the 7th Infantry Division, however, casualties were concentrated in the first 10 days of the period. The distribution of those casualties is summarized in Table 85.

Table 85 — Unspecified Battle Near Chup'a-ri, 7th Infantry Division

	KIA	WIA	POW Returned	POW Died	MIA Returned	MIA Died	Unit Total
7th Infantry Division							
17th Inf, 7th Inf Div	114	427	2			2	545
32nd Inf, 7th Inf Div	36	93	2				131
31st Inf, 7th Inf Div	21	63	3				87
Other 7th Div Units (5)	2	11					13
Total 08/26–09/04/51	173	594	7			2	776

One member of the 7th Division was awarded the Medal of Honor for his heroism in this engagement

MEDAL OF HONOR: WILLIAM F. LYELL

Awarded to: Corporal William F. Lyell, Old Hickory, TN, U.S. Army, Company F, 17th Infantry Regiment, 7th Infantry Division. Near Chup'a-ri, Korea, 31 August 1951.

> Cpl. Lyell, a member of Company F, distinguished himself by conspicuous gallantry and outstanding courage above and beyond the call of duty

in action against the enemy. When his platoon leader was killed, Cpl. Lyell assumed command and led his unit in an assault on strongly fortified enemy positions located on commanding terrain. When his platoon came under vicious, raking fire which halted the forward movement, Cpl. Lyell seized a 57mm. recoilless rifle and unhesitatingly moved ahead to a suitable firing position from which he delivered deadly accurate fire completely destroying an enemy bunker, killing its occupants. He then returned to his platoon and was resuming the assault when the unit was again subjected to intense hostile fire from 2 other bunkers. Disregarding his personal safety, armed with grenades he charged forward hurling grenades into 1 of the enemy emplacements, and although painfully wounded in this action he pressed on destroying the bunker and killing 6 of the foe. He then continued his attack against a third enemy position, throwing grenades as he ran forward, annihilating 4 enemy soldiers. He then led his platoon to the north slope of the hill where positions were occupied from which effective fire was delivered against the enemy in support of friendly troops moving up. Fearlessly exposing himself to enemy fire, he continuously moved about directing and encouraging his men until he was mortally wounded by enemy mortar fire. Cpl. Lyell's extraordinary heroism, indomitable courage, and aggressive leadership reflect great credit on himself and are in keeping with the highest traditions of the military service.

Although the losses by some units engaged in the fighting at this time could not be identified with specific battles, the numbers of their casualties indicate that the day-to-day combat they were engaged in remained ferocious. This is clearly demonstrated by three Medals of Honor awarded in this period to men in those units, one from the 3rd Infantry Division and two from the 25th Infantry Division.

Medal of Honor Jerry K. Crump

Awarded to: Corporal Jerry K. Crump, Forest City, NC, U.S. Army, Company L, 7th Infantry Regiment, 3d Infantry Division. Near Chorwon, Korea, 6 and 7 September 1951.

Cpl. Crump, a member of Company L, distinguished himself by conspicuous gallantry and outstanding courage above and beyond the call of duty in action against the enemy. During the night a numerically superior hostile force launched an assault against his platoon on Hill 284, overrunning friendly positions and swarming into the sector. Cpl. Crump repeatedly exposed himself to deliver effective fire into the ranks of the assailants, inflicting numerous casualties. Observing 2 enemy soldiers endeavoring to capture a friendly machinegun, he charged and killed both with his bayonet, regaining control of the weapon. Returning to his position, now occupied by 4 of his wounded comrades, he continued his accurate fire into enemy troops surrounding his emplacement. When a hostile soldier hurled a grenade into the position, Cpl. Crump immediately flung himself over the missile, absorbing the blast with his body and saving his comrades from death or serious injury. His aggressive actions had so inspired his comrades that a spirited counterattack drove the enemy from the perimeter. Cpl. Crump's heroic devotion to duty, indomitable fighting spirit, and willingness to sacrifice himself to save his comrades reflect the highest credit upon himself, the infantry and the U.S. Army.

Cpl. Crump, who had been wounded in action three months earlier and returned to duty after six weeks of rehabilitation, was not killed in this action. However, his wounds were serious enough to require his evacuation to the States, where he was eventually returned to duty.

MEDAL OF HONOR: BILLIE G. KANELL

Awarded to: Private Billie G. Kanell, Poplar Bluff, MO, U.S. Army, Company I, 35th Infantry Regiment, 25th Infantry Division. Near Pyongyang, Korea, 7 September 1951.

> Pvt. Kanell, a member of Company I, distinguished himself by conspicuous gallantry and outstanding courage above and beyond the call of duty in action against the enemy. A numerically superior hostile force had launched a fanatical assault against friendly positions, supported by mortar and artillery fire, when Pvt. Kanell stood in his emplacement exposed to enemy observation and action and delivered accurate fire into the ranks of the assailants. An enemy grenade was hurled into his emplacement and Pvt. Kanell threw himself upon the grenade, absorbing the blast with his body to protect 2 of his comrades from serious injury and possible death. A few seconds later another grenade was thrown into the emplacement and, although seriously wounded by the first missile, he summoned his waning strength to roll toward the second grenade and used his body as a shield to again protect his comrades. He was mortally wounded as a result of his heroic actions. His indomitable courage, sustained fortitude against overwhelming odds, and gallant self-sacrifice reflect the highest credit upon himself, the infantry, and the U.S. Army.

MEDAL OF HONOR: JEROME A. SUDUT

Awarded to: Second Lieutenant Jerome A. Sudut, Wausau, WI, U.S. Army, Company B, 27th Infantry Regiment, 25th Infantry Division. Near Kumhwa, Korea, 12 September 1951

> 2d Lt. Sudut distinguished himself by conspicuous gallantry above and beyond the call of duty in action against the enemy. His platoon, attacking heavily fortified and strategically located hostile emplacements, had been stopped by intense fire from a large bunker containing several firing posts. Armed with submachinegun, pistol, and grenades, 2d Lt. Sudut charged the emplacement alone through vicious hostile fire, killing 3 of the occupants and dispersing the remainder. Painfully wounded, he returned to reorganize his platoon, refused evacuation and led his men in a renewed attack. The enemy had returned to the bunker by means of connecting trenches from other emplacements and the platoon was again halted by devastating fire. Accompanied by an automatic-rifleman 2d Lt. Sudut again charged into close-range fire to eliminate the position. When the rifleman was wounded, 2d Lt. Sudut seized his weapon and continued alone, killing 3 of the 4 remaining occupants. Though mortally wounded and his ammunition exhausted, he jumped into the emplacement and killed the remaining enemy soldier with his trench knife. His single-handed assaults so inspired his comrades that they continued the attack and drove the enemy from the hill, securing the objective. 2d Lt. Sudut's consummate fighting

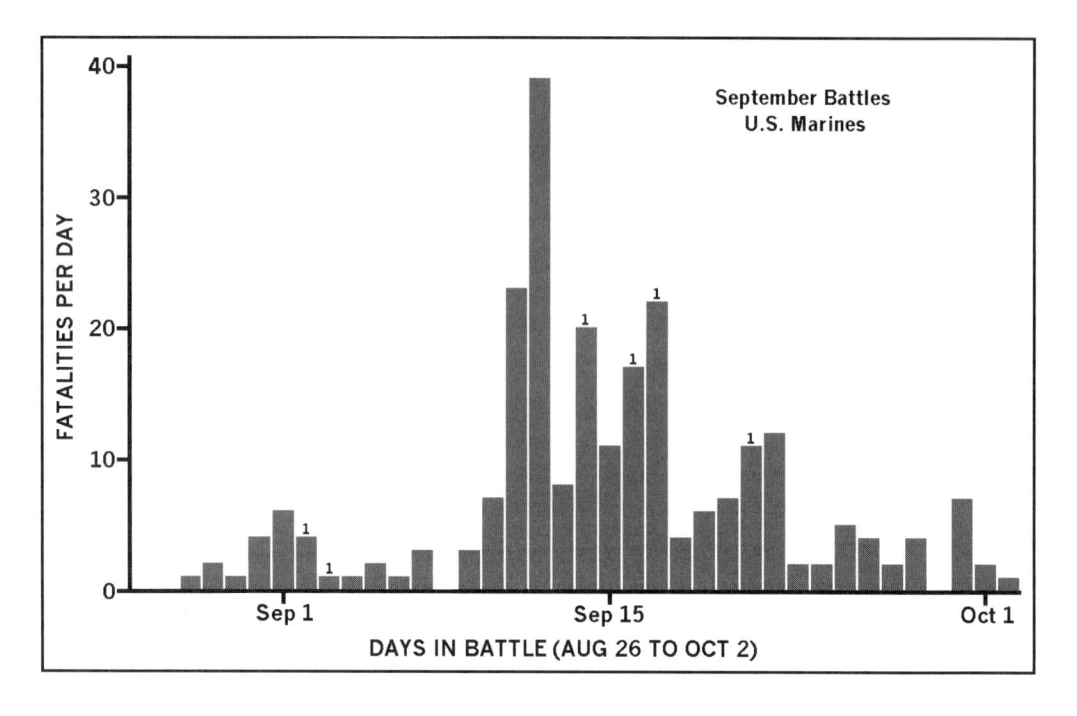

Figure 20. Daily fatalities for U.S. Marine units during the September Battles. The numbers over the bars on some dates indicate the number of presumed Navy corpsmen killed in ground action on those days.

spirit, outstanding leadership, and gallant self-sacrifice are in keeping with the finest traditions of the infantry and the U.S. Army.

U. S. Marine losses in the September Battles are shown in Figure 20.

Two U.S. 1st Marine Division battles have been identified during the period shown in Figure 20: The assault on Hill 749 between September 15 and 19 and Operation Summit on September 21, in which a company of Marines became the first American combat unit to be deployed in helicopters.

Total marine losses in the period shown were 245 killed, two of which were pilots lost in fixed wing crashes over land. Five marines earned Medals of Honor in these battles.

Medal of Honor: Frank W. Mausert, III

Awarded to: Sergeant Frank W. Mausert III, Dresher, PA, U.S. Marine Corps, Company B, 1st Battalion, 7th Marines, 1st Marine Division (Rein.) Songnap-yong, Korea, 12 September 1951.

> For conspicuous gallantry and intrepidity at the risk of his life above and beyond the call of duty while serving as a squad leader in Company B, in action against enemy aggressor forces. With his company pinned down and suffering heavy casualties under murderous machinegun, rifle, artillery,

and mortar fire laid down from heavily fortified, deeply entrenched hostile strongholds on Hill 673, Sgt. Mausert unhesitatingly left his covered position and ran through a heavily mined and fire-swept area to bring back 2 critically wounded men to the comparative safety of the lines. Staunchly refusing evacuation despite a painful head wound sustained during his voluntary act, he insisted on remaining with his squad and, with his platoon ordered into the assault moments later, took the point position and led his men in a furious bayonet charge against the first of a literally impregnable series of bunkers. Stunned and knocked to the ground when another bullet struck his helmet, he regained his feet and resumed his drive, personally silencing the machinegun and leading his men in eliminating several other emplacements in the area. Promptly reorganizing his unit for a renewed fight to the final objective on top of the ridge, Sgt. Mausert boldly left his position when the enemy's fire gained momentum and, making a target of himself, boldly advanced alone into the face of the machinegun, drawing the fire away from his men and enabling them to move into position to assault. Again severely wounded when the enemy's fire found its mark, he still refused aid and continued spearheading the assault to the topmost machinegun nest and bunkers, the last bulwark of the fanatic aggressors. Leaping into the wall of fire, he destroyed another machinegun with grenades before he was mortally wounded by bursting grenades and machinegun fire. Stouthearted and indomitable, Sgt. Mausert, by his fortitude, great personal valor, and extraordinary heroism in the face of almost certain death, had inspired his men to sweep on, overrun and finally secure the objective. His unyielding courage throughout reflects the highest credit upon himself and the U.S. Naval Service. He gallantly gave his life for his country.

MEDAL OF HONOR: GEORGE H. RAMER

Awarded to: Second Lieutenant George H. Ramer, Lewisburg, PA, U.S. Marine Corps Reserve, Company I, 3d Battalion, 7th Marines, 1st Marine Division (Rein.). Korea, 12 September 1951

For conspicuous gallantry and intrepidity at the risk of his life above and beyond the call of duty as leader of the 3d Platoon in Company I, in action against enemy aggressor forces. Ordered to attack and seize hostile positions atop a hall, vigorously defended by well-entrenched enemy forces delivering massed small-arms mortar, and machinegun fire, 2d Lt. Ramer fearlessly led his men up the steep slopes and although he and the majority of his unit were wounded during the ascent, boldly continued to spearhead the assault. With the terrain becoming more precipitous near the summit and the climb more perilous as the hostile forces added grenades to the devastating hail of fire, he staunchly carried the attack to the top, personally annihilated 1 enemy bunker with grenade and carbine fire and captured the objective with his remaining 8 men. Unable to hold the position against an immediate, overwhelming hostile counterattack, he ordered his group to withdraw and single-handedly fought the enemy to furnish cover for his men and for the evacuation of 3 fatally wounded marines. Severely wounded a second time, 2d Lt. Ramer refused aid when his men returned to help him and, after ordering them to seek shelter, courageously manned his post until the hostile troops overran his position and he fell mortally wounded. His indomitable fighting spirit, inspiring leadership and unselfish concern for others in the face of death, reflect the highest credit upon 2d Lt. Ramer and the U.S. Naval Service. He gallantly gave his life for his country.

Medal of Honor: Edward Gomez

Awarded to: Private First Class Edward Gomez, Omaha, NE, U.S. Marine Corps, Reserve, Company E, 2d Battalion, 1st Marines, 1st Marine Division (Rein.). Korea, Hill 749, 14 September 1951.

> For conspicuous gallantry and intrepidity at the risk of his life above and beyond the call of duty while serving as an ammunition bearer in Company E, in action against enemy aggressor forces. Bolding advancing with his squad in support of a group of riflemen assaulting a series of strongly fortified and bitterly defended hostile positions on Hill 749, Pfc. Gomez consistently exposed himself to the withering barrage to keep his machinegun supplied with ammunition during the drive forward to seize the objective. As his squad deployed to meet an imminent counterattack, he voluntarily moved down an abandoned trench to search for a new location for the gun and, when a hostile grenade landed between himself and his weapon, shouted a warning to those around him as he grasped the activated charge in his hand. Determined to save his comrades, he unhesitatingly chose to sacrifice himself and, diving into the ditch with the deadly missile, absorbed the shattering violence of the explosion in his body. By his stouthearted courage, incomparable valor, and decisive spirit of self-sacrifice, Pfc. Gomez inspired the others to heroic efforts in subsequently repelling the outnumbering foe, and his valiant conduct throughout sustained and enhanced the finest traditions of the U.S. Naval Service. He gallantly gave his life for his country.

Medal of Honor: Joseph Vittori

Awarded to: Corporal Joseph Vittori, Beverly, MA, U.S. Marine Corps Reserve, Company F, 2d Battalion, 1st Marines, 1st Marine Division (Rein.). Hill 749, Korea, 15 and 16 September 1951.

> For conspicuous gallantry and intrepidity at the risk of his life above and beyond the call of duty while serving as an automatic-rifleman in Company F, in action against enemy aggressor forces. With a forward platoon suffering heavy casualties and forced to withdraw under a vicious enemy counterattack as his company assaulted strong hostile forces entrenched on Hill 749, Cpl. Vittori boldly rushed through the withdrawing troops with 2 other volunteers from his reserve platoon and plunged directly into the midst of the enemy. Overwhelming them in a fierce hand-to-hand struggle, he enabled his company to consolidate its positions to meet further imminent onslaughts. Quick to respond to an urgent call for a rifleman to defend a heavy machinegun positioned on the extreme point of the northern flank and virtually isolated from the remainder of the unit when the enemy again struck in force during the night, he assumed position under the devastating barrage and, fighting a single-handed battle, leaped from 1 flank to the other, covering each foxhole in turn as casualties continued to mount manning a machinegun when the gunner was struck down and making repeated trips through the heaviest shellfire to replenish ammunition.

With the situation becoming extremely critical, reinforcing units to the rear pinned down under the blistering attack and foxholes left practically void by dead and wounded for a distance of 100 yards, Cpl. Vittori continued his valiant stand, refusing to give ground as the enemy penetrated to within feet of his position, simulating strength in the line and denying the foe physical occupation of the ground. Mortally wounded by the enemy machinegun and rifle bullets while persisting in his magnificent defense of the sector where approximately 200 enemy dead were found the following morning, Cpl. Vittori, by his fortitude, stouthearted courage, and great personal valor, had kept the point position intact despite the tremendous odds and undoubtedly prevented the entire battalion position from collapsing. His extraordinary heroism throughout the furious nightlong battle reflects the highest credit upon himself and the U.S. Naval Service. He gallantly gave his life for his country.

MEDAL OF HONOR: JACK A. DAVENPORT

Awarded to: Corporal Jack A. Davenport, Mission, KS, U.S. Marine Corps, Company G, 3d Battalion, 5th Marines, 1st Marine Division (Rein.). Vicinity of Songnae-Dong, Korea, 21 September 1951.

For conspicuous gallantry and intrepidity at the risk of his life above and beyond the call of duty while serving as a squad leader in Company G, in action against enemy aggressor forces, early in the morning. While expertly directing the defense of his position during a probing attack by hostile forces attempting to infiltrate the area, Cpl. Davenport, acting quickly when an enemy grenade fell into the foxhole which he was occupying with another marine, skillfully located the deadly projectile in the dark and, undeterred by the personal risk involved, heroically threw himself over the live missile, thereby saving his companion from serious injury or possible death. His cool and resourceful leadership were contributing factors in the successful repulse of the enemy attack and his superb courage and admirable spirit of self-sacrifice in the face of almost certain death enhance and sustain the highest traditions of the U.S. Naval Service. Cpl. Davenport gallantly gave his life for his country.

U.S. Navy losses in this period included four pilots lost in fixed-wing crashes over land, all lost early in the period and all reported KIA. Also lost were five sailors killed from explosive devices at sea, one on September 27 and four on October 2. Four of the five were never found and were declared dead.

Losses by the U.S. Air Force in the period are summarized in Table 86.

Table 86 — September 1951 Battles, U.S. Air Force

Fixed Wing Crash Over Land	
Pilot, Killed in Action	6
Pilot, Died while Missing	22
Aircrew, Killed in Action	3
Aircrew, Died while Missing	18
Aircrew, Died in Captivity	1
Non-Aircrew, Killed in Action	2
Non-Aircrew, Died while Missing	4
Total 08/26–10/02/51	56

One of these airmen earned the Medal of Honor for his valor in action.

Medal of Honor: John S. Walmsley

Awarded to: Captain John S. Walmsley, Baltimore, MD, U.S. Air Force, 8th Bombardment Squadron, 3d Bomb Group. Near Yangdok, Korea, 14 September 1951.

Capt. Walmsley, distinguished himself by conspicuous gallantry and intrepidity at the risk of his life above and beyond the call of duty. While flying a B-26 aircraft on a night combat mission with the objective of developing new tactics, Capt. Walmsley sighted an enemy supply train which had been assigned top priority as a target of opportunity. He immediately attacked, producing a strike which disabled the train, and, when his ammunition was expended, radioed for friendly aircraft in the area to complete destruction of the target. Employing the searchlight mounted on his aircraft, he guided another B-26 aircraft to the target area, meanwhile constantly exposing himself to enemy fire. Directing an incoming B-26 pilot, he twice boldly aligned himself with the target, his searchlight illuminating the area, in a determined effort to give the attacking aircraft full visibility. As the friendly aircraft prepared for the attack, Capt. Walmsley descended into the valley in a low level run over the target with searchlight blazing, selflessly exposing himself to vicious enemy antiaircraft fire. In his determination to inflict maximum damage on the enemy, he refused to employ evasive tactics and valiantly pressed forward straight through an intense barrage, thus insuring complete destruction of the enemy's vitally needed war cargo. While he courageously pressed his attack Capt. Walmsley's plane was hit and crashed into the surrounding mountains, exploding upon impact. His heroic initiative and daring aggressiveness in completing this important mission in the face of overwhelming opposition and at the risk of his life, reflects the highest credit upon himself and the U.S. Air Force.

October Operations

Figure 21 shows the daily casualty count in all U.S. Army units for the last six weeks of major offensive action in 1951 before peace talks began.

Hidden among the significant losses in the early days of this period were those from the 2nd Division's continuing effort to secure Heartbreak Ridge. From 2nd Division casualty figures, it appears that the resumption of the battle began on about October 5, continued at fairly high intensity for about the next week and then subsided rapidly to the expected level of day-to-day combat. Table 87 shows the distribution of 2nd Division losses in this phase of the battle, when reports suggest that the division finally captured the objective.

I. The Peninsular War

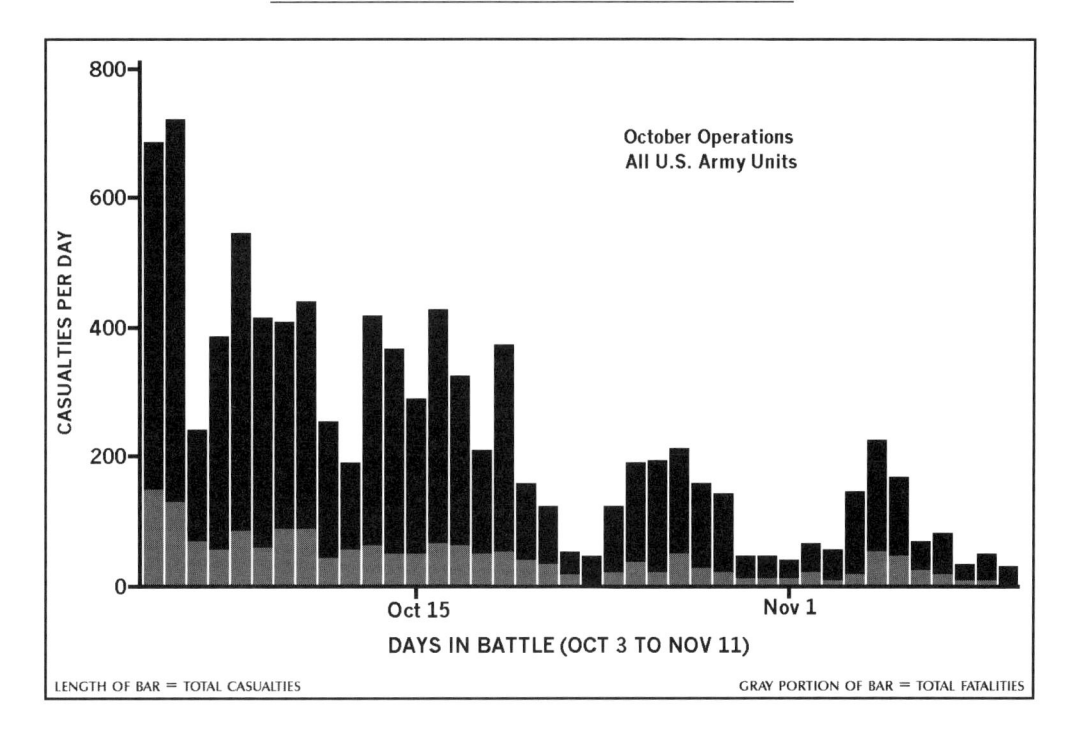

Figure 21. Daily casualties for all U.S. Army units during October Operations.

Table 87 — Heartbreak Ridge Continued, 2nd Infantry Division

	KIA	WIA	POW Returned	POW Died	MIA Returned	MIA Died	Unit Total
2nd Infantry Division							
38th Inf, 2nd Div	103	509				1	613
23rd Inf, 2nd Div	67	338					405
9th Inf, 2nd Div	58	284	1				343
Other 2nd Div Units (11)	13	67	1				81
Total 10/05–10/14/51	241	1198	2			1	1442

One of the participants in this battle was awarded the Medal of Honor for his gallantry.

MEDAL OF HONOR: TONY K. BURRIS

Awarded to: Sergeant First Class Tony K. Burris, Blanchard, OK, U.S. Army, Company L, 38th Infantry Regiment, 2d Infantry Division. vicinity of Mundung-ni, Korea 8 and 9 October 1951

> Sfc. Burris, a member of Company L, distinguished himself by conspicuous gallantry and outstanding courage above and beyond the call of duty. On 8 October, when his company encountered intense fire from an entrenched hostile force, Sfc. Burris charged forward alone, throwing grenades into the position and destroying approximately 15 of the enemy. On the following day, spearheading a renewed assault on enemy positions

on the next ridge, he was wounded by machinegun fire but continued the assault, reaching the crest of the ridge ahead of his unit and sustaining a second wound. Calling for a 57mm. recoilless rifle team, he deliberately exposed himself to draw hostile fire and reveal the enemy position. The enemy machinegun emplacement was destroyed. The company then moved forward and prepared to assault other positions on the ridge line. Sfc. Burris, refusing evacuation and submitting only to emergency treatment, joined the unit in its renewed attack but fire from hostile emplacement halted the advance. Sfc. Burris rose to his feet, charged forward and destroyed the first emplacement with its heavy machinegun and crew of 6 men. Moving out to the next emplacement, and throwing his last grenade which destroyed this position, he fell mortally wounded by enemy fire. Inspired by his consummate gallantry, his comrades renewed a spirited assault which overran enemy positions and secured Hill 605, a strategic position in the battle for "Heartbreak Ridge," Sfc. Burris' indomitable fighting spirit, outstanding heroism, and gallant self-sacrifice reflect the highest glory upon himself, the infantry and the U.S. Army.

Sfc. Burris had been wounded in February of 1951 and was returned to duty after six weeks in recovery.

Operation Commando, beginning on October 3, was intended to secure a defense line called Jamestown. Three U.S. Divisions were reported to have been involved in the operation; the 1st Cavalry Division, the 3rd Infantry Division and the 25th Infantry Division. From casualty figures, it is clear that the 1st Cav took the brunt of the punishment in the operation. Figure 22 shows the distribution of 1st Cav casualties by day during the period shown in Figure 21.

Operation Commando was reported to have concluded on October 9. Table 88 summarizes the losses in the participating divisions during the operation.

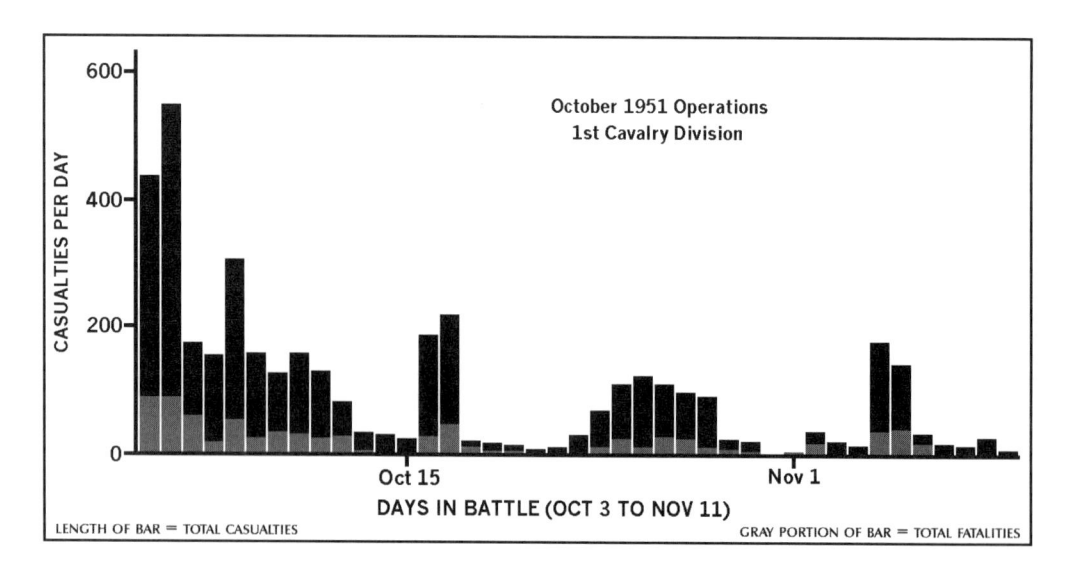

Figure 22. Daily casualties in the U.S. 1st Cavalry Division during October Operations.

I. The Peninsular War

Table 88 — Operation Commando, 1st Cavalry Division and Others

	KIA	WIA	POW Returned	POW Died	MIA Returned	MIA Died	Unit Total
1st Cavalry Division							
5th Cav, 1st Cav Div	122	497		1		3	623
7th Cav, 1st Cav Div	146	742	1				889
8th Cav, 1st Cav Div	73	251					324
16th Recon Co, 1st Cav Div	10	18					28
Other 1st Cav Units (7)	10	30					40
Total 1st Cav 10/03–10/09/51	361	1538	1	1		3	1904
3rd Infantry Division							
7th Inf 3rd Inf Div	25	85					110
15th Inf, 3rd Inf Div	53	144					197
65th Inf, 3rd Inf Div	3	9					12
Other 3rd Div Units (3)	5	7					12
Total 3rd Div 10/03–10/09/51	86	245					331
25th Infantry Division							
Total 25th Div 10/03–10/09/51	15	67	4			2	88
Total 10/03–10/09/51	462	1850	5	1		5	2323

Because so many different operations were being carried on at the same time all along the 120-mile battle front, it is impossible to identify which non-divisional units may have been involved — and reported casualties — in any specific operation.

Two other October operations, called Nomad and Polar, were undertaken to secure a defense line called Missouri. These operations took place between October 13 and 22 and were carried out primarily by the 24th Infantry Division, although other units were undoubtedly involved. Table 89 summarizes 24th Division losses in this operation.

Table 89 — Operations Nomad and Polar, 24th Infantry Division

	KIA	WIA	POW Returned	POW Died	MIA Returned	MIA Died	Unit Total
19th Inf, 24th Inf Div	129	605					734
21st Inf, 24th Inf Div	76	414					490
26th AAA Bn, 24th Inf Div	4	15					19
70th Med Tk Bn, 24th Inf Div	3	12	1			1	17
Other 24th Div Units (8)	11	17					28
Total 10/13–10/22/51	223	1063	1			1	1288

From Figure 22, it is apparent that 1st Cavalry Division involvement in October operations did not end with the completion of Operation Commando. Almost half of the division's losses in the period were sustained subsequent to that operation. In one of those battles, a member of the 1st Cav was awarded the Medal of Honor for his actions.

MEDAL OF HONOR: LLOYD L. BURKE

Awarded to: First Lieutenant Lloyd L. Burke, Stuttgart, AR, U.S. Army, Company G, 5th Cavalry Regiment, 1st Cavalry Division. Near Chong-dong, Korea, 28 October 1951.

1st Lt. Burke, distinguished himself by conspicuous gallantry and outstanding courage above and beyond the call of duty in action against the enemy. Intense enemy fire had pinned down leading elements of his company committed to secure commanding ground when 1st Lt. Burke left the command post to rally and urge the men to follow him toward 3 bunkers impeding the advance. Dashing to an exposed vantage point he threw several grenades at the bunkers, then, returning for an Ml rifle and adapter, he made a lone assault, wiping out the position and killing the crew. Closing on the center bunker he lobbed grenades through the opening and, with his pistol, killed 3 of its occupants attempting to surround him. Ordering his men forward he charged the third emplacement, catching several grenades in midair and hurling them back at the enemy. Inspired by his display of valor his men stormed forward, overran the hostile position, but were again pinned down by increased fire. Securing a light machinegun and 3 boxes of ammunition, 1st Lt. Burke dashed through the impact area to an open knoll, set up his gun and poured a crippling fire into the ranks of the enemy, killing approximately 75. Although wounded, he ordered more ammunition, reloading and destroying 2 mortar emplacements and a machinegun position with his accurate fire. Cradling the weapon in his arms he then led his men forward, killing some 25 more of the retreating enemy and securing the objective. 1st Lt. Burke's heroic action and daring exploits inspired his small force of 35 troops. His unflinching courage and outstanding leadership reflect the highest credit upon himself, the infantry, and the U.S. Army.

There is no record in the database reporting Lt. Burke as wounded in action.

Table 90 is a summary of all U.S. Army casualties in the period of October operations.

Table 90 — October 1951 Operations, All U.S. Army Units

	KIA	WIA	POW Returned	POW Died	MIA Returned	MIA Died	Unit Total
1st Cavalry Division	730	3156	43	3		66	3998
2nd Infantry Division	265	1324	3			1	1593
3rd Infantry Division	106	292	2				400
7th Infantry Division	57	285				2	344
24th Infantry Division	312	1455	4			3	1774
25th Infantry Division	54	332	4			3	393
11th Airborne Division	8	3					11
5th RCT	85	414					499
Other Units (45)	16	120	1	2			139
Total 10/03–11/11/51	**1633**	**7381**	**57**	**5**		**75**	**9151**

There were no major conflicts during October operations in which the U.S. Marines are identified as a participant. In fact, marine losses in the period were minimal, totaling 93 fatalities in 40 days. This total includes 11 pilots lost in fixed-wing air crashes over land, one of which was never found and declared dead. One other marine airman was killed in an aircraft loss on the ground. One sailor, presumed to be a corpsman, was killed in ground action in the period.

Other U.S. Navy losses in the period are shown in Table 91.

Table 91—October Operations, U.S. Navy

Fixed Wing Crash Over Land	
Pilot, Killed in Action	3
Fixed Wing Crash at Sea	
Pilot, Killed in Action	1
Aircrew, Killed in Action	1
Sea Casualty	
Explosive Device, Killed in Action	8
Explosive Device, Died of Wounds	1
Total 10/03–11/11/51	14

U.S. Airforce losses in the period would have been consistent with reports from earlier actions, except for "Black Tuesday." On October 23, three B-29 bombers were shot down and four were force to crash land. A total of 28 airmen lost their lives on that day; eight pilots, 14 aircrew and 6 non-aircrew. Table 92 summarizes all U.S. Air Force losses in the period.

Table 92—October Operations, U.S. Air Force

Fixed Wing Crash Over Land	
Pilot, Killed in Action	5
Pilot, Died while Missing	27
Aircrew, Killed in Action	8
Aircrew, Died while Missing	17
Non-Aircrew, Killed in Action	3
Non-Aircrew, Died while Missing	8
Fixed Wing Crash at Sea	
Pilot, Killed in Action	1
Total 10/03–11/11/51	69

On November 12, 1951, with peace talks beginning, UN offensive operations cease and the 8th Army begins what is called "active defense."

II

ACTIVE DEFENSE

Anticipating peace talks and a negotiated settlement of the war, UN commanders had spent most of the past six months capturing territory that would provide good defensive positions for their troops to wait out the negotiations. The cost in casualties had been tremendous. Now, with the cessation of offensive operations, the 8th Army had the opportunity to re-man, re-supply and to improve defenses. Apparently, communist forces were equally willing to curb their offensive efforts, and the tenor of fighting in the combat zone decreased substantially. The numbers of U.S. losses diminished — but not totally, and not immediately. For about two weeks after "Active Defense" was undertaken on November 12, skirmishes continued to produce some significant losses in American units. From the distribution of the casualties, it appears that these conflicts involved units all across the defense line, although the U.S. 3rd and 7th Divisions reported the greatest number of losses.

For some units, combat remained intense as "active defense" began. This is made clear by three Medal of Honor awards to men engaged in this fighting.

MEDAL OF HONOR: MACK A. JORDON

Awarded to: Private First Class Mack A. Jordon, Collins, MS, U.S. Army, Company K, 21st Infantry Regiment, 24th Infantry Division. Near Kumsong, Korea, 15 November 1951.

> Pfc. Jordan, a member of Company K, distinguished himself by conspicuous gallantry and indomitable courage above and beyond the call of duty in action against the enemy. As a squad leader of the 3d Platoon, he was participating in a night attack on key terrain against a fanatical hostile force when the advance was halted by intense small-arms and automatic-weapons fire and a vicious barrage of hand grenades. Upon orders for the platoon to withdraw and reorganize, Pfc. Jordan voluntarily remained behind to provide covering fire. Crawling toward an enemy machinegun emplacement, he threw 3 grenades and neutralized the gun. He then rushed the position delivering a devastating hail of fire, killing several of the enemy and forcing the remainder to fall back to new positions. He courageously attempted to move forward to silence another machinegun but, before he could leave his position, the ruthless foe hurled explo-

sives down the hill and in the ensuing blast both legs were severed. Despite mortal wounds, he continued to deliver deadly fire and held off the assailants until the platoon returned. Pfc. Jordan's unflinching courage and gallant self-sacrifice reflect lasting glory upon himself and uphold the noble traditions of the infantry and the military service.

MEDAL OF HONOR: JAMES L. STONE

Awarded to: First Lieutenant James L. Stone, Houston, TX, U.S. Army, Company E, 8th Cavalry Regiment, 1st Cavalry Division. Near Sokkogae, Korea, 21 and 22 November 1951.

> 1st Lt. Stone, distinguished himself by conspicuous gallantry and indomitable courage above and beyond the call of duty in action against the enemy. When his platoon, holding a vital outpost position, was attacked by overwhelming Chinese forces, 1st Lt. Stone stood erect and exposed to the terrific enemy fire calmly directed his men in the defense. A defensive flame-thrower failing to function, he personally moved to its location, further exposing himself, and personally repaired the weapon. Throughout a second attack, 1st Lt. Stone; though painfully wounded, personally carried the only remaining light machinegun from place to place in the position in order to bring fire upon the Chinese advancing from 2 directions. Throughout he continued to encourage and direct his depleted platoon in its hopeless defense. Although again wounded, he continued the fight with his carbine, still exposing himself as an example to his men. When this final overwhelming assault swept over the platoon's position his voice could still be heard faintly urging his men to carry on, until he lost consciousness. Only because of this officer's driving spirit and heroic action was the platoon emboldened to make its brave but hopeless last ditch stand.

Lt. Stone was captured in this action and remained in captivity for almost two years. He was released on September 2, 1953. There is no record in the database of his wounds.

MEDAL OF HONOR: NOAH O. KNIGHT

Awarded to: Private First Class Noah O. Knight, Jefferson, SC, U.S. Army, Company F, 7th Infantry Regiment, 3d Infantry Division. Near Kowang-San, Korea, 23 and 24 November 1951.

> Pfc. Knight, a member of Company F, distinguished himself by conspicuous gallantry and indomitable courage above and beyond the call of duty in action against the enemy. He occupied a key position in the defense perimeter when waves of enemy troops passed through their own artillery and mortar concentrations and charged the company position. Two direct hits from an enemy emplacement demolished his bunker and wounded him. Disregarding personal safety, he moved to a shallow depression for a better firing vantage. Unable to deliver effective fire from his defilade position, he left his shelter, moved through heavy fire in full view of the enemy and, firing into the ranks of the relentless assailants, inflicted numerous casualties, momentarily stemming the attack. Later during another vicious onslaught, he observed an enemy squad infiltrating the position and, coun-

terattacking, killed or wounded the entire group. Expending the last of his ammunition, he discovered 3 enemy soldiers entering the friendly position with demolition charges. Realizing the explosives would enable the enemy to exploit the breach, he fearlessly rushed forward and disabled 2 assailants with the butt of his rifle when the third exploded a demolition charge killing the 3 enemy soldiers and mortally wounding Pfc. Knight. Pfc. Knight's supreme sacrifice and consummate devotion to duty reflect lasting glory on himself and uphold the noble traditions of the military service.

Table 93 summarizes U.S. Army casualties during the first two weeks of "active defense."

Table 93 — Early Active Defense, All U.S. Army Units

	KIA	WIA	POW Returned	POW Died	MIA Returned	MIA Died	Unit Total
1st Cavalry Division	43	83	8			3	137
2nd Infantry Division	1	3	1			1	6
3rd Infantry Division	91	288	1				380
7th Infantry Division	58	223	1	1		6	289
24th Infantry Division	17	79	1				97
25th Infantry Division	19	84	5				108
5th RCT		21				1	22
Other Units (13)	6	24					30
Total 11/12–11/26/51	235	805	17	1		11	1069

For the next six months, as peace talks continued, conflict along the Korean battle line remained at a low level, interrupted only rarely by some brief flare-up. Casualties continued to accumulate, of course, but at much reduced rates. Table 94 summarizes all U.S. Army casualties over the next 197 days.

Table 94 — Active Defense, All U.S. Army Units

	KIA	WIA	POW Returned	POW Died	MIA Returned	MIA Died	Unit Total
1st Cavalry Division	2	16					18
2nd Infantry Division	57	353	3			5	418
3rd Infantry Division	123	549	9			23	704
7th Infantry Division	137	653	4			2	796
24th Infantry Division	32	171	4				207
25th Infantry Division	119	556	5		1	1	682
40th Infantry Division	82	284	2			2	370
45th Infantry Division	123	544	13			6	686
5th RCT	21	110					131
Other Units (62)	48	155	4			3	210
Total 11/27/51–06/05/52	744	3391	44		1	42	4222

Note that two new American units have been added to UN forces, the 40th Infantry Division and the 45th Infantry Division. The first 45th Division casualty recorded in the database was on December 11, 1951. The first 40th Division casualty was reported on January 16, 1952.

On the ground, the half-year-long interval of "active defense" was characterized by perpetual mortar and artillery exchanges and occasional incursions by one side or the other into enemy territory. None of these incursions rose to the level of being identified as a major battle, but the fighting that took place in them was no less intense. One of them produced the most costly day in casualties of any day in the period of "active defense" (114), and it produced the first Medal of Honor of the new year.

MEDAL OF HONOR: RONALD E. ROSSER

Awarded to: Corporal Ronald E. Rosser, Crooksville, OH, U.S. Army, Heavy Mortar Company, 38th Infantry Regiment, 2d Infantry Division. Vicinity of Ponggilli, Korea, 12 January 1952.

> Cpl. Rosser, distinguished himself by conspicuous gallantry above and beyond the call of duty. While assaulting heavily fortified enemy hill positions, Company L, 38th Infantry Regiment, was stopped by fierce automatic-weapons, small-arms, artillery, and mortar fire. Cpl. Rosser, a forward observer was with the lead platoon of Company L, when it came under fire from 2 directions. Cpl. Rosser turned his radio over to his assistant and, disregarding the enemy fire, charged the enemy positions armed with only carbine and a grenade. At the first bunker, he silenced its occupants with a burst from his weapon. Gaining the top of the hill, he killed 2 enemy soldiers, and then went down the trench, killing 5 more as he advanced. He then hurled his grenade into a bunker and shot 2 other soldiers as they emerged. Having exhausted his ammunition, he returned through the enemy fire to obtain more ammunition and grenades and charged the hill once more. Calling on others to follow him, he assaulted 2 more enemy bunkers. Although those who attempted to join him became casualties, Cpl. Rosser once again exhausted his ammunition obtained a new supply, and returning to the hilltop a third time hurled grenades into the enemy positions. During this heroic action Cpl. Rosser single-handedly killed at least 13 of the enemy. After exhausting his ammunition he accompanied the withdrawing platoon, and though himself wounded, made several trips across open terrain still under enemy fire to help remove other men injured more seriously than himself. This outstanding soldier's courageous and selfless devotion to duty is worthy of emulation by all men. He has contributed magnificently to the high traditions of the military service.

There is no record of Cpl. Rosser's wounds in the database.

The total number of casualties sustained by UN units in the period makes it clear that the Korean war zone during "active defense" was still very dangerous. Yet, compared to the numbers reported for earlier actions, it was a much safer place than it had been. Casualties per day averaged only 22 and fatalities averaged only four per day. When you consider that an estimated 102,000 enemy mortar and artillery rounds were fired on UN forces in the month of May 1952 alone, these casualty averages are remarkably small.

Clearly, in some cases, the casualty counts would have been much greater had it not been for the gallant acts of some fighting men. One of those men, an Army medic, earned the Medal of Honor for his self-sacrifice in behalf of his comrades.

Medal of Honor: Bryant E. Womack

Awarded to: Private First Class Bryant E. Womack, Mill Springs, NC, U.S. Army, Medical Company, 14th Infantry Regiment, 25th Infantry Division. Near Sokso-ri, Korea, 12 March 1952.

> Pfc. Womack distinguished himself by conspicuous gallantry above and beyond the call of duty in action against the enemy. Pfc. Womack was the only medical aid man attached to a night combat patrol when sudden contact with a numerically superior enemy produced numerous casualties. Pfc. Womack went immediately to their aid, although this necessitated exposing himself to a devastating hail of enemy fire, during which he was seriously wounded. Refusing medical aid for himself, he continued moving among his comrades to administer aid. While he was aiding 1 man, he was again struck by enemy mortar fire, this time suffering the loss of his right arm. Although he knew the consequences should immediate aid not be administered, he still refused aid and insisted that all efforts be made for the benefit of others that were wounded. Although unable to perform the task himself, he remained on the scene and directed others in first aid techniques. The last man to withdraw, he walked until he collapsed from loss of blood, and died a few minutes later while being carried by his comrades. The extraordinary heroism, outstanding courage, and unswerving devotion to his duties displayed by Pfc. Womack reflect the utmost distinction upon himself and uphold the esteemed traditions of the U.S. Army.

For the 1st Marine Division, the casualty pattern during "active defense" was much the same as that of the Army units—extended periods with few fatalities, interrupted by brief skirmishes that produced slight increases in reported deaths. The division reported 263 total fatalities from ground action in the period from November 12, 1951, to June 5, 1952, an average of slightly more than one per day. In addition, 2 marine pilots died in fixed wing crashes over land and two at sea. Four others died in aircraft losses on the ground. A total of 13 sailors, presumed to be corpsmen, were also killed in ground action in the period

During one skirmish, Cpl. Duane Dewey earned the Medal of Honor for his bravery and self-sacrifice.

Medal of Honor: Duane E. Dewey

Awarded to: Corporal Duane E. Dewey, Muskegon, MI, U.S. Marine Corps Reserve, Company E, 2d Battalion, 5th Marines, 1st Marine Division (Rein.). Near Panmunjon, Korea, 16 April 1952.

> For conspicuous gallantry and intrepidity at the risk of his life above and beyond the call of duty while serving as a gunner in a machinegun platoon of Company E, in action against enemy aggressor forces. When an enemy grenade landed close to his position while he and his assistant gunner were receiving medical attention for their wounds during a fierce night attack by numerically superior hostile forces, Cpl. Dewey, although suffering intense pain, immediately pulled the corpsman to the ground and, shouting a warning to the other marines around him. bravely smothered the deadly missile with his body, personally absorbing the full force of the explosion to save his comrades from possible injury or death. His indomitable

courage, outstanding initiative, and valiant efforts in behalf of others in the face of almost certain death reflect the highest credit upon Cpl. Dewey and enhance the finest traditions of the U.S. Naval Service.

Although no specific battle is mentioned in the chronology, the database shows significantly increased Marine Corps casualties in the period May 28 to 31, with a total of 25 fatalities on those four days. On one of those days, two of the fatalities were marines that earned the Medal of Honor for their heroism

Medal of Honor: David B. Champagne

Awarded to: Corporal David B. Champagne, Wakefield, RI, U.S. Marine Corps, Company A 1st Battalion, 7th Marines, 1st Marine Division (Rein.). Korea, 28 May 1952.

> For conspicuous gallantry and intrepidity at the risk of his life above and beyond the call of duty while serving as a fire team leader of Company A, in action against enemy aggressor forces. Advancing with his platoon in the initial assault of the company against a strongly fortified and heavily defended hill position, Cpl. Champagne skillfully led his fire team through a veritable hail of intense enemy machinegun, small-arms, and grenade fire, overrunning trenches and a series of almost impregnable bunker positions before reaching the crest of the hill and placing his men in defensive positions. Suffering a painful leg wound while assisting in repelling the ensuing hostile counterattack, which was launched under cover of a murderous hail of mortar and artillery fire, he steadfastly refused evacuation and fearlessly continued to control his fire team When the enemy counterattack increased in intensity, and a hostile grenade landed in the midst of the fire team, Cpl. Champagne unhesitatingly seized the deadly missile and hurled it in the direction of the approaching enemy. As the grenade left his hand, it exploded blowing off his hand and throwing him out of the trench. Mortally wounded by enemy mortar fire while in this exposed position, Cpl. Champagne, by his valiant leadership, fortitude, and gallant spirit of self-sacrifice in the face of almost certain death, undoubtedly saved the lives of several of his fellow marines. His heroic actions served to inspire all who observed him and reflect the highest credit upon himself and the U.S. Naval Service. He gallantly gave his life for his country.

Medal of Honor: John D. Kelly

Awarded to: Private First Class John D. Kelly, Homestead, PA, U.S. Marine Corps, Company C, 1st Battalion, 7th Marines, 1st Marine Division (Rein.). Korea, 28 May 1952.

> For conspicuous gallantry and intrepidity at the risk of his life above and beyond the call of duty while serving as a radio operator of Company C, in action against enemy aggressor forces. With his platoon pinned down by a numerically superior enemy force employing intense mortar, artillery, small-arms and grenade fire, Pfc. Kelly requested permission to leave his radio in the care of another man and to participate in an assault on enemy key positions. Fearlessly charging forward in the face of a murderous hail of machinegun fire and handgrenades, he initiated a daring attack against a hostile strongpoint and personally neutralized the position, killing 2 of the enemy.

Unyielding in the fact of heavy odds, he continued forward and single-handedly assaulted a machinegun bunker. Although painfully wounded, he bravely charged the bunker and destroyed it, killing 3 of the enemy. Courageously continuing his 1-man assault, he again stormed forward in a valiant attempt to wipe out a third bunker and boldly delivered pointblank fire into the aperture of the hostile emplacement. Mortally wounded by enemy fire while carrying out this heroic action, Pfc. Kelly, by his great personal valor and aggressive fighting spirit, inspired his comrades to sweep on, overrun and secure the objective. His extraordinary heroism in the face of almost certain death reflects the highest credit upon himself and enhances the finest traditions of the U.S. Naval Service. He gallantly gave his life for his country.

Navy losses during "active defense" are summarized in Table 95.

Table 95 — Active Defense, U.S. Navy

Fixed Wing Crash Over Land	
Pilot, Killed in Action	18
Pilot, Died while Missing	4
Aircrew, Killed in Action	4
Fixed Wing Crash At Sea	
Pilot, Killed in Action	2
Sea Casualty	
Small-arms Fire, Killed in Action	1
Explosive Device, Killed in Action	24
Multiple Fragmentation Wounds, Killed in Action	1
Misadventure, Killed in Action	2
Drowned/Suffocated, Killed in Action	2
Artillery/Rocket, Died of Wounds	1
Vehicle Crash, Died while Missing	2
Drowned/Suffocated, Died while Missing	2
Total 11/12/51–06/05/52	63

On April 21, 1952, the U.S. Navy Cruiser *St. Paul* experienced a powder fire with the reported loss of 30 lives. Among the fatalities reported above are 24 that were reported on April 21. Of these, 22 were caused by an explosive device and two were attributed to misadventures. Presumably these individuals died as a result of the powder fire on the *St. Paul*. It is not known what became of the other six reported deaths from that accident.

In the air, the declaration of "active defense" didn't seem to change things much from the way they had been when the fighting on the ground was more intense. Air losses remained substantial, whatever the situation on the ground. U.S. Air Force fatalities in the period are summarized in Table 96.

Table 96 — Active Defense, U.S. Air Force

Fixed Wing Crash Over Land	
Pilot, Killed in Action	14
Pilot, Died of Wounds	1
Pilot, Died while Missing	112
Aircrew, Died while Missing	51
Aircrew, Died in Captivity	2
Non-Aircrew, Died while Missing	5
Total 11/12/51–06/05/52	185

One of these fatalities was Maj. George Davis, who was awarded the Medal of Honor for his gallantry under fire.

MEDAL OF HONOR: GEORGE ANDREW DAVIS, JR.

Awarded to: Major George Andrew Davis, Jr., Lubbock, TX, U.S. Air Force, CO, 334th Fighter Squadron, 4th Fighter Group, 5th Air Force. Near Sinuiju-Yalu River area, Korea, 10 February 1952.

> Maj. Davis distinguished himself by conspicuous gallantry and intrepidity at the risk of his life above and beyond the call of duty. While leading a flight of 4 F-86 Saberjets on a combat aerial patrol mission near the Manchurian border, Maj. Davis' element leader ran out of oxygen and was forced to retire from the flight with his wingman accompanying him. Maj. Davis and the remaining F-86's continued the mission and sighted a formation of approximately 12 enemy MIG-15 aircraft speeding southward toward an area where friendly fighter-bombers were conducting low level operations against the Communist lines of communications. With selfless disregard for the numerical superiority of the enemy, Maj. Davis positioned his 2 aircraft, then dove at the MIG formation. While speeding through the formation from the rear he singled out a MIG-15 and destroyed it with a concentrated burst of fire. Although he was now under continuous fire from the enemy fighters to his rear, Maj. Davis sustained his attack. He fired at another MIG-15 which, bursting into smoke and flames, went into a vertical dive. Rather than maintain his superior speed and evade the enemy fire being concentrated on him, he elected to reduce his speed and sought out still a third MIG-15. During this latest attack his aircraft sustained a direct hit, went out of control, then crashed into a mountain 30 miles south of the Yalu River. Maj. Davis' bold attack completely disrupted the enemy formation, permitting the friendly fighter-bombers to successfully complete their interdiction mission. Maj. Davis, by his indomitable fighting spirit, heroic aggressiveness, and superb courage in engaging the enemy against formidable odds exemplified valor at its highest.

"Active defense" was a time of "wait and see," but neither side wanted to allow the other to gain any military advantage while they waited. Front-line GIs continued to hope that the negotiations going on in Panmunjom would produce an end to the fighting, but the negotiators found themselves drifting irrevocably toward an impasse—and commanders on the ground grew increasingly more impatient with the lack of resolution to the military stalemate. The scene was set for the War of the Hills.

III

The War of the Hills

History does not tell us when the War of the Hills began. Like spontaneous combustion, it just smoldered for a while and then finally burst into flame. Peace talks were going nowhere and, as the increasing activity of "active defense" was beginning to indicate, military commanders on both sides were itching to get back into the fray. For the discussions that follows, the beginning of this phase of the war is set on June 6, 1952, as this was when the first substantial increase in U.S. Army casualties occurred. Thereafter, although specific battles and operations can sometimes be identified, fighting often took place at the same time over large sections of the Main Line of Resistance (MLR) and involved a number of different units. Thus, it is not always easy to identify which casualties were associated with which operations.

The first period of prolonged increase in casualty counts lasted through the month of June. Figure 23 shows the distribution of U.S. Army casualties in this period.

A New War Begins

The first major operation that shifted the level of combat to a significantly higher intensity began on June 6, 1952, west of Chorwon. In Operation Counter, the U.S. 45th Division launched a series of attacks to establish 11 patrol bases (outposts) in that area. One of these outposts was in a particularly critical location and was the site of many costly battles throughout the rest of the war. The GIs in the area named it "Old Baldy." The attacks and counterattacks in this engagement continued through June 29.

Other units experienced increased losses in the same period, although not at the level of the 45th. Casualties in all units during the period are summarized in Table 97.

During these actions, another U.S. Army medic earned the Medal of Honor for his courage and self-sacrifice.

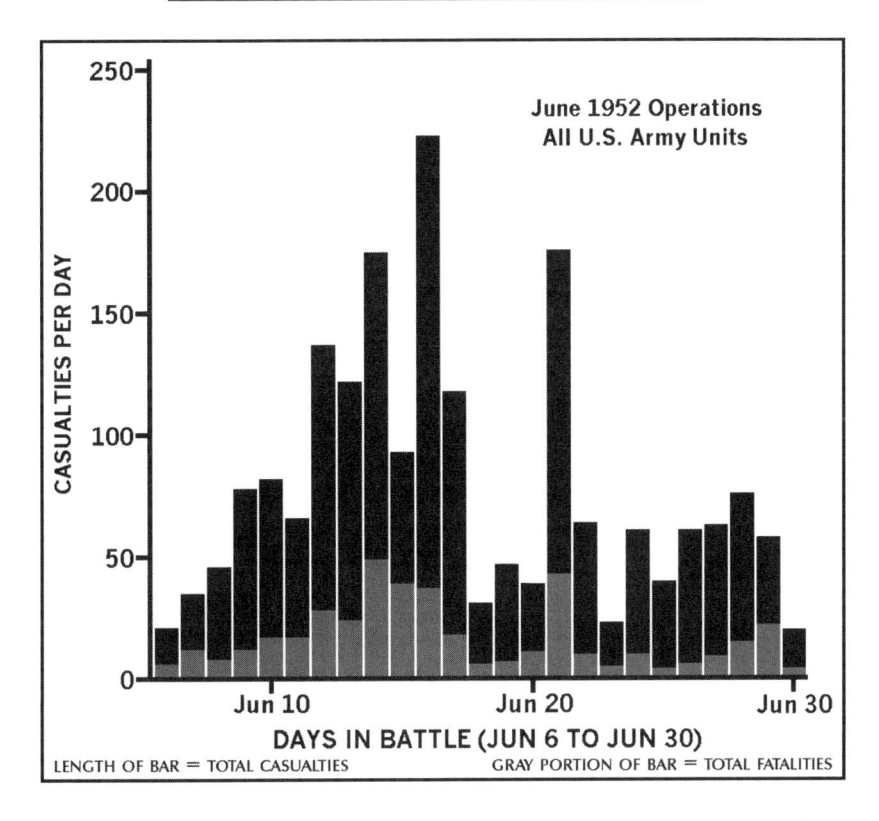

Figure 23. Daily casualties for all U.S. Army units during June 1952 Operations.

Table 97 — June 1952 Operations, All U.S. Army Units

	KIA	WIA	POW Returned	POW Died	MIA Returned	MIA Died	Unit Total
45th Infantry Division							
179th Inf, 45th Inf Div	135	486	7			12	640
180th Inf, 45th Inf Div	97	336				4	437
279th Inf, 45th Inf Div	10	119				3	132
Other 45th Div Units (11)	5	52					57
Total 45th Div	247	993	7			19	1266
7th Infantry Division	29	120	1			2	152
25th Infantry Division	15	115					130
40th Infantry Division	41	171	6			8	226
5th RCT	12	60				3	75
Other Units (28)	15	47					62
Total 06/06–06/30/52	360	1505	14			32	1911

Medal of Honor: David B. Bleak

Awarded to: Sergeant David B. Bleak, Shelly, ID, U.S. Army, Medical Company 223d Infantry Regiment, 40th Infantry Division. Vicinity of Minari-gol, Korea, 14 June 1952.

Sgt. Bleak, a member of the medical company, distinguished himself by conspicuous gallantry and indomitable courage above and beyond the call of duty in action against the enemy. As a medical aidman, he volunteered to accompany a reconnaissance patrol committed to engage the enemy and capture a prisoner for interrogation. Forging up the rugged slope of the key terrain, the group was subjected to intense automatic weapons and small arms fire and suffered several casualties. After administering to the wounded, he continued to advance with the patrol. Nearing the military crest of the hill, while attempting to cross the fire-swept area to attend the wounded, he came under hostile fire from a small group of the enemy concealed in a trench. Entering the trench he closed with the enemy, killed 2 with bare hands and a third with his trench knife. Moving from the emplacement, he saw a concussion grenade fall in front of a companion and, quickly shifting his position, shielded the man from the impact of the blast. Later, while ministering to the wounded, he was struck by a hostile bullet but, despite the wound, he undertook to evacuate a wounded comrade. As he moved down the hill with his heavy burden, he was attacked by 2 enemy soldiers with fixed bayonets. Closing with the aggressors, he grabbed them and smacked their heads together, then carried his helpless comrade down the hill to safety. Sgt. Bleak's dauntless courage and intrepid actions reflect utmost credit upon himself and are in keeping with the honored traditions of the military service.

After being hospitalized for treatment of his wounds, Sgt. Bleak returned to duty on July 9, 1952.

In what was possibly the same action, another member of the 223rd Infantry was awarded the Medal of Honor.

MEDAL OF HONOR: CLIFTON T. SPEICHER

Awarded to: Corporal Clifton T. Speicher, Gray, PA, U.S. Army, Company F, 223d Infantry Regiment, 40th Infantry Division. Near Minarigol, Korea, 14 June 1952.

Cpl. Speicher distinguished himself by conspicuous gallantry and indomitable courage above and beyond the call of duty in action against the enemy. While participating in an assault to secure a key terrain feature, Cpl. Speicher's squad was pinned down by withering small-arms mortar, and machinegun fire. Although already wounded he left the comparative safety of his position, and made a daring charge against the machinegun emplacement. Within 10 yards of the goal, he was again wounded by small-arms fire but continued on, entered the bunker, killed 2 hostile soldiers with his rifle, a third with his bayonet, and silenced the machinegun. Inspired by this incredible display of valor, the men quickly moved up and completed the mission. Dazed and shaken, he walked to the foot of the hill where he collapsed and died. Cpl. Speicher's consummate sacrifice and unflinching devotion to duty reflect lasting glory upon himself and uphold the noble traditions of the military service.

The U.S. Marines experienced a similar increase in the level of fighting, and losses, as the War of the Hills began. During the period indicated in Figure 23, the 1st Marine Division lost 63 men in ground action, plus two sailors presumed to be corpsmen. The marines also lost three pilots killed in fixed-wing plane crashes over land and one killed in an aircraft loss on the ground.

Navy losses in the period are summarized in Table 98.

Table 98 — June 1952 Operations, U.S. Navy

Fixed Wing Crash Over Land	
Pilot, Killed in Action	3
Pilot, Died while Missing	1
Fixed Wing Crash At Sea	
Pilot, Killed in Action	1
Aircrew, Died while Missing	1
Helicopter Crash Over Land	
Non-Aircrew, Died while Missing	1
Total 06/06–06/30/52	7

On June 10, 1952, three U.S. Air Force bombers were shot down in a raid over Kwaksan. The database shows 12 airmen killed on that date, 11 of them reported as "died while missing." The following day, database records show 13 airmen who were also reported as missing and never found. It may be that all of these 24 records— 6 pilots, 15 aircrew and 3 non-aircrew—represent the airmen lost in those crashes. Table 99 is a summary of all U.S. Air Force losses in the period.

Table 99 — June 1952 Operations, U.S. Air Force

Fixed Wing Crash Over Land	
Pilot, Killed in Action	4
Pilot, Died while Missing	9
Aircrew, Died while Missing	15
Non-Aircrew, Killed in Action	1
Non-Aircrew, Died while Missing	3
Ground Casualty	
Other Weapon, Killed in Action	1
Total 06/06–06/30/52	33

July Operations

In the War of the Hills, not every operation had a title, nor every hill a name. This war, at least in its early stages, involved on-and-off contests all across the 120-mile front, with one side or the other, at one location or another, attempting to gain control of some locally important high ground. In the absence of specific identification of these contests, the best way to determine that they occurred is by inspecting the casualty patterns. The pattern of U.S. Army losses in July operations is shown in Figure 24.

To get a really accurate picture of the nature of the combat represented in Figure 24, we would almost need to evaluate the situation day by day. For example, the peak of casualties shown for early July looks like it might represent the losses in a single battle in one location. In fact, it represents a number of different units, each in a different battle situation. Of the casualties on July 3, most were in the 17th Infantry Regiment of the 7th Division. Yet, the losses the next day were primarily in the 279th Regiment of the 45th Division, and the day after that mostly in the 5th RCT.

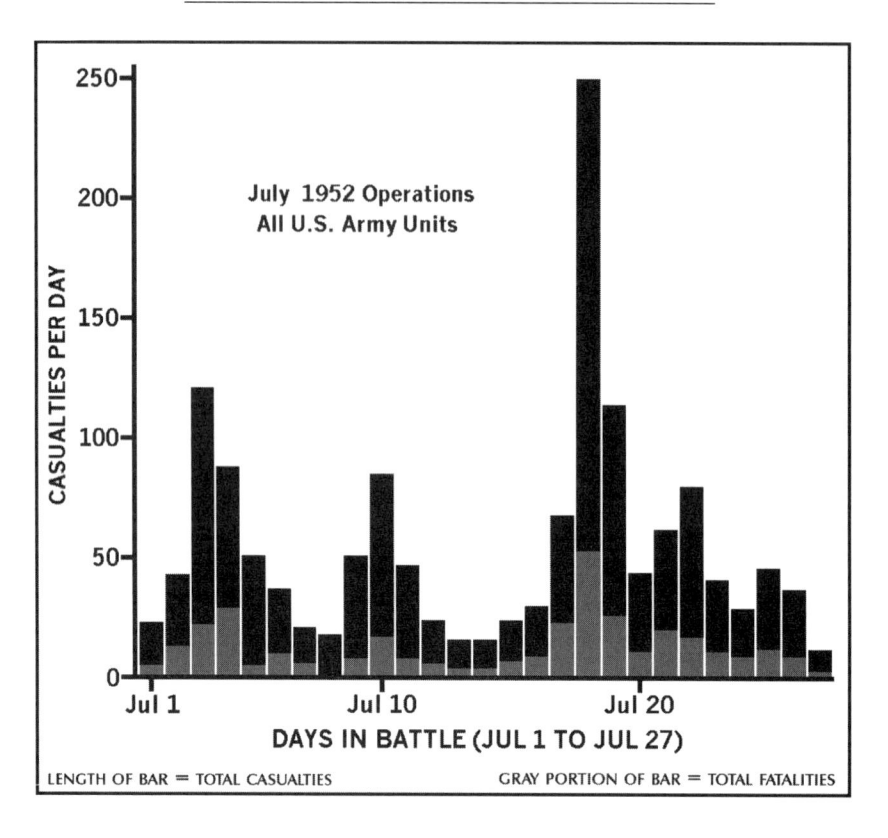

Figure 24. Daily casualties for all U.S. Army units during July 1952 Operations.

On July 17, according to reports, a major battle broke out, as the 23rd Infantry Regiment of the 2nd Division contested with the enemy over Old Baldy. This battle was reported to have continued for almost three weeks. However, after the first few days, casualties in the regiment were basically no different from those of other units along the front. On one day in those three weeks, the regiment reported no casualties at all. Certainly, the 23rd suffered significant losses in the battle, particularly on July 18 (and later on August 1). But, like many engagements in the War of the Hills, its battle for Old Baldy was an on-again/off-again contest that really defies being pinned down in terms of when it was on, when it was off and how long it lasted. In the case of Old Baldy, in fact, it could be argued that the battle really did not end till the termination of hostilities in July of 1953.

So, unless it is obvious that the losses are from a given unit in a given situation, casualty summaries will be presented over convenient periods, divided at times when casualties are low. In Table 100, casualties are summarized for the period shown in Figure 24.

III. The War of the Hills

Table 100 — July 1952 Operations, All U.S. Army Units

	KIA	WIA	POW Returned	POW Died	MIA Returned	MIA Died	Unit Total
2nd Infantry Division							
23rd Inf, 2nd Div	90	274	6			13	383
Other 2nd Div Units (12)	11	32	1			2	46
Total 2nd Division	101	306	7			15	429
3rd Infantry Division	38	163				6	207
7th Infantry Division	50	214	6			2	272
25th Infantry Division	34	158					192
45th Infantry Division	58	203				2	263
5th RCT	12	57					69
Other Units (11)	3	15	1				19
Total 07/01–07/27/52	296	1116	14			25	1451

Virtually all of the casualties in the 23rd Infantry Regiment occurred after July 17. Casualties in the 45th Division occurred almost totally prior to that date.

Casualties in the 1st Marine Division were highest in the first week of the period, and then decreased to relatively low levels through the rest of the month. The total of marine ground casualties in the 27 days was 75. Seven pilots died in fixed-wing crashes over land, two of them missing and never found.

One marine earned the Medal of Honor for his heroism in action.

Medal of Honor: William E. Shuck

Awarded to: Staff Sergeant William E. Shuck, Jr., Cumberland, MD, U.S. Marine Corps, Company G, 3d Battalion, 7th Marines, 1st Marine Division (Rein.). Korea, 3 July 1952.

> For conspicuous gallantry and intrepidity at the risk of his life above and beyond the call of duty while serving as a squad leader of Company G, in action against enemy aggressor forces. When his platoon was subjected to a devastating barrage of enemy small-arms, grenade, artillery, and mortar fire during an assault against strongly fortified hill positions well forward of the main line of resistance, S/Sgt. Shuck, although painfully wounded, refused medical attention and continued to lead his machinegun squad in the attack. Unhesitatingly assuming command of a rifle squad when the leader became a casualty, he skillfully organized the 2 squads into an attacking force and led 2 more daring assaults upon the hostile positions. Wounded a second time, he steadfastly refused evacuation and remained in the foremost position under heavy fire until assured that all dead and wounded were evacuated. Mortally wounded by an enemy sniper bullet while voluntarily assisting in the removal of the last casualty, S/Sgt. Shuck, by his fortitude and great personal valor in the face of overwhelming odds, served to inspire all who observed him. His unyielding courage throughout reflects the highest credit upon himself and the U.S. Naval Service. He gallantly gave his life for his country.

The U.S. Navy lost four pilots and one aircrew in fixed-wing crashes over land during the period. Two of the pilots and the aircrewman were reported missing and never found. There were no Navy ground casualties in the period.

U.S. Air Force losses in the period are summarized in Table 101.

Table 101—July 1952 Operations, U.S. Air Force

Fixed Wing Crash Over Land	
Pilot, Killed in Action	1
Pilot, Died while Missing	10
Aircrew, Died while Missing	6
Non-Aircrew, Died while Missing	3
Fixed Wing Crash at Sea	
Pilot, Died while Missing	1
Total 07/01–07/27/52	21

The Summer of 1952

For the next month and a half, the on-and-off nature of combat along the MLR in Korea continued. The only major operations reported in the period were the continuing battle by the 23rd Infantry over Old Baldy and some U.S. Marine operations that will be discussed later. Figure 25 shows the pattern of casualties in all U.S. Army units during these summer engagements.

In the matter of the battle for Old Baldy, reports suggest that it continued through August 4, but casualty counts show only one day in that period in which the 23rd Infantry reported an unusually large proportion of all the losses—63 out of 77 on August 1. On July 31, the most costly day in the period, the majority of casualties were from the 15th Infantry of the 3rd Division. On August 4, a total of 29 casualties were distributed among 15 different units.

An analysis of the casualty patterns shown in Figure 25 suggests that the "on and off" scenario dominated the combat all across the battle line. Seldom during the period, for example, did one unit report the highest number of casualties for two days in a row. On August 24, only three casualties were reported among all Army units. Table 102 summarizes all U.S. Army casualties in the period.

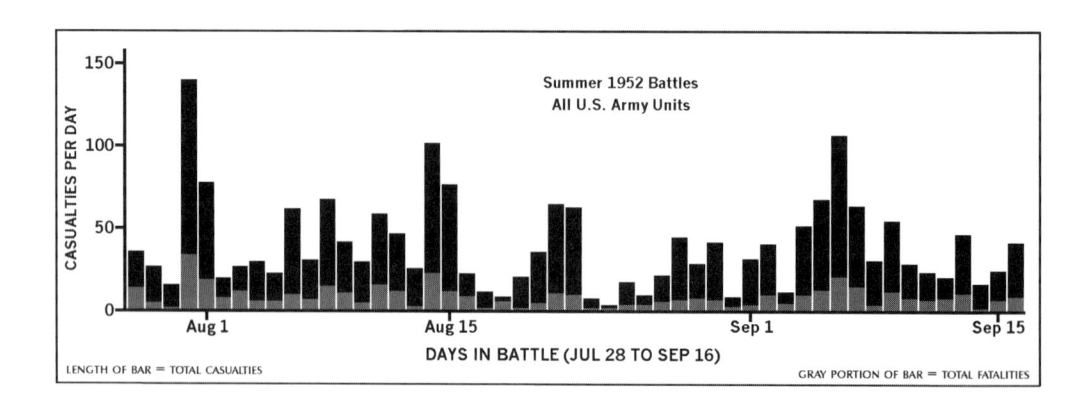

Figure 25. Daily casualties for all U.S. Army units during Summer 1952 Operations.

Table 102 — Summer 1952 Battles, All U.S. Army Units

	KIA	WIA	POW Returned	POW Died	MIA Returned	MIA Died	Unit Total
2nd Infantry Division	74	360	1			12	447
3rd Infantry Division	103	363	1			7	474
7th Infantry Division	39	205	1			6	251
25th Infantry Division	88	311	1			1	401
187th Airborne Regt/RCT	7	75	1		1		84
5th RCT	41	179				3	223
Other Units (33)	21	72					93
Totals 07/28–09/16/52	373	1565	5		1	29	1973

The number of casualties summarized in this table is not trivial. A lot of GIs were killed and wounded in these skirmishes. It was simply in the nature of the combat at that time that the engagements were neither long enough or intense enough to attract much attention. One thing was not missing in these battles: the courageous acts of men in the middle of the fighting. Three of those men earned the Medal of Honor for their valor.

MEDAL OF HONOR: LESTER HAMMOND, JR.

Awarded to: Corporal Lester Hammond, Jr., Quincy, IL, U.S. Army, Company A, 187th Airborne Regimental Combat Team. Near Kumwha, Korea, 14 August 1952.

> Cpl. Hammond, a radio operator with Company A, distinguished himself by conspicuous gallantry and outstanding courage above and beyond the call of duty in action against the enemy. Cpl. Hammond was a member of a 6 man reconnaissance patrol which had penetrated approximately 3,500 yards into enemy-held territory. Ambushed and partially surrounded by a large hostile force, the small group opened fire, then quickly withdrew up a narrow ravine in search of protective cover. Despite a wound sustained in the initial exchange of fire and imminent danger of being overrun by the numerically superior foe, he refused to seek shelter and, remaining in an exposed place, called for artillery fire to support a defensive action. Constantly vulnerable to enemy observation and action, he coordinated and directed crippling fire on the assailants, inflicting heavy casualties and repulsing several attempts to overrun friendly positions. Although wounded a second time, he remained steadfast and maintained his stand until mortally wounded. His indomitable fighting spirit set an inspiring example of valor to his comrades and, through his actions, the onslaught was stemmed, enabling a friendly platoon to reach the beleaguered patrol, evacuate the wounded, and effect a safe withdrawal to friendly lines. Cpl. Hammond's unflinching courage and consummate devotion to duty reflect lasting glory on himself and uphold the finest traditions of the military service.

MEDAL OF HONOR: BENITO MARTINEZ

Awarded to: Corporal Benito Martinez, Ft. Hancock, TX, U.S. Army, Company A, 27th Infantry Regiment, 25th Infantry Division. Near Satae-ri Korea, 6 September 1952.

> Cpl. Martinez, a machine gunner with Company A, distinguished himself by conspicuous gallantry and outstanding courage above and beyond the call of duty in action against the enemy. While manning a listening post forward of the main line of resistance, his position was attacked by a hostile force of reinforced company strength. In the bitter fighting which ensued, the enemy infiltrated the defense perimeter and, realizing that encirclement was imminent, Cpl. Martinez elected to remain at his post in an attempt to stem the onslaught. In a daring defense, he raked the attacking troops with crippling fire, inflicting numerous casualties. Although contacted by sound power phone several times, he insisted that no attempt be made to rescue him because of the danger involved. Soon thereafter, the hostile forces rushed the emplacement, forcing him to make a limited withdrawal with only an automatic rifle and pistol to defend himself. After a courageous 6-hour stand and shortly before dawn, he called in for the last time, stating that the enemy was converging on his position His magnificent stand enabled friendly elements to reorganize, attack, and regain the key terrain. Cpl. Martinez' incredible valor and supreme sacrifice reflect lasting glory upon himself and are in keeping with the honored traditions of the military service.

MEDAL OF HONOR: DONN F. PORTER

Awarded to: Sergeant Donn F. Porter, Baltimore, MD, U.S. Army, Company G, 14th Infantry Regiment, 25th Infantry Division. Near Mundung-ni Korea, 7 September 1952.

> Sgt. Porter, a member of Company G, distinguished himself by conspicuous gallantry and outstanding courage above and beyond the call of duty in action against the enemy. Advancing under cover of intense mortar and artillery fire, 2 hostile platoons attacked a combat outpost commanded by Sgt. Porter, destroyed communications, and killed 2 of his 3-man crew. Gallantly maintaining his position, he poured deadly accurate fire into the ranks of the enemy, killing 15 and dispersing the remainder. After falling back under a hail of fire, the determined foe reorganized and stormed forward in an attempt to overrun the outpost. Without hesitation, Sgt. Porter jumped from his position with bayonet fixed and, meeting the onslaught and in close combat, killed 6 hostile soldiers and routed the attack. While returning to the outpost, he was killed by an artillery burst, but his courageous actions forced the enemy to break off the engagement and thwarted a surprise attack on the main line of resistance. Sgt. Porter's incredible display of valor, gallant self-sacrifice, and consummate devotion to duty reflect the highest credit upon himself and uphold the noble traditions of the military service.

The 1st Marine Division spent much of this period in battle with the communists over Bunker Hill and Outpost Bruce on the western end of the MLR. Bunker Hill at 122 meters (about 400 ft.) and Outpost Bruce at 149 meters (about 490 ft) were small compared to places in the east like Heartbreak Ridge (931 meters), but that did not make the fighting all that much easier. Figure 26 shows the distribution of U.S. Marine Corps losses in this period.

The chronology suggests that the Battle of Bunker Hill occurred in two stages; the first between August 12 and 16, the second between September 5 and 15. Cer-

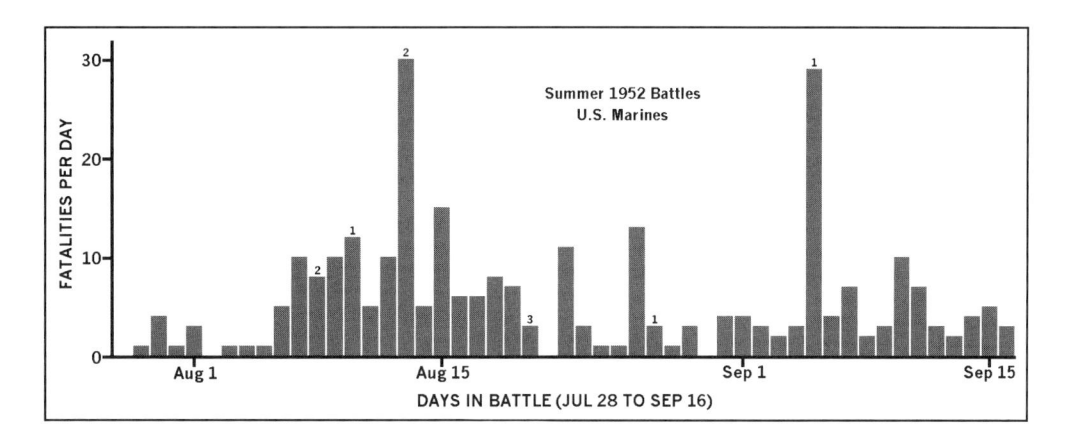

Figure 26. Daily fatalities for U.S. Marine units during the Summer 1952 Battles. The numbers over the bars on some dates indicate the number of presumed Navy corpsmen killed in ground action on those days.

tainly the days with the greatest losses were early in each of those stages. However, the September stage overlapped with Outpost Bruce (September 6 to 9)—and many losses occurred when neither of these battles was supposed to be ongoing—so it is not possible from these data to identify accurately which of the casualties shown in Fig 27 might be attributable to these two battles and which to other operations that are not specifically identified. The data do tell us that there were a total of 283 Marine fatalities in the period. Of these, 272 were killed in ground action, one of whom died while missing and another died in captivity. The remaining 11 were all marine pilots, one KIA in a fixed-wing crash at sea and the rest killed in fixed-wing crashes over land, one of whom was never found. As Figure 26 indicates, ten sailors (corpsmen) were killed in ground action in the period, two of whom were awarded the Medal of Honor for their valor and self-sacrifice.

Medal of Honor: John E. Kilmer

Hospital Corpsman John E. Kilmer, Houston, TX, U.S. Navy, attached to duty as a medical corpsman with a Marine rifle company in the 1st Marine Division. Korea, 13 August 1952.

> For conspicuous gallantry and intrepidity at the risk of his life above and beyond the call of duty in action against enemy aggressor forces. With his company engaged in defending a vitally important hill position well forward of the main line of resistance during an assault by large concentrations of hostile troops, HC Kilmer repeatedly braved intense enemy mortar, artillery, and sniper fire to move from 1 position to another, administering aid to the wounded and expediting their evacuation. Painfully wounded himself when struck by mortar fragments while moving to the aid of a casualty, he persisted in his efforts and inched his way to the side of the stricken marine through a hail of enemy shells falling around him. Undaunted by the devastating hostile fire, he skillfully administered first aid to his comrade and, as another mounting barrage of enemy fire shattered the imme-

diate area, unhesitatingly shielded the wounded man with his body. Mortally wounded by flying shrapnel while carrying out this heroic action, HC Kilmer, by his great personal valor and gallant spirit of self-sacrifice in saving the life of a comrade, served to inspire all who observed him. His unyielding devotion to duty in the face of heavy odds reflects the highest credit upon himself and enhances the finest traditions of the U.S. Naval Service. He gallantly gave his life for another.

MEDAL OF HONOR: EDWARD C. BENFORD

Awarded to: Hospital Corpsman Third Class Edward C. Benford, Philadelphia, PA, U.S. Navy, attached to a company in the 1st Marine Division. Korea, 5 September 1952.

> For gallantry and intrepidity at the risk of his life above and beyond the call of duty while serving in operations against enemy aggressor forces. When his company was subjected to heavy artillery and mortar barrages, followed by a determined assault during the hours of darkness by an enemy force estimated at battalion strength, HC3c. Benford resolutely moved from position to position in the face of intense hostile fire, treating the wounded and lending words of encouragement. Leaving the protection of his sheltered position to treat the wounded when the platoon area in which he was working was attacked from both the front and rear, he moved forward to an exposed ridge line where he observed 2 marines in a large crater. As he approached the 2 men to determine their condition, an enemy soldier threw 2 grenades into the crater while 2 other enemy charged the position. Picking up a grenade in each hand, HC3c. Benford leaped out of the crater and hurled himself against the on-rushing hostile soldiers, pushing the grenades against their chests and killing both the attackers. Mortally wounded while carrying out this heroic act, HC3c. Benford, by his great personal valor and resolute spirit of self-sacrifice in the face of almost certain death, was directly responsible for saving the lives of his 2 comrades. His exceptional courage reflects the highest credit upon himself and enhances

Three marines were also awarded the Medal of Honor for their heroism in these battles.

MEDAL OF HONOR: ROBERT E. SIMANEK

Awarded to: Private First Class Robert E. Simanek, Detroit, MI, U.S. Marine Corps, Company F, 2d Battalion, 5th Marines, 1st Marine Division (Rein.). Korea, 17 August 1952.

> For conspicuous gallantry and intrepidity at the risk of his life above and beyond the call of duty while serving with Company F, in action against enemy aggressor forces. While accompanying a patrol en route to occupy a combat outpost forward of friendly lines, Pfc. Simanek exhibited a high degree of courage and a resolute spirit of self-sacrifice in protecting the lives of his fellow marines. With his unit ambushed by an intense concentration of enemy mortar and small-arms fire, and suffering heavy casualties, he was forced to seek cover with the remaining members of the patrol in a nearby trench line. Determined to save his comrades when a hostile grenade

was hurled into their midst, he unhesitatingly threw himself on the deadly missile absorbing the shattering violence of the exploding charge in his body and shielding his fellow marines from serious injury or death. Gravely wounded as a result of his heroic action, Pfc. Simanek, by his daring initiative and great personal valor in the face of almost certain death, served to inspire all who observed him and upheld the highest traditions of the U.S. Naval Service.

MEDAL OF HONOR: ALFORD L. MCLAUGHLIN

Awarded to: Private First Class Alford L. McLaughlin, Leeds, AL, U.S. Marine Corps Company L, 3d Battalion, 5th Marines, 1st Marine Division (Rein.) Korea, 4 and 5 September 1952.

> For conspicuous gallantry and intrepidity at the risk of his life above and beyond the call of duty while serving as a machine gunner of Company L, in action against enemy aggressor forces on the night of 4–5 September 1952. Volunteering for his second continuous tour of duty on a strategic combat outpost far in advance of the main line of resistance, Pfc. McLaughlin, although operating under a barrage of enemy artillery and mortar fire, set up plans for the defense of his position which proved decisive in the successful defense of the outpost. When hostile forces attacked in battalion strength during the night, he maintained a constant flow of devastating fire upon the enemy, alternately employing 2 machineguns, a carbine, and hand grenades. Although painfully wounded, he bravely fired the machineguns from the hip until his hands became blistered by the extreme heat from the weapons and, placing the guns on the ground to allow them to cool, continued to defend the position with his carbine and grenades. Standing up in full view, he shouted words of encouragement to his comrades above the din of battle and, throughout a series of fanatical enemy attacks, sprayed the surrounding area with deadly fire, accounting for an estimated 150 enemy dead and 50 wounded. By his indomitable courage, superb leadership, and valiant fighting spirit in the face of overwhelming odds, Pfc. McLaughlin served to inspire his fellow marines in their gallant stand against the enemy and was directly instrumental in preventing the vital outpost from falling into the hands of a determined and numerically superior hostile force. His outstanding heroism and unwavering devotion to duty reflect the highest credit upon himself and enhance the finest traditions of the U.S. Naval Service.

MEDAL OF HONOR: FERNANDO LUIS GARCIA

Awarded to: Private First Class Fernando Luis Garcia, San Juan, PR, U.S. Marine Corps, Company I, 3d Battalion, 5th Marines, 1st Marine Division (Rein.). Korea, 5 September 1952.

> For conspicuous gallantry and intrepidity at the risk of his life above and beyond the call of duty while serving as a member of Company I, in action against enemy aggressor forces. While participating in the defense of a combat outpost located more than 1 mile forward of the main line of resistance during a savage night attack by a fanatical enemy force employing grenades, mortars, and artillery, Pfc. Garcia, although suffering painful

wounds, moved through the intense hail of hostile fire to a supply point to secure more hand grenades. Quick to act when a hostile grenade landed nearby, endangering the life of another marine, as well as his own, he unhesitatingly chose to sacrifice himself and immediately threw his body upon the deadly missile, receiving the full impact of the explosion. His great personal valor and cool decision in the face of almost certain death sustain and enhance the finest traditions of the U.S. Naval Service. He gallantly gave his life for his country.

The chronology indicates that the ocean tug *Sarsi* was sunk by a mine off Hungnam on August 30, 1952, with four sailors killed in the action. The database shows no U.S. Navy losses on that date. However, database records do show four Navy fatalities at sea from an explosive device three days earlier, on August 27. One was listed as KIA; the other three as missing and never found. Records also show the loss of five sailors from an explosive device at sea on September 16, two of whom were KIA and three missing and never found. The cause of these losses is unknown.

These and other U.S. Navy losses in the period (except ground casualties) are summarized in Table 103.

Table 103 — Summer 1952 Battles, U.S. Navy

Fixed Wing Crash Over Land	
Pilot, Killed in Action	3
Aircrew, Killed in Action	2
Fixed Wing Crash At Sea	
Aircrew, Killed in Action	1
Sea Casualty	
Explosive Device, Killed in Action	6
Explosive Device, Died while Missing	5
Total 07/28–09/16/52	17

U.S. Air Force losses in the period are summarized in Table 104.

Table 104 — Summer 1952 Battles, U.S. Air Force

Fixed Wing Crash Over Land	
Pilot, Killed in Action	4
Pilot, Died while Missing	21
Aircrew, Died while Missing	17
Non-Aircrew, Died while Missing	5
Total 07/28–09/16/52	47

Raising the Volume

It could be reasonably expected that, as each side in this war made bolder incursions into enemy territory, the other side would respond in kind. And it could also be expected that the intensity of the combat in these incursions would rise to a higher level with each response. So it was that the coming of fall to the Korean war zone in 1952 brought with it an elevation in the level of fighting, and an increase in American casualties. Figure 27 shows the distribution of U.S. Army casualties in the first month of higher level combat.

III. The War of the Hills

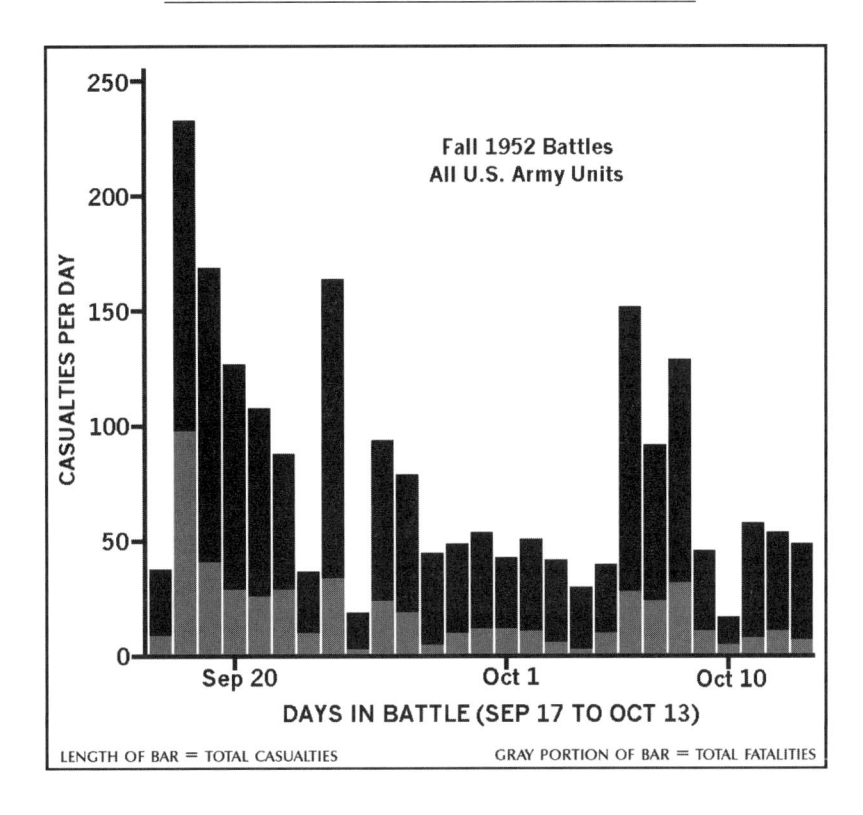

Figure 27. Daily casualties for all U.S. Army units during Fall 1952 Battles.

From September 17 to 24, the 65 Infantry Regiment of the 3rd Infantry Division was besieged on Outpost Kelly by CCF forces, and recorded 334 casualties. A summary of those casualties is shown in Table 105.

Table 105 — Outpost Kelly, 65th Infantry Regiment

	KIA	WIA	POW Returned	POW Died	MIA Returned	MIA Died	Unit Total
65th Infantry, 3rd Division Total 09/17–09/24/52	38	210	12		1	73	334

Concurrent with this action, the 38th Regiment of the 2nd Division, now responsible for the sector occupied by Old Baldy, were in renewed combat with the enemy over that outpost. A summary of that unit's losses from September 18 to 21 is shown in Table 106.

Table 106 — Old Baldy, 38th Infantry Regiment

	KIA	WIA	POW Returned	POW Died	MIA Returned	MIA Died	Unit Total
38th Infantry, 2nd Division Total 09/18–09/21/52	88	234	4			3	329

Of course, other Army units were taking casualties as well. In fact, 40 different units reported losses that week. But, over two-thirds of all reported casualties and over three-fourths of all fatalities were in the 65th and the 38th.

Following these outpost battles, casualty reports resumed the "on and off" pattern that had become characteristic of the War of the Hills, with many different units sharing the dubious honor of reporting the most daily losses. Then, beginning on October 6, the CCF mounted attacks in the west central sector of the MLR. The primary American units defending against these assaults were in Army's 2nd and 7th Divisions and the 1st Marine Division. Although 45 different Army units reported a total of 589 casualties that week, the 17th Infantry of the 7th Division took the biggest hit. That regiment's losses are summarized in Table 107.

Table 107 — 7th Division Outpost, 17th Infantry Regiment

	KIA	WIA	POW Returned	POW Died	MIA Returned	MIA Died	Unit Total
17th Infantry, 7th Division Total 10/06–10/13/52	46	171				6	223

Among the 45 units that reported losses that week was the 14th Infantry Regiment of the 25th Division. Although units like the 14th reported fewer casualties than some, their combat was no less intense, a fact that is exemplified in the Medal of Honor award to one of its members.

MEDAL OF HONOR: ERNEST E. WEST

Awarded to: Private First Class Ernest E. West, Wurtland, KY, U.S. Army, Company L, 14th Infantry Regiment, 25th Infantry Division. Near Sataeri, Korea, 12 October 1952.

> Pfc. West distinguished himself by conspicuous gallantry above and beyond the call of duty in action against the enemy. He voluntarily accompanied a contingent to locate and destroy a reported enemy outpost. Nearing the objective, the patrol was ambushed and suffered numerous casualties. Observing his wounded leader lying in an exposed position, Pfc. West ordered the troops to withdraw, then braved intense fire to reach and assist him. While attempting evacuation, he was attacked by 3 hostile soldiers employing grenades and small-arms fire. Quickly shifting his body to shelter the officer, he killed the assailants with his rifle, then carried the helpless man to safety. He was critically wounded and lost an eye in this action. but courageously returned through withering fire and bursting shells to assist the wounded. While evacuating 2 comrades, he closed with and killed 3 more of the foe. Pfc. West's indomitable spirit, consummate valor, and intrepid actions inspired all who observed him, reflect the highest credit on himself, and uphold the honored traditions of the military service.

Pfc. West was evacuated to the States and separated from the service. The officer he saved, assumed from the record to be 1st Lt. George M. Gividen, was evacuated to the States and returned to duty there. There were only 14 casualties in the 14th Infantry that day, none of them fatal, for which Pfc. West was unquestionably due some considerable credit.

III. The War of the Hills

During the month of combat shown in Figure 27, more than 2,000 casualties were reported by U.S. Army Units. A summary of those losses is shown in Table 108.

Table 108 — Fall 1952 Battles, All U.S. Army Units

	KIA	WIA	POW Returned	POW Died	MIA Returned	MIA Died	Unit Total
2nd Infantry Division	155	452	6	1		5	619
3rd Infantry Division	70	319	19		1	77	486
7th Infantry Division	68	342	2			6	418
25th Infantry Division	16	131				1	148
45th Infantry Division	49	156					205
187th Airborne Regt/RCT	5	20					25
5th RCT	18	85				3	106
Other Units (23)	14	53	5			1	73
Total 09/17–10/13/52	395	1558	32	1	1	93	2080

Marines, Navy and Air Force

During this month, the 1st Marine Division continued to hold positions in the western sector of the MLR, a scant 30 miles north of Seoul. They were the primary defense against an enemy thrust that could endanger the South Korean capital. Figure 28 shows the distribution of Marine Corps casualties in the period.

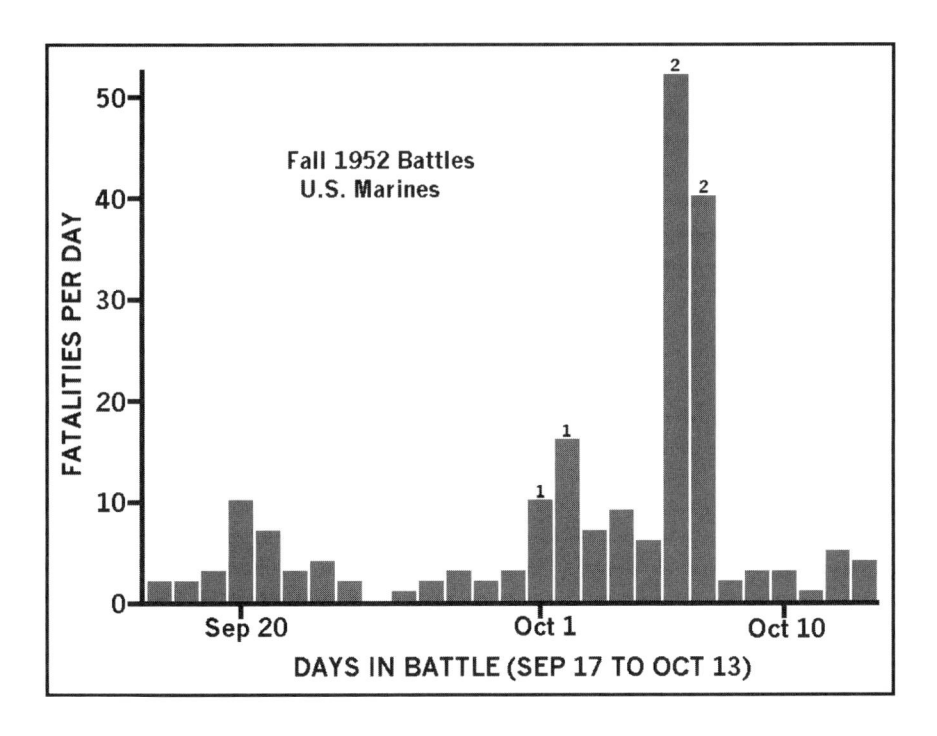

Figure 28. Daily fatalities for U.S. Marine Corps units in the Fall 1952 Battles. The numbers over the bars on some dates indicate the number of presumed Navy corpsmen killed on those days.

When the CCF attacks began in the western and central sectors on October 6, the marines were already in a major fight to hold their positions on the line. This fact is substantiated by the award of the Medal of Honor to one marine who was in the middle of it.

Medal of Honor: William Jack Kelso

Awarded to: Private First Class William Jack Kelso, Caruthers, CA, U.S. Marine Corps, Company I, 3d Battalion, 7th Marines, 1st Marine Division (Rein.). Korea, 2 October 1952.

> For conspicuous gallantry and intrepidity at the risk of his life above and beyond the call of duty while serving as a rifleman of Company I, in action against enemy aggressor forces. When both the platoon commander and the platoon sergeant became casualties during the defense of a vital outpost against a numerically superior enemy force attacking at night under cover of intense small-arms, grenade, and mortar fire, Pfc. Kelso bravely exposed himself to the hail of enemy fire in a determined effort to reorganize the unit and to repel the onrushing attackers. Forced to seek cover, along with 4 other marines, in a nearby bunker which immediately came under attack, he unhesitatingly picked up an enemy grenade which landed in the shelter, rushed out into the open and hurled it back at the enemy. Although painfully wounded when the grenade exploded as it left his hand, and again forced to seek the protection of the bunker when the hostile fire became more intensified Pfc. Kelso refused to remain in his position of comparative safety and moved out into the fire-swept area to return the enemy fire, thereby permitting the pinned-down marines in the bunker to escape. Mortally wounded while providing covering fire for his comrades, Pfc. Kelso, by his valiant fighting spirit, aggressive determination, and self-sacrificing efforts in behalf of others, served to inspire all who observed him. His heroic actions sustain and enhance the highest traditions of the U.S. Naval Service. He gallantly gave his life for his country.

Five days later, after the CCF offensive had started in earnest, another marine hero was awarded the Medal of Honor for his part in helping his comrades hold their ground.

Medal of Honor: Lewis G. Watkins

Awarded to: Staff Sergeant Lewis G. Watkins, Seneca, SC, U.S. Marine Corps, Company I, 3d Battalion, 7th Marines, 1st Marine Division (Rein.). Korea, 7 October 1952.

> For conspicuous gallantry and intrepidity at the risk of his life above and beyond the call of duty while serving as a guide of a rifle platoon of Company I, in action against enemy aggressor forces during the hours of darkness on the morning of 7 October 1952. With his platoon assigned the mission of retaking an outpost which had been overrun by the enemy earlier in the night, S/Sgt. Watkins skillfully led his unit in the assault up the designated hill. Although painfully wounded when a well-entrenched hostile force at the crest of the hill engaged the platoon with intense small-

arms and grenade fire, he gallantly continued to lead his men. Obtaining an automatic rifle from 1 of the wounded men, he assisted in pinning down an enemy machinegun holding up the assault. When an enemy grenade landed among S/Sgt. Watkins and several other marines while they were moving forward through a trench on the hill crest, he immediately pushed his companions aside, placed himself in a position to shield them and picked up the deadly missile in an attempt to throw it outside the trench. Mortally wounded when the grenade exploded in his hand, S/Sgt. Watkins, by his great personal valor in the face of almost certain death, saved the lives of several of his comrades and contributed materially to the success of the mission. His extraordinary heroism, inspiring leadership, and resolute spirit of self-sacrifice reflect the highest credit upon himself and enhance the finest traditions of the U.S. Naval Service. He gallantly gave his life for his country.

The marines lost a total of 202 men killed in the period, 196 on the ground and 6 pilots lost in fixed-wing crashes over land. Of the ground casualties, 17 were reported missing and never found and one died in captivity. As Figure 28 indicates, six sailors (corpsmen) were also lost in ground action.

Other U.S. Navy losses in the period included one pilot and one aircrew killed in fixed-wing air crashes over land, one sailor lost as a sea casualty due to an explosive device and one sailor as a sea casualty due to drowning.

In Table 109 is an accounting of U.S. Air Force losses in the period.

Table 109 — Fall 1952 Battles, U.S. Air Force

Fixed Wing Crash Over Land	
Pilot, Killed in Action	1
Pilot, Died while Missing	7
Aircrew, Died while Missing	2
Non-Aircrew, Died while Missing	1
Total 09/17–10/13/52	11

Showdown

On October 14, 1952, the boldest American offensive of the War of the Hills was undertaken by the U.S. 7th Infantry Division. Called Operation Showdown, its purpose was to capture Triangle Hill (Hill 598) and two adjacent elevations, Pikes Peak and Jane Russell. Initially planned to be secured by two battalions in five days, it ultimately required the commitment of the entire division. When it was not yet consolidated after 12 days and over 1,500 American casualties, the objective was turned over to the ROK army, who could not hold it. Reports suggest that CCF commanders consider the defense of Triangle Hill to be their greatest victory of the war.

For the 31st Infantry, the assault regiment, the first day of Operation Showdown became its most costly single day of casualties in the entire war (96 KIA, 337 WIA). Losses would probably have been even greater if it were not for the fact that, for the first time in history, every member of the assault force was wearing an armored vest.

Figure 29 shows the distribution of casualties in all U.S. Army units during the time of Operation Showdown and the two weeks following.

Figure 30 shows casualties for the same period reported by the 7th Division only.

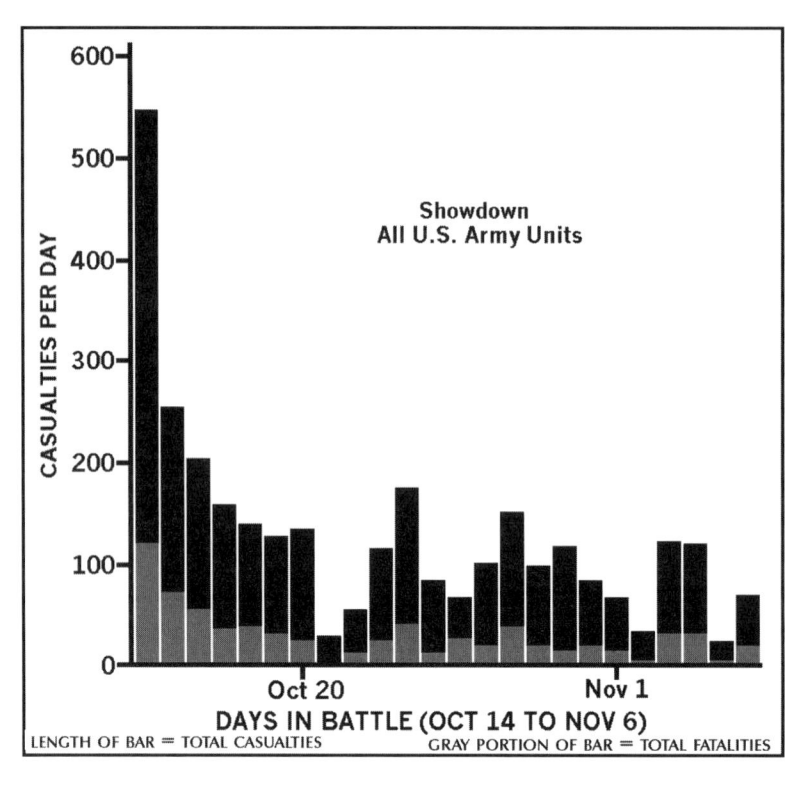

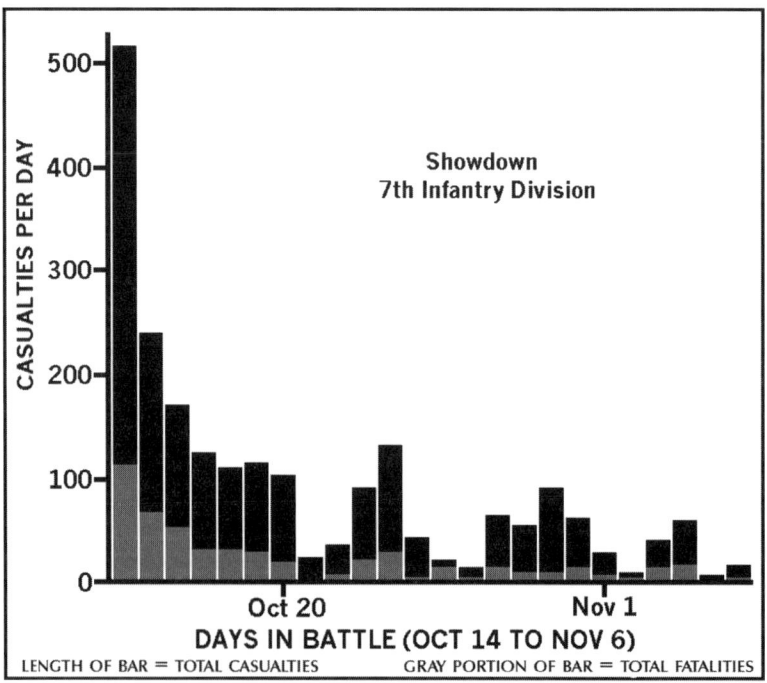

Figure 29. (*top*) Daily casualties for all U.S. Army units during the time of Operation Showdown. Figure 30. (*bottom*) Daily casualties for the U.S. 7th Infantry Division during the time of Operation Showdown.

III. The War of the Hills

In the period of time the 7th Division was engaged in Operation Showdown (October 14 to 25), the division reported 85 percent of all Army casualties and 88 percent of all Army fatalities. However, not all of the 7th division casualties in that period were due to the action on Triangle Hill. Recall from discussions earlier in the chapter that, on October 6, the CCF had mounted an offensive in the west-central sector of the MLR and that the 7th Division's 17th Infantry was one of the defending units in that offensive. So, all the while it was engaged in Operation Showdown, the 7th Division had to continue its defense of the western end of its sector, which it accomplished by rotating units between Triangle and the west sector.

For this reason, it is difficult to determine the exact count of losses in Operation Showdown. Total 7th Division losses during the time of the operation are summarized in Table 110.

Table 110 — Operation Showdown, 7th Infantry Division

	KIA	WIA	POW Returned	POW Died	MIA Returned	MIA Died	Unit Total
7th Infantry Division							
31st Inf, 7th Inf Div	141	509				37	687
32nd Inf, 7th Inf Div	119	487	1			17	624
17th Inf, 7th Inf Div	55	250				8	313
13th Engr Bn, 7th Inf Div	5	12					17
48th FA Bn, 7th Inf Div	3	10					13
57th FA Bn, 7th Inf Div	1	8				1	10
Other 7th Div Units (7)	5	22	1				28
Total 10/14–10/25/52	**329**	**1298**	**2**			**63**	**1692**

From estimates of which units were committed to the operation at which times, the best guess of 7th Division losses in the battle is 365 killed and 1,174 wounded.

Two Medals of Honor were awarded to men for their heroic actions in Operation Showdown.

MEDAL OF HONOR: EDWARD R. SCHOWALTER, JR.

Awarded to: First Lieutenant Edward R. Schowalter, Jr., Metairie, LA, U.S. Army, Company A, 31st Infantry Regiment, 7th Infantry Division. Near Kumhwa, Korea, 14 October 1952.

> 1st Lt. Schowalter, commanding, Company A, distinguished himself by conspicuous gallantry and indomitable courage above and beyond the call of duty in action against the enemy. Committed to attack and occupy a key-approach to the primary objective, the 1st Platoon of his company came under heavy vicious small-arms, grenade, and mortar fire within 50 yards of the enemy-held strongpoint, halting the advance and inflicting several casualties. The 2d Platoon moved up in support at this juncture, and although wounded, 1st Lt. Schowalter continued to spearhead the assault. Nearing the objective he was severely wounded by a grenade fragment but, refusing medical aid, he led his men into the trenches and began routing the enemy from the bunkers with grenades. Suddenly from a burst of fire from a hidden cove off the trench he was again wounded. Although suffering from his wounds, he refused to relinquish command and continued issu-

ing orders and encouraging his men until the commanding ground was secured and then he was evacuated. 1st Lt. Schowalter's unflinching courage, extraordinary heroism, and inspirational leadership reflect the highest credit upon himself and are in keeping with the highest traditions of the military service.

1st Lt. Schowalter was evacuated to the States and returned to duty there on February 17, 1953.

MEDAL OF HONOR: RALPH E. POMEROY

Awarded to: Private First Class Ralph E. Pomeroy, Quinwood, WV, U.S. Army, Company E, 31st Infantry Regiment, 7th Infantry Division. Near Kumhwa, Korea, 15 October 1952.

Pfc. Pomeroy, a machine gunner with Company E, distinguished himself by conspicuous gallantry and indomitable courage above and beyond the call of duty in action against the enemy. While his comrades were consolidating on a key terrain feature, he manned a machinegun at the end of a communication trench on the forward slope to protect the platoon flank and prevent a surprise attack. When the enemy attacked through a ravine leading directly to his firing position, he immediately opened fire on the advancing troops inflicting a heavy toll in casualties and blunting the assault. At this juncture the enemy directed intense concentrations of artillery and mortar fire on his position in an attempt to neutralize his gun. Despite withering fire and bursting shells, he maintained his heroic stand and poured crippling fire into the ranks of the hostile force until a mortar burst severely wounded him and rendered the gun mount inoperable. Quickly removing the hot, heavy weapon, he cradled it in his arms and, moving forward with grim determination, raked the attacking forces with a hail of fire. Although wounded a second time he pursued his relentless course until his ammunition was expended within 10 feet of the foe and then, using the machinegun as a club, he courageously closed with the enemy in hand-to-hand combat until mortally wounded. Pfc. Pomeroy's consummate valor, inspirational actions and supreme sacrifice enabled the platoon to contain the attack and maintain the integrity of the perimeter, reflecting lasting glory upon himself and upholding the noble traditions of the military service.

Meanwhile, other U.S. Army units continued to engage the enemy in their sectors of the MLR and report casualties from those actions. In one of those actions, on November 3rd, the 160th Regiment of the 40th Division was attacked by the NKPA on Heartbreak Ridge. The chronology lists 19 KIA and 54 WIA in that battle. The database records 12 KIA and 31 WIA in the 160th that day. However, on the following day the regiment reported 8 KIA and 19 WIA. Between the two days, the casualties approximate the figures in the chronology. Table 111 summarizes all Army casualties in the period shown in Figure 29.

Table 111—October Outpost Battles, All U.S. Army Units

	KIA	WIA	POW Returned	POW Died	MIA Returned	MIA Died	Unit Total
2nd Infantry Division	25	118	1				144
3rd Infantry Division	27	127	3			5	162
7th Infantry Division	424	1646	5	2		69	2146
25th Infantry Division	11	54				2	67
40th Infantry Division	73	226	1				300
45th Infantry Division	20	120				4	144
5th RCT	7	36				2	45
Other Units (21)	7	31				1	39
Total 10/14–11/06/52	594	2358	10	2		83	3047

Marines, Navy and Air Force

Through most of this period, U.S. Marine losses on the ground continued at much the same level they had been at the end of the previous period (see Figure 28). In the middle of that relative tranquility, however, came the Battle of the Hook. On October 26 to 28, the 7th Marine Regiment engaged the enemy in ferocious combat in the marine's ongoing contest over outposts in the western sector of the MLR. In that battle, the chronology lists marine losses as 70 KIA, 386 WIA, 12 MIA and 27 POW. The database records 95 marine ground fatalities in the period, two of which were missing and never found. In addition, one marine flyer was killed in a fixed-wing crash over land. There were no recorded Navy ground casualties in the battle.

Total U.S. Marine casualties for the period shown in Figure 29 were 147, including 3 pilots lost in fixed-wing crashes over land and one airman killed in an aircraft loss on the ground. Three of the marine ground casualties were reported missing and never found.

Two marine officers were awarded the Medal of Honor for their bravery in action during the Battle of the Hook.

MEDAL OF HONOR: SHERROD E. SKINNER, JR.

Awarded to: Second Lieutenant Sherrod E. Skinner, Jr., East Lansing, MI, U.S. Marine Corps Reserve, Battery F, 2d Battalion, 11th Marines, 1st Marine Division (Rein.). Korea, 26 October 1952

> For conspicuous gallantry and intrepidity at the risk of his life above and beyond the call of duty as an artillery forward observer of Battery F, in action against enemy aggressor forces on the night of 26 October 1952. When his observation post in an extremely critical and vital sector of the main line of resistance was subjected to a sudden and fanatical attack by hostile forces, supported by a devastating barrage of artillery and mortar fire which completely severed communication lines connecting the outpost with friendly firing batteries, 2d Lt. Skinner, in a determined effort to hold his position, immediately organized and directed the surviving personnel in the defense of the outpost, continuing to call down fire on the enemy by means of radio alone until his equipment became damaged beyond repair. Undaunted by the intense hostile barrage and the rapidly-closing attackers, he twice left the protection of his bunker in order to direct accurate machinegun fire and to replenish the depleted supply of ammunition

and grenades. Although painfully wounded on each occasion, he steadfastly refused medical aid until the rest of the men received treatment. As the ground attack reached its climax, he gallantly directed the final defense until the meager supply of ammunition was exhausted and the position overrun. During the 3 hours that the outpost was occupied by the enemy, several grenades were thrown into the bunker which served as protection for 2d Lt. Skinner and his remaining comrades. Realizing that there was no chance for other than passive resistance, he directed his men to feign death even though the hostile troops entered the bunker and searched their persons. Later, when an enemy grenade was thrown between him and 2 other survivors, he immediately threw himself on the deadly missile in an effort to protect the others, absorbing the full force of the explosion and sacrificing his life for his comrades. By his indomitable fighting spirit, superb leadership, and great personal valor in the face of tremendous odds, 2d Lt. Skinner served to inspire his fellow marines in their heroic stand against the enemy and upheld the highest traditions of the U.S. Naval Service. He gallantly gave his life for his country.

MEDAL OF HONOR: GEORGE H. O'BRIEN, JR.

Awarded to: Second Lieutenant George H. O'Brien, Jr., Big Spring, TX, U.S. Marine Corps Reserve, Company H, 3d Battalion, 7th Marines, 1st Marine Division (Rein.). Korea, 27 October, 1952.

For conspicuous gallantry and intrepidity at the risk of his life above and beyond the call of duty as a rifle platoon commander of Company H, in action against enemy aggressor forces. With his platoon subjected to an intense mortar and artillery bombardment while preparing to assault a vitally important hill position on the main line of resistance which had been overrun by a numerically superior enemy force on the preceding night, 2d Lt. O'Brien leaped from his trench when the attack signal was given and, shouting for his men to follow, raced across an exposed saddle and up the enemy-held hill through a virtual hail of deadly small-arms, artillery, and mortar fire. Although shot through the arm and thrown to the ground by hostile automatic-weapons fire as he neared the well-entrenched enemy position, he bravely regained his feet, waved his men onward, and continued to spearhead the assault, pausing only long enough to go to the aid of a wounded marine. Encountering the enemy at close range, he proceeded to hurl hand grenades into the bunkers and, utilizing his carbine to best advantage in savage hand-to-hand combat, succeeded in killing at least 3 of the enemy. Struck down by the concussion of grenades on 3 occasions during the subsequent action, he steadfastly refused to be evacuated for medical treatment and continued to lead his platoon in the assault for a period of nearly 4 hours, repeatedly encouraging his men and maintaining superb direction of the unit. With the attack halted he set up a defense with his remaining forces to prepare for a counterattack, personally checking each position, attending to the wounded and expediting their evacuation. When a relief of the position was effected by another unit, he remained to cover the withdrawal and to assure that no wounded were left behind. By his exceptionally daring and forceful leadership in the face of overwhelming odds, 2d Lt. O'Brien served as a constant source of inspiration to all who observed him and was greatly instrumental in the recapture of a strategic position on the main line of resistance. His indomitable determination and valiant fighting spirit reflect the highest credit upon himself and enhance the finest traditions of the U.S. Naval Service.

On October 21, the USS *Lewis* was hit by fire from a shore battery off Wonsan. The chronology lists 7 KIA in the action. The database records 4 sea casualties KIA on that date. However, three sailors were recorded as killed in ground action on October 21. As only one marine was killed on that date, this low level of ground combat would not likely have caused the death of three corpsmen. It seems more likely that these were recorded as ground casualties when they should have been sea casualties. This would account for the additional three KIAs in the chronology. No other ground casualties of seamen were recorded in the period.

U.S. Air Force losses in the period are summarized in Table 112.

Table 112 — October Outpost Battles, U.S. Air Force

Fixed Wing Crash Over Land	
Pilot, Killed in Action	1
Pilot, Died while Missing	6
Non-Aircrew, Killed in Action	1
Fixed Wing Crash At Sea	
Pilot, Died while Missing	1
Total 10/14–11/06/52	9

Active Defense Resumed

Activity on the MLR during the next four months of the war was not officially called "active defense," but the fact is, the end of 1952 and the beginning of 1953 were just about carbon copies of what had happened the year before. There were no major battles, and fighting tended to ebb and flow as it had during active defense. No single unit reported large numbers of casualties and all units that were committed to combat reported some. Active fighting continued across the no-man's-land that separated the two sides in the war, but the level was generally more subdued than it had been.

Through the month of November casualties remained somewhat higher as the participants began to back away from the more costly incursions that had punctuated the opening months of the War of the Hills. For the remainder of November, casualties averaged about 32 per day. Table 113 summarizes the distribution of casualties among U.S. Army units in action during November 1952.

Table 113 — November 1952 actions, All U.S. Army Units

	KIA	WIA	POW Returned	POW Died	MIA Returned	MIA Died	Unit Total
2nd Infantry Division	18	83				4	105
3rd Infantry Division	24	135	1			1	161
7th Infantry Division	6	33				3	42
25th Infantry Division	14	64	1				79
40th Infantry Division	28	155	1				184
45th Infantry Division	27	140	2			1	170
Other Units (16)	6	32					38
Total 11/7–11/30/52	123	642	5			9	779

One participant in these engagements was awarded the Medal of Honor for his valor and self-sacrifice.

MEDAL OF HONOR: CHARLES GEORGE

Awarded to: Private First Class Charles George, Whittier, NC, U.S. Army, Company C, 179th Infantry Regiment, 45th Infantry Division. Near Songnae-dong, Korea, 30 November 1952.

> Pfc. George, a member of Company C, distinguished himself by conspicuous gallantry and outstanding courage above and beyond the call of duty in action against the enemy on the night of 30 November 1952. He was a member of a raiding party committed to engage the enemy and capture a prisoner for interrogation. Forging up the rugged slope of the key terrain feature, the group was subjected to intense mortar and machine-gun fire and suffered several casualties. Throughout the advance, he fought valiantly and, upon reaching the crest of the hill, leaped into the trenches and closed with the enemy in hand-to-hand combat. When friendly troops were ordered to move back upon completion of the assignment, he and 2 comrades remained to cover the withdrawal. While in the process of leaving the trenches a hostile soldier hurled a grenade into their midst. Pfc. George shouted a warning to 1 comrade, pushed the other soldier out of danger, and, with full knowledge of the consequences, unhesitatingly threw himself upon the grenade, absorbing the full blast of the explosion. Although seriously wounded in this display of valor, he refrained from any outcry which would divulge the position of his companions. The 2 soldiers evacuated him to the forward aid station and shortly thereafter he succumbed to his wound. Pfc. George's indomitable courage, consummate devotion to duty, and willing self-sacrifice reflect the highest credit upon himself and uphold the finest traditions of the military service.

Beginning the first of December, and through the month of January 1953 — except for some increased activity around Christmas 1952 and Operation Smack, a one-day incursion in late January — casualties averaged about 18 per day. The increased casualties over Christmas began on December 22 and ended six days later. Six different U.S. Army divisions (plus the 1st Marine Division) reported losses in that period, so the increased activity obviously occurred all across the front. Table 114 is a summary of all U.S. Army losses during these six days.

Table 114 — Christmas 1952, All U.S. Army Units

	KIA	WIA	POW Returned	POW Died	MIA Returned	MIA Died	Unit Total
38th Inf, 2nd Div	16	42					58
223rd Inf, 40th Inf Div	9	40					49
179th Inf, 45th Inf Div	8	25					33
279th Inf, 45th Inf Div	2	13	2				17
7th Inf, 3rd Inf Div	3	7	1				11
35th Inf, 25th Inf Div	2	6					8
Other Units (9)	9	17					26
Total 12/22–12/27/52	49	150	3				202

III. The War of the Hills

Operation Smack was an assault conducted by the 31st Infantry on January 25, 1953. Its stated goal was the capture of Spud Hill, a low-lying appendage at the far south end of a hill complex west of Chorwon know as "T-bone." In fact, according to eyewitnesses, its real purpose was to put on a big show for UN brass. If it were not for that fact, this minor operation with only 57 casualties would deserve no greater mention than those listed in Table 114 above. However, because these men were lost solely in the interest of high-level vanity, their sacrifice deserves to be recognized more specifically.

The eyewitness account of the operation begins early on D-day with high-ranking UN officers being chauffeured to front-line OP's (observations posts) by 31st Infantry drivers. At H-hour, the objective was hit by a massive artillery and mortar bombardment, followed by air strikes by both Air Force and Marine flyers. Soon after the attack started, the assault company was pinned down by well-entrenched CCF solders on the crest of the hill. The GIs remained pinned down for the rest of the day—even after being reinforced by a reserve company—slowly being decimated by small-arms fire and grenades delivered by the enemy above them.

At the end of the day, the assault force withdrew. Of the 57 casualties that day, two were killed in action and three died of their wounds. An additional 10 were wounded seriously enough to be evacuated to the States. The remainder of the wounded were subsequently returned to duty in the Far East.

Table 115 is a summary of all U.S. Army casualties in December 1952 and January 1953, including the Christmas incursions and Operation Smack.

Table 115 — Active Defense Resumed, All U.S. Army Units

	KIA	WIA	POW Returned	POW Died	MIA Returned	MIA Died	Unit Total
2nd Infantry Division	26	103				1	130
3rd Infantry Division	18	96	2	1		3	120
7th Infantry Division	47	200	2			6	255
25th Infantry Division	13	111	1				125
40th Infantry Division	66	247	3			4	320
45th Infantry Division	19	97	2			1	119
5th RCT	17	79				2	98
Other Units (19)	21	32					53
Total 12/01/52–01/31/53	227	965	10	1		17	1220

For the most part, the pattern of U.S. Marine casualties from November 1952 through January 1953 was much the same as it was for Army units; consistent losses, but a low levels. Periodically, losses might increase slightly for a single day, but for the most part, they remained around two or three per day. On one day in the period, during the Christmas incursions, they reached a high of 18.

Total losses for the marines in the period were 193, including four pilots lost in fixed-wing crashes at sea, five lost in fixed-wing crashes over land and one killed in the loss of an aircraft on the ground. Three sailors (corpsmen) were lost in ground action during the period.

Other U.S. Navy losses in the period are summarized in Table 116.

Table 116 — Active Defense Resumed, U.S. Navy

Fixed Wing Crash Over Land	
Pilot, Killed in Action	3
Pilot, Died while Missing	5
Aircrew, Killed in Action	1
Aircrew, Died while Missing	3
Non-Aircrew, Died while Missing	1
Fixed Wing Crash At Sea	
Pilot, Killed in Action	1
Aircrew, Died while Missing	3
Helicopter Crash Over Land	
Pilot, Killed in Action	1
Total 11/01/52–01/31/53	18

During these three months, the U.S. Air Force continued to report casualty numbers that greatly exceeded what might be expected from the level of fighting on the ground. They are summarized in Table 117.

Table 117 — Active Defense Resumed, U.S. Air Force

Fixed Wing Crash Over Land	
Pilot, Killed in Action	1
Pilot, Died while Missing	24
Aircrew, Killed in Action	1
Aircrew, Died while Missing	33
Non-Aircrew, Died while Missing	9
Total 11/01/52–01/31/53	68

One U.S. Air Force pilot was awarded the Medal of Honor for his heroism and self-sacrifice during a combat mission in late November.

MEDAL OF HONOR: CHARLES J. LORING, JR.

Awarded to: Major Charles J. Loring, Jr., Portland, ME, U.S. Air Force, 80th Fighter-Bomber Squadron, 8th Fighter-Bomber Wing. Near Sniper Ridge, North Korea, 22 November 1952.

Maj. Loring distinguished himself by conspicuous gallantry and intrepidity at the risk of his life above and beyond the call of duty. While leading a night of 4 F-80 type aircraft on a close support mission, Maj. Loring was briefed by a controller to dive-bomb enemy gun positions which were harassing friendly ground troops. After verifying the location of the target, Maj. Loring rolled into his dive bomb run. Throughout the run, extremely accurate ground fire was directed on his aircraft. Disregarding the accuracy and intensity of the ground fire, Maj. Loring aggressively continued to press the attack until his aircraft was hit. At approximately 4,000 feet, he deliberately altered his course and aimed his diving aircraft at active gun emplacements concentrated on a ridge northwest of the briefed target, turned his aircraft 45 degrees to the left, pulled up in a deliberate, controlled maneuver, and elected to sacrifice his life by diving his aircraft directly into the midst of the enemy emplacements. His selfless and heroic action completely destroyed the enemy gun emplacement and eliminated a dangerous threat to United Nations ground forces. Maj. Loring's noble spirit, superlative courage, and conspicuous self-sacrifice in inflicting maximum damage on the enemy exemplified valor of the highest degree and his actions were in keeping with the finest traditions of the U.S. Air Force.

Sometime after the beginning of 1953, body armor (flak jackets) became more abundant and were required apparel—at all times—for all combatants in frontline units. No data are available on exactly when, or over how long a period, this transition took place. Nothing in the casualty data sheds any light in the issue. It might be expected that, with all combatants on the U.S. side protected in this way, at least the incidence of fatalities would be reduced. But, a comparison of the percentage of fatalities between the earlier days of the war and the figures from 1953 do not clarify the question. Just too many other variables enter into the issue. There is probably no question that casualties (at least fatalities) on the U.S. side after flak jackets were put into regular use would have been much greater without them.

More of the Same

For the next month and a half, the pattern remained much the same; consistent losses at relatively low levels, with a lot of on again/off again skirmishes but few battles that made it into the history books. U.S. Army casualty levels tended to be a bit higher in February, but not exceptionally so. Four Army divisions and the 5th RCT reported significant casualties in the period, but the 2nd Division and the 7th Division clearly took the brunt of the punishment.

The chronology mentions two encounters from which army units reported significantly higher then average losses. In the first, it was reported that a 7th Division 34-man patrol was ambushed on March 9 with the loss of 20 KIA, 2 MIA and 12 WIA. The database does show similar losses by the division's 31st Infantry on that date. The exact figures were 19 KIA, one missing and never found, 13 WIA and one captured.

On the same day, the chronology reports that a 2nd Division patrol was also ambushed with the loss of 12 KIA and 5 MIA. The database, however, indicates only one 2nd Division soldier WIA that day.

Another encounter in this period with significant U.S. Army losses was the battle for Little Gibralter (Hill 355), in which 9th Infantry Regiment of the 2nd Division was attacked by CCF forces on March 17. The database records the losses in the 9th Infantry that day as 29 KIA and 84 WIA.

Total U.S. Army casualties in the period are summarized in Table 118.

Table 118 — Feburary/March 1953 Actions, All U.S. Army Units

	KIA	WIA	POW Returned	POW Died	MIA Returned	MIA Died	Unit Total
2nd Infantry Division							
9th Inf, 2nd Div	81	201	8			2	292
38th Inf, 2nd Div	23	107	3				133
2nd Recon Co, 2nd Inf Div	5	16					21
2nd Engr Bn, 2nd Inf Div	2	14					16
Other 2nd Div Units (4)		11				1	12
Total 2nd Division	111	349	11			3	474
7th Infantry Division							
17th Inf, 7th Inf Div	34	102	2			1	139
32nd Inf, 7th Inf Div	32	114	3			3	152
31st Inf, 7th Inf Div	37	72	3			1	113
Other 7th Div Units (10)	4	12	1				17
Total 7th Division	107	300	9			5	421
3rd Infantry Division	32	130				1	163
45th Infantry Division	30	142					172
5th RCT	6	51					57
Other Units (21)	11	29					40
Total 02/01–03/21/53	297	1001	20			9	1327

The 1st Marine Division started off the month of February with a raid on Hill 101. The chronology reports 15 KIA and 55 WIA. The database confirms the 15 fatalities. Although the chronology reports no specific Marine Corps battles through the remainder of the period, the database shows elevated losses between February 22 and 27, and between March 19 and 21. The latter action, in which the Marines reported 26 fatalities in three days, may have been a low-key preview of the battle of the Nevada Cities, which began a few days later. Total U.S. Marine Corps losses in the period were 137, five of which were pilots lost in fixed-wing crashes, four over land and one at sea. Three sailors (corpsmen?) were killed in ground action.

For his valor in the action on Hill 101, one marine officer was awarded the Medal of Honor.

MEDAL OF HONOR: RAYMOND G. MURPHY

Awarded to: Second Lieutenant Raymond G. Murphy, Pueblo, CO, U.S. Marine Corps Reserve, Company A, 1st Battalion, 5th Marines, 1st Marine Division (Rein.). Korea, 3 February 1953.

> For conspicuous gallantry and intrepidity at the risk of his life above and beyond the call of duty as a platoon commander of Company A, in action against enemy aggressor forces. Although painfully wounded by fragments from an enemy mortar shell while leading his evacuation platoon in support of assault units attacking a cleverly concealed and well-entrenched hostile force occupying commanding ground, 2d Lt. Murphy steadfastly refused medical aid and continued to lead his men up a hill through a withering barrage of hostile mortar and small-arms fire, skillfully maneuvering his force from one position to the next and shouting words of encouragement. Undeterred by the increasing intense enemy fire, he imme-

diately located casualties as they fell and made several trips up and down the fire-swept hill to direct evacuation teams to the wounded, personally carrying many of the stricken marines to safety. When reinforcements were needed by the assaulting elements, 2d Lt. Murphy employed part of his unit as support and, during the ensuing battle, personally killed 2 of the enemy with his pistol. With all the wounded evacuated and the assaulting units beginning to disengage, he remained behind with a carbine to cover the movement of friendly forces off the hill and, though suffering intense pain from his previous wounds, seized an automatic rifle to provide more firepower when the enemy reappeared in the trenches. After reaching the base of the hill, he organized a search party and again ascended the slope for a final check on missing marines, locating and carrying the bodies of a machinegun crew back down the hill. Wounded a second time while conducting the entire force to the line of departure through a continuing barrage of enemy small-arms, artillery, and mortar fire, he again refused medical assistance until assured that every one of his men, including all casualties, had preceded him to the main lines. His resolute and inspiring leadership, exceptional fortitude, and great personal valor reflect the highest credit upon 2d Lt. Murphy and enhance the finest traditions of the U.S. Naval Service.

Navy losses other than ground casualties were all pilots killed in fixed-wing crashes, five over land and one at sea. One was reported missing and never found. U.S. Air Force losses in the period are summarized in Table 119.

Table 119 — Feburary/March 1953 Actions, U.S. Air Force

Fixed Wing Crash Over Land	
Pilot, Killed in Action	2
Pilot, Died while Missing	8
Aircrew, Died while Missing	3
Total 02/01–03/21/53	13

The Outpost Battles

By March of 1953, the Main Line of Resistance (MLR) across central Korea had been well established for months. Each side was now solidly dug in across the 120-mile front, with a no-man's-land between them varying in width from a few hundred yards to a mile or more. Situated in that no-man's-land were hills in strategic locations that could serve either side as sites for better observing enemy activity and for defending against unexpected enemy assaults on front-line positions. Possession of these hills also had political value as bargaining chips in the ongoing peace talks at Panmunjom. These were the outposts—hills that had already become famous in the popular press with names like Old Baldy, Pork Chop, Reno and Vegas.

Since its beginning, much of the War of the Hills had been fought over outposts like these, but never with the intensity or level of losses that came to characterize the combat on these hills throughout the last months of the war. In March and April 1953, these battles were concentrated on Old Baldy and Pork Chop in the 7th Infantry Division sector west of Chorwon and the Nevada Cities in the 1st Marine Division

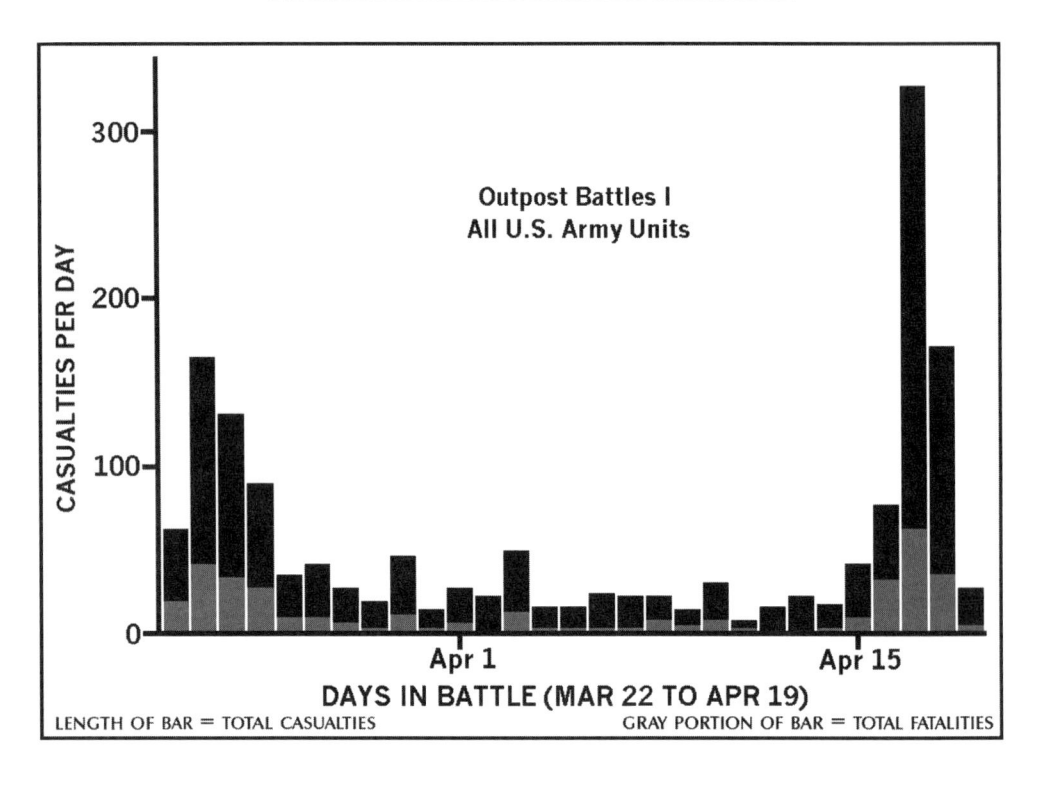

Figure 31. Daily casualties for all U.S. Army units during the first Outpost Battles.

sector north of Seoul. Figure 31 shows the distribution of U.S. Army casualties over the four weeks between the battles for Old Baldy and Pork Chop.

Because these two outpost were held at the time by elements of the 7th Infantry Division, the vast majority of the casualties in the periods March 23 to 25 and April 16 to 18 were in that division. Table 120 shows a summary of all U.S. Army casualties during the three days of the battle for Old Baldy.

Table 120 — Old Baldy, 7th Infantry Division

	KIA	WIA	POW Returned	POW Died	MIA Returned	MIA Died	Unit Total
7th Infantry Division							
17th Inf, 7th Inf Div	10	15					25
31st Inf, 7th Inf Div	39	107	2			1	149
32nd Inf, 7th Inf Div	30	97				8	135
57th FA Bn, 7th Inf Div	1	10	1				12
Other 7th Div Units (3)	2	11					13
7th Division Total	82	240	3			9	334
2nd Infantry Division	5	7					12
3rd Infantry Division	2	20					22
45th Infantry Division	1	10					11
Other Units (3)		4					4
Total 03/23–03/25/53	90	281	3			9	383

III. The War of the Hills

These figures, however, still do not tell the whole story of losses during the battle for the outpost. When CCF forces attacked the hill on March 23, Old Baldy was being held primarily by elements from a battalion of Colombians that were attached to the 31st Infantry of the 7th Division. The bulk of the casualties when the outpost was taken by the Chinese that night were Colombians, for which no casualty figures are available. Most U.S. losses in the battle were sustained in unsuccessful efforts to retake the hill. Casualties in the other divisions shown were from actions in other sectors of the MLR, and are included in the table simply to show the dominance of 7th Division losses over these three days.

Four weeks later, the CCF attempted to take Pork Chop. This time they were unsuccessful, but the cost in American casualties was high. Table 121 summarizes those casualties for the period of the battle.

Table 121 — Pork Chop, 7th Infantry Division

	KIA	WIA	POW Returned	POW Died	MIA Returned	MIA Died	Unit Total
7th Infantry Division							
17th Inf, 7th Inf Div	29	157				2	188
31st Inf, 7th Inf Div	61	195	2			3	261
32nd Inf, 7th Inf Div	8	24					32
13th Engr Bn, 7th Inf Div	5	14					19
Other 7th Div Units (3)	4	14					18
7th Division Total	107	404	2			5	518
3rd Infantry Division	10	20	1				31
40th Infantry Division	2	6					8
45th Infantry Division	3	7					10
Other Units (4)		5					5
Total 04/16–04/18/53	122	442	3			5	572

The numbers of casualties reported by units other than the 7th Division in these two battles are fairly representative of the losses shown in Figure 32 during the interim between them. In general, units all across the front shared in those losses. Table 122 summarizes all U.S. Army losses in the period shown in Figure 32.

Table 122 — Outpost Battles I, All U.S. Army Units

	KIA	WIA	POW Returned	POW Died	MIA Returned	MIA Died	Unit Total
2nd Infantry Division	42	136	2			3	183
3rd Infantry Division	34	138	1			1	174
7th Infantry Division	221	758	5			15	999
40th Infantry Division	5	17					22
45th Infantry Division	14	84					98
5th RCT	3	31					34
Other Units (19)	14	31	1				46
Total 03/22–04/19/53	333	1195	9			19	1556

The Nevada Cities

At about the time the battle for Old Baldy ended, a series of outposts held by the 1st Marine Division in the west came under ferocious attack from CCF. These outposts (Vegas, Reno, Carson), dubbed "The Nevada Cities" by the marines, were located well forward of the MLR and served to provide advance warning of possible attacks on front line positions. Figure 32 shows the distribution of U.S. Marine losses during the four weeks that included this outpost battle.

The chronology lists Marine casualties in the five days of the Nevada Cities battle as 156 KIA and 901 WIA. The database records 161 Marine ground fatalities in that period, plus the 3 Navy men presumed to be corpsmen. For the entire period shown in Figure 32, total marine fatalities were 284, including 1 pilot lost in a fixed-wing crash over land and 1 airman killed in an aircraft loss on the ground. Of the ground casualties, three were recorded as missing and never found and one died in captivity.

One marine and one of the Navy corpsmen killed in the Nevada Cities battle were awarded the Medal of Honor for their valor in the action. Another corpsman, who survived his wounds, also received the award.

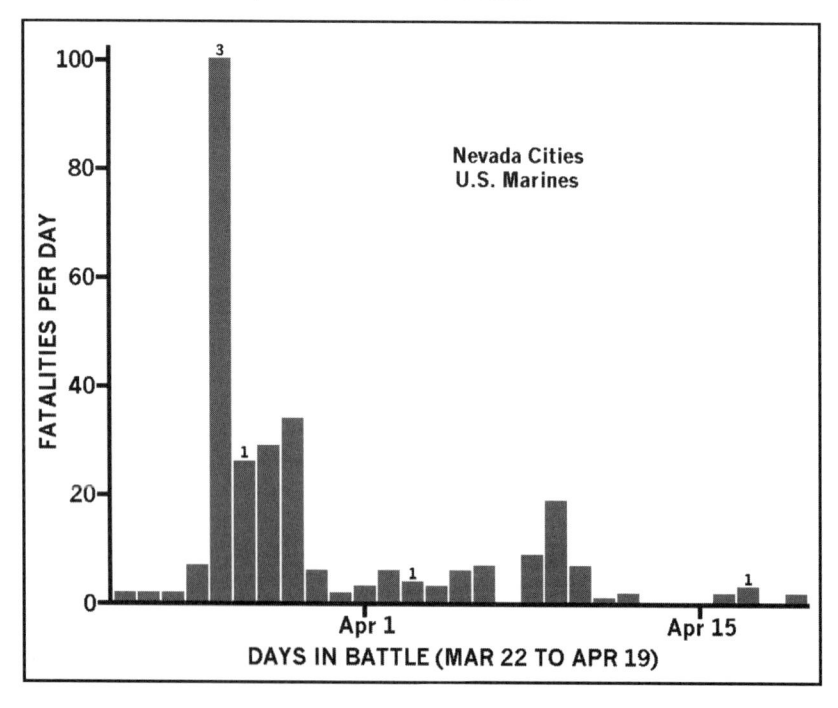

Figure 32. Daily fatalities for U.S. Marine Corps units in the battles of the Nevada Cities. The numbers over the bars on some dates indicate the number of presumed Navy corpsmen killed on those days.

Medal of Honor: Francis C. Hammond

Awarded to: Hospital Corpsman Francis C. Hammond, Alexandria, VA, U.S. Navy, attached as a medical corpsman to 1st Marine Division, Korea, 26–27 March 1953.

For conspicuous gallantry and intrepidity at the risk of his life above and beyond the call of duty as a HC serving with the 1st Marine Division in action against enemy aggressor forces on the night of 26–27 March 1953. After reaching an intermediate objective during a counterattack against a heavily entrenched and numerically superior hostile force occupying ground on a bitterly contested outpost far in advance of the main line of resistance. HC Hammond's platoon was subjected to a murderous barrage of hostile mortar and artillery fire, followed by a vicious assault by onrushing enemy troops. Resolutely advancing through the veritable curtain of fire to aid his stricken comrades, HC Hammond moved among the stalwart garrison of marines and, although critically wounded himself, valiantly continued to administer aid to the other wounded throughout an exhausting 4-hour period. When the unit was ordered to withdraw, he skillfully directed the evacuation of casualties and remained in the fire-swept area to assist the corpsmen of the relieving unit until he was struck by a round of enemy mortar fire and fell, mortally wounded. By his exceptional fortitude, inspiring initiative and self-sacrificing efforts, HC Hammond undoubtedly saved the lives of many marines. His great personal valor in the face of overwhelming odds enhances and sustains the finest traditions of the U.S. Naval Service. He gallantly gave his life for his country.

Medal of Honor: William R. Charette

Awarded to: Hospital Corpsman Third Class William R. Charette, Ludington, MI, U.S. Navy Medical Corpsman serving with a marine rifle company. Korea, 27 March 1953.

For conspicuous gallantry and intrepidity at the risk of his life above and beyond the call of duty in action against enemy aggressor forces during the early morning hours. Participating in a fierce encounter with a cleverly concealed and well-entrenched enemy force occupying positions on a vital and bitterly contested outpost far in advance of the main line of resistance, HC3c. Charette repeatedly and unhesitatingly moved about through a murderous barrage of hostile small-arms and mortar fire to render assistance to his wounded comrades. When an enemy grenade landed within a few feet of a marine he was attending, he immediately threw himself upon the stricken man and absorbed the entire concussion of the deadly missile with his body. Although sustaining painful facial wounds, and undergoing shock from the intensity of the blast which ripped the helmet and medical aid kit from his person, HC3c. Charette resourcefully improvised emergency bandages by tearing off part of his clothing, and gallantly continued to administer medical aid to the wounded in his own unit and to those in adjacent platoon areas as well. Observing a seriously wounded comrade whose armored vest had been torn from his body by the blast from an exploding shell, he selflessly removed his own battle vest and placed it upon the helpless man although fully aware of the added jeopardy to himself. Moving to the side of another casualty who was suffering excruciating pain from a serious leg wound, HC3c. Charette stood upright in the trench line and exposed himself to a deadly hail of enemy fire in order to lend more effective aid to the victim and to alleviate his anguish while being removed to a position of safety. By his indomitable courage and inspiring efforts in behalf of his wounded comrades, HC3c. Charette was directly responsible for saving many lives. His great personal valor reflects the highest credit upon himself and enhances the finest traditions of the U.S. Naval Service.

MEDAL OF HONOR: DANIEL P. MATTHEWS

Awarded to: Sergeant Daniel P. Matthews, Van Nuys, CA, U.S. Marine Corps, Company F, 2d Battalion, 7th Marines, 1st Marine Division (Rein.). Vegas Hill, Korea, 28 March 1953.

> For conspicuous gallantry and intrepidity at the risk of his life above and beyond the call of duty while serving as a squad leader of Company F, in action against enemy aggressor forces. Participating in a counterattack against a firmly entrenched and well-concealed hostile force which had repelled 6 previous assaults on a vital enemy-held outpost far forward of the main line of resistance Sgt. Matthews fearlessly advanced in the attack until his squad was pinned down by a murderous sweep of fire from an enemy machinegun located on the peak of the outpost. Observing that the deadly fire prevented a corpsman from removing a wounded man lying in an open area fully exposed to the brunt of the devastating gunfire, he worked his way to the base of the hostile machinegun emplacement, leaped onto the rock fortification surrounding the gun and, taking the enemy by complete surprise, single-handedly charged the hostile emplacement with his rifle. Although severely wounded when the enemy brought a withering hail of fire to bear upon him, he gallantly continued his valiant l-man assault and, firing his rifle with deadly effectiveness, succeeded in killing 2 of the enemy, routing a third, and completely silencing the enemy weapon, thereby enabling his comrades to evacuate the stricken marine to a safe position. Succumbing to his wounds before aid could reach him, Sgt. Matthews, by his indomitable fighting spirit, courageous initiative, and resolute determination in the face of almost certain death, served to inspire all who observed him and was directly instrumental in saving the life of his wounded comrade. His great personal valor reflects the highest credit upon himself and enhances the finest traditions of the U.S. Naval Service. He gallantly gave his life for his country.

Other than corpsmen, the only Navy fatality in this period was one pilot lost in a fixed-wing crash over land.

Air Force losses in the period included seven pilots, 2 aircrew and 1 non-aircrew all lost in fixed wing crashes over land.

Interlude

After the battle for Pork Chop, activity along the MLR resumed the pattern it had followed between the two 7th Division outpost battles (see Figure 31). For the next five weeks, casualties averaged about 25 per day, with all front-line units sharing in the losses. There undoubtedly were battles on outposts along the MLR, but there were no major disputes over them. Table 123 summarizes the losses in all U.S. Army units during this interlude.

Table 123 — Outpost Battle Interlude, All U.S. Army Units

	KIA	WIA	POW Returned	POW Died	MIA Returned	MIA Died	Unit Total
2nd Infantry Division	8	13					21
3rd Infantry Division	57	255	1				313
7th Infantry Division	48	172					220
25th Infantry Division	25	85	2				112
40th Infantry Division	16	103					119
45th Infantry Division	16	92	1				109
5th RCT	4	24					28
Other Units (16)	4	27				1	32
Total 04/20–05/27/53	178	771	4			1	954

For the Marines, the interlude was longer and more tranquil than that of the Army. In the five-week period the Marines lost 21 KIA, including four pilots lost in fixed-wing crashes over land.

The Navy lost three pilots and two aircrew in fixed-wing crashes over land. One pilot and one aircrew were reported missing and never found.

Air Force losses in this period were comparatively abundant. They are summarized in Table 124.

Table 124 — Outpost Battles Interlude, U.S. Air Force

Fixed Wing Crash Over Land	
Pilot, Killed in Action	1
Pilot, Died while Missing	9
Aircrew, Killed in Action	2
Aircrew, Died while Missing	3
Non-Aircrew, Died while Missing	2
Total 04/20–05/27/53	17

Operation Little Switch

During the week of April 20 to 26, the chronology lists the exchange of 149 sick and wounded POWs in an operation that became know as Little Switch (in contrast to Big Switch, in which most remaining POWs were exchanged after hostilities ceased). A search of the database produced the names of 127 U.S. Army POWs who were released in that week. The other 22 individuals most likely were from the other services and could not be identified because that database lists only fatalities.

Among the 127 GIs repatriated in Little Switch, 27 had been wounded prior to their capture. Many of these had been captured early in the war (one of them on July 6, 1950), so it might reasonably be expected that they had recovered from those wounds. Only five of these 27 repatriates were reported as wounded and captured in 1953, so it is likely that the vast majority of the 127 were included in the switch because they were sick.

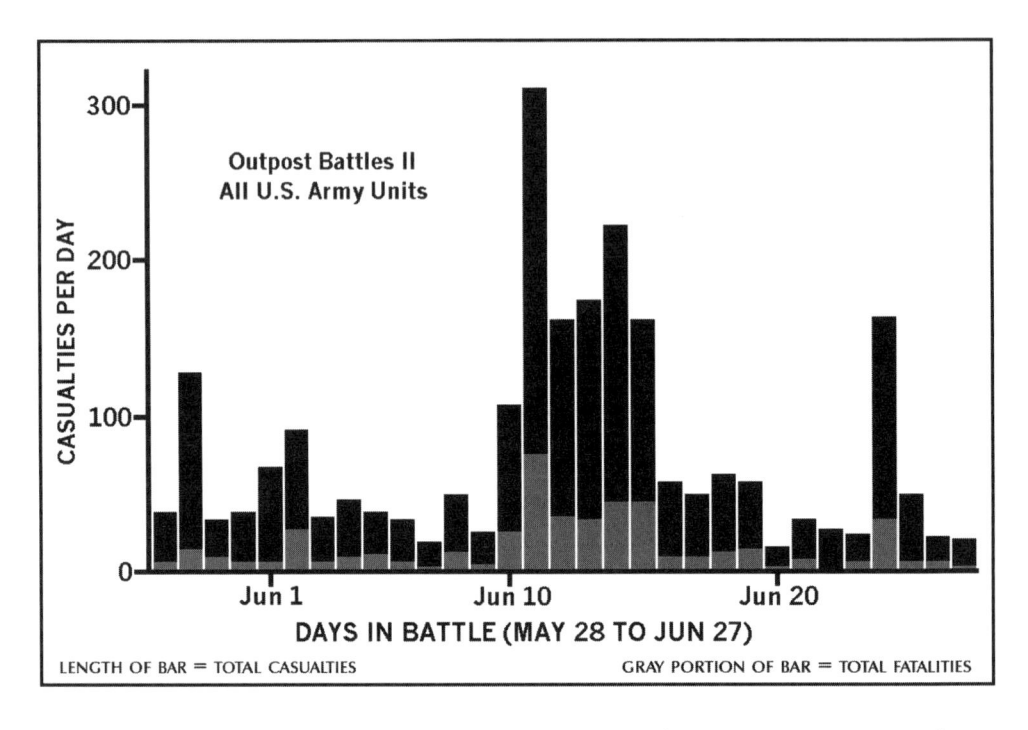

Fig 33. Daily casualties for all U.S. Army units during the June 1953 Outpost Battles.

Renewed Outpost Offensives

The end of May and the beginning June brought renewed offensive action in the outpost war. Figure 33 shows daily casualties for all U.S. Army units during the month after these offensives began.

The chronology reports a CCF attack launched on May 28 against the 25th Division, now defending in the area of the Nevada Cities and the Hook. Although the battle was reported to continue for three days, casualty figures suggest that on only one of those days, May 29, did any U.S. Army unit report an extraordinary number of losses. On that day, the 14th Infantry of the 25th Division reported 98 of 127 total Army casualties, 9 KIA and 89 WIA.

Following this engagement, casualty patterns returned for a brief time to levels that had become common between major battles. However, the combat during these periods was anything but ordinary, as can be seen in the award of the Medal of Honor to a defender of one of the outposts, Pork Chop Hill.

Medal of Honor: Charles H. Barker

Awarded to: Private First Class (then Pvt.), Charles H. Barker, Pickens County, SC, U.S. Army, Company K, 17th Infantry Regiment, 7th Infantry Division. Near Sokkogae, Korea, 4 June 1953.

> Pfc. Barker, a member of Company K, distinguished himself by conspicuous gallantry and indomitable courage above and beyond the call of

duty in action against the enemy. While participating in a combat patrol engaged in screening an approach to "Pork-Chop Outpost," Pfc. Barker and his companions surprised and engaged an enemy group digging emplacements on the slope. Totally unprepared, the hostile troops sought cover. After ordering Pfc. Barker and a comrade to lay down a base of fire, the patrol leader maneuvered the remainder of the platoon to a vantage point on higher ground. Pfc. Barker moved to an open area firing his rifle and hurling grenades on the hostile positions. As enemy action increased in volume and intensity, mortar bursts fell on friendly positions, ammunition was in critical supply, and the platoon was ordered to withdraw into a perimeter defense preparatory to moving back to the outpost. Voluntarily electing to cover the retrograde movement, he gallantly maintained a defense and was last seen in close hand-to-hand combat with the enemy. Pfc. Barker's unflinching courage, consummate devotion to duty, and supreme sacrifice enabled the patrol to complete the mission and effect an orderly withdrawal to friendly lines, reflecting lasting glory upon himself and upholding the highest traditions of the military service.

Pfc. Barker was reported missing on the day of this action and was declared dead a year later.

Outpost Harry

In the chronology, this battle is reported to have carried on for nine days, beginning on Jun 10. The primary defenders of Outpost Harry are reported to have been the 15th Infantry Regiment of the 3rd Division and the 5th RCT. However, analysis of casualty reports indicates that the 15th Infantry reported extraordinary losses only between the 10th and the 15th, and the 5th RCT only between the 11th and the 13th. In addition, as can be seen in the summary of casualties during the period (Table 125), other 3rd Division units—and possibly some non-divisional units—reported significant losses, some possibly sustained in the battle for Outpost Harry.

Table 125 — Outpost Harry, All U.S. Army Units

	KIA	WIA	POW Returned	POW Died	MIA Returned	MIA Died	Unit Total
3rd Infantry Division							
7th Inf 3rd Inf Div	36	127					163
15th Inf, 3rd Inf Div	98	313				11	422
65th Inf, 3rd Inf Div	24	130	2			2	158
10th Engr Bn, 3rd Inf Div	5	16					21
39th FA Bn, 3rd Inf Div	5	11					16
Other 3rd Div Units (8)	3	17				1	20
Total 3rd Division	**171**	**614**	**2**			**14**	**801**
5th RCT	29	125				1	155
2nd Infantry Division	5	19					24
7th Infantry Division	19	92	1				112
25th Infantry Division	5	55				1	61
40th Infantry Division	6	18					24
45th Infantry Division	8	28					36

(continued on next page)

Table 125 (*cont.*)

	KIA	WIA	POW Returned	POW Died	MIA Returned	MIA Died	Unit Total
Other Units							
461st Inf Bn, Hv Mortars	5	16	4			1	26
92nd FA Bn	2	12					14
176th FA Bn	3	5					8
987th FA Bn	2		1			3	6
235th FA Bn, Obs	2	2	2				6
Additional Other Units (14)	3	21					24
Total Other Units	17	56	7			4	84
Total 06/10–06/18/53	260	1007	10			20	1297

One member of the 15th Infantry earned the Medal of Honor for his gallant actions on Outpost Harry.

MEDAL OF HONOR: OLA L. MIZE

Awarded to: Master Sergeant (then Sgt.) Ola L. Mize, Gadsden, AL, U.S. Army, Company K, 15th Infantry Regiment, 3d Infantry Division. Near Surang-ni, Korea, 10 to 11 June 1953.

> M/Sgt. Mize, a member of Company K, distinguished himself by conspicuous gallantry and outstanding courage above and beyond the call of duty in action against the enemy. Company K was committed to the defense of "Outpost Harry", a strategically valuable position, when the enemy launched a heavy attack. Learning that a comrade on a friendly listening post had been wounded he moved through the intense barrage, accompanied by a medical aid man, and rescued the wounded soldier. On returning to the main position he established an effective defense system and inflicted heavy casualties against attacks from determined enemy assault forces which had penetrated into trenches within the outpost area. During his fearless actions he was blown down by artillery and grenade blasts 3 times but each time he dauntlessly returned to his position, tenaciously fighting and successfully repelling hostile attacks. When enemy onslaughts ceased he took his few men and moved from bunker to bunker, firing through apertures and throwing grenades at the foe, neutralizing their positions. When an enemy soldier stepped out behind a comrade, prepared to fire, M/Sgt. Mize killed him, saving the life of his fellow soldier. After rejoining the platoon, moving from man to man, distributing ammunition, and shouting words of encouragement he observed a friendly machinegun position overrun. He immediately fought his way to the position, killing 10 of the enemy and dispersing the remainder. Fighting back to the command post, and finding several friendly wounded there, he took a position to protect them. Later, securing a radio, he directed friendly artillery fire upon the attacking enemy's routes of approach. At dawn he helped regroup for a counterattack which successfully drove the enemy from the outpost. M/Sgt. Mize's valorous conduct and unflinching courage reflect lasting glory upon himself and uphold the noble traditions of the military service.

The chronology indicates a renewed CCF offensive on June 24. A significant increase in casualties can be seen in Figure 33 for that date. There is no identification in the chronology concerning which unit or units might have been involved in that battle. However, a search of the database indicates that the majority of casualties on that day were reported by the 7th Infantry of the 3rd Division, with 106 of the 162 total reported; 24 KIA and 82 WIA. No details are available concerning the combat in which these casualties occurred.

Table 126 is a summary of all U.S. Army casualties in this period.

Table 126 — Outpost Battles II, All U.S. Army Units

	KIA	WIA	POW Returned	POW Died	MIA Returned	MIA Died	Unit Total
2nd Infantry Division	9	35					44
3rd Infantry Division	222	840	10			15	1087
7th Infantry Division	48	214	1			3	266
25th Infantry Division	54	304	3			4	365
40th Infantry Division	32	119					151
45th Infantry Division	26	105					131
5th RCT	31	130				1	162
Other Units (32)	23	92	11			4	130
Total 05/28–06/27/53	422	1747	14			23	2206

Marine losses in the period were minimal; 7 fatalities total, all ground casualties.

The Navy lost one pilot in the period. He went down in a fixed-wing crash over land, was reported missing and was never found.

Air Force losses in the period are summarized in Table 127.

Table 127 — Outpost Battles II, U.S. Air Force

Fixed Wing Crash Over Land	
Pilot, Killed in Action	3
Pilot, Died while Missing	11
Aircrew, Killed in Action	1
Aircrew, Died while Missing	4
Total 05/28–06/27/53	19

Grand Finale

Figure 34 shows the pattern of U.S. Army casualties through the remainder of the war. After about a week of reduced casualties, the Outpost War resumed with a vengeance and continued until hostilities ended.

The last battle for Pork Chop Hill began on July 6. It ended six days later when the defending forces finally abandoned the outpost. Elements of the 7th Division's 17th Infantry were defending the outpost when the enemy siege began. By the time it was over, the 32nd Infantry had also been committed in an effort to hold the hill. The last 7th Division troops were withdrawn from the outpost on July 11. Many of their comrades had been evacuated earlier as they fell victims to the fury of the enemy assault. A summary of all U.S. Army casualties in this six-day period is shown in Table 128.

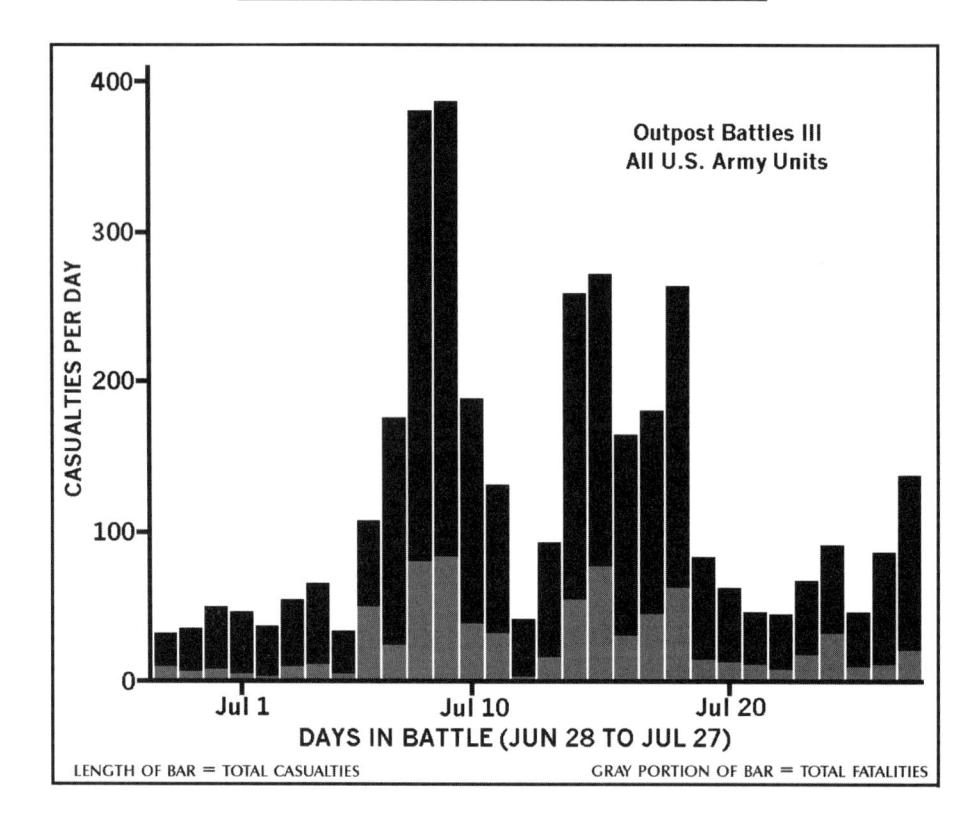

Figure 34. Daily casualties for all U.S. Army units during the July 1953 Outpost Battles.

Table 128 — Port Chop Hill, 7th Infantry Division and All Other Units

	KIA	WIA	POW Returned	POW Died	MIA Returned	MIA Died	Unit Total
7th Infantry Division							
17th Inf, 7th Inf Div	108	551	11			61	731
32nd Inf, 7th Inf Div	50	249				11	310
31st Inf, 7th Inf Div	3	10					13
13th Engr Bn, 7th Inf Div	5	20				1	26
48th FA Bn, 7th Inf Div	5	8					13
57th FA Bn, 7th Inf Div	5	8					13
15th AAA Bn, 7th Inf Div	5	6					11
73rd Tank Bn, 7th Inf Div	1	9					10
49th FA Bn, 7th Inf Div	3	5				1	9
Other 7th Div Units (9)	1	24					25
Total 7th Division	186	890	11			74	1161
2nd Infantry Division	3	24					27
3rd Infantry Division	7	44	2			6	59
25th Infantry Division	2	12				1	15
40th Infantry Division	2	11					13
45th Infantry Division	20	54					74
Other Units (10)	2	14				1	17
Total 07/06–07/11/53	222	1049	13			82	1366

Two members of the 7th Division earned Medals of Honor for their valor in the defense of Pork Chop Hill.

Medal of Honor: Richard T. Shea Jr.

Awarded to: First Lieutenant Richard T. Shea, Jr., Portsmouth, VA, U.S. Army, Company A 17th Infantry Regiment, 7th Infantry Division. Near Sokkogae, Korea, 6 to 8 July 1953.

> 1st Lt. Shea, executive officer, Company A, distinguished himself by conspicuous gallantry and indomitable courage above and beyond the call of duty in action against the enemy. On the night of 6 July, he was supervising the reinforcement of defensive positions when the enemy attacked with great numerical superiority. Voluntarily proceeding to the area most threatened, he organized and led a counterattack and, in the bitter fighting which ensued, closed with and killed 2 hostile soldiers with his trench knife. Calmly moving among the men, checking positions, steadying and urging the troops to hold firm, he fought side by side with them throughout the night. Despite heavy losses, the hostile force pressed the assault with determination, and at dawn made an all-out attempt to overrun friendly elements. Charging forward to meet the challenge, 1st Lt. Shea and his gallant men drove back the hostile troops. Elements of Company G joined the defense on the afternoon of 7 July, having lost key personnel through casualties. Immediately integrating these troops into his unit, 1st Lt. Shea rallied a group of 20 men and again charged the enemy. Although wounded in this action, he refused evacuation and continued to lead the counterattack. When the assaulting element was pinned down by heavy machine-gun fire, he personally rushed the emplacement and, firing his carbine and lobbing grenades with deadly accuracy, neutralized the weapon and killed 3 of the enemy. With forceful leadership and by his heroic example, 1st Lt. Shea coordinated and directed a holding action throughout the night and the following morning. On 8 July, the enemy attacked again. Despite additional wounds, he launched a determined counterattack and was last seen in close hand-to-hand combat with the enemy. 1st Lt. Shea's inspirational leadership and unflinching courage set an illustrious example of valor to the men of his regiment, reflecting lasting glory upon himself and upholding the noble traditions of the military service.

Medal of Honor: Dan D. Schoonover

Awarded to: Corporal Dan D. Schoonover, Boise, ID, U.S. Army, Company A, 13th Engineer Combat Battalion, 7th Infantry Division. Near Sokkogae, Korea, 8 to 10 July 1953

> Cpl. Schoonover, distinguished himself by conspicuous gallantry and outstanding courage above and beyond the call of duty in action against the enemy. He was in charge of an engineer demolition squad attached to an infantry company which was committed to dislodge the enemy from a vital hill. Realizing that the heavy fighting and intense enemy fire made it impossible to carry out his mission, he voluntarily employed his unit as a rifle squad and, forging up the steep barren slope, participated in the assault

on hostile positions. When an artillery round exploded on the roof of an enemy bunker, he courageously ran forward and leaped into the position, killing 1 hostile infantryman and taking another prisoner. Later in the action, when friendly forces were pinned down by vicious fire from another enemy bunker, he dashed through the hail of fire, hurled grenades in the nearest aperture, then ran to the doorway and emptied his pistol, killing the remainder of the enemy. His brave action neutralized the position and enabled friendly troops to continue their advance to the crest of the hill. When the enemy counterattacked he constantly exposed himself to the heavy bombardment to direct the fire of his men and to call in an effective artillery barrage on hostile forces. Although the company was relieved early the following morning, he voluntarily remained in the area, manned a machinegun for several hours, and subsequently joined another assault on enemy emplacements. When last seen he was operating an automatic rifle with devastating effect until mortally wounded by artillery fire. Cpl. Schoonover's heroic leadership during 2 days of heavy fighting, superb personal bravery, and willing self-sacrifice inspired his comrades and saved many lives, reflecting lasting glory upon himself and upholding the honored traditions of the military service

The last major CCF offensive of the war was directed at what was called the Kumsong River Salient (or prominence). This was an area in the Kumsong River valley east of Kumhwa, where the MLR bulged prominently to the north. At the time, the salient was defended by elements of the ROK Army. When the defenders were unable to hold the position against an onslaught of some 80,000 CCF troops, the U.S. 3rd Division was moved into the breach and the 187th Airborne RCT was airlifted from Japan to reinforce the line. Before the engagement ended on July 20, elements of the 40th and 45 Divisions, and the 5th RCT all had become involved in the fighting.

Because the forces at the point of the original attack were not U.S. infantry, significant losses in infantry units were not recorded until about the third day of the battle. However, U.S. Army support units were in the path of the offensive and some of them were hit hard on the first two days. Table 129 is a summary of U.S. Army losses on those two days.

Table 129 — Kumsong River Opening Days, Non-divisional Units

	KIA	WIA	POW Returned	POW Died	MIA Returned	MIA Died	Unit Total
Day 1							
461st Inf Bn, Hv Mortars		24	1			2	27
555th FA Bn, 5th RCT		3	3				6
987th FA Bn		2					2
424th FA Bn			2				2
176th FA Bn		2					2
92nd FA Bn		1					1
235th FA Bn, Obs	1					1	2
2nd FA Bty, 5 in	3	1					4
Total Non-divisional Units	4	33	6			3	46
All U.S. Infantry Divisions	8	38					46
Total 07/13/53	12	71	6			3	92

(continued on next page)

Table 129 (*cont.*)

	KIA	WIA	POW Returned	POW Died	MIA Returned	MIA Died	Unit Total
Day 2							
555th FA Bn, 5th RCT	2	19	46		2	20	89
8219th Map Service	3	36					39
92nd FA Bn	3	20	6			2	31
300th FA Bn	1	3	7				11
2nd FA Bty, 5 in		4	4				8
955th FA Bn		2			1	2	5
235th FA Bn, Obs			5				5
461st Inf Bn, Hv Mortars	2					1	3
8202nd Mil Missions Comm.			2			1	3
937th FA Bn	1	1					2
424th FA Bn	2						2
953rd FA Bn						1	1
Total Non-divisional Units	14	85	70		3	27	199
All U.S. Infantry Divisions	12	44	3			1	60
Total 07/14/53	26	129	73	3		28	259

It is unlikely, of course, that all of these non-divisional losses were sustained in the battle at the Kumsong River. After all, fighting continued all along the MLR. However, considering the levels and kinds of losses—plus the fact that this was *the* major offensive being carried on at the time and divisional losses were so low by comparison—it is likely that most of them were the result of this battle.

Two of these units have been encountered and commented on in earlier discussions. The star-crossed "Triple Nickel," the 555th FA Battalion, had been overrun twice before, with disastrous losses; first on August 12, 1950, soon after it arrived in Korea to aid in the defense of the Pusan Perimeter, and again on April 25, 1951, right after the opening of the first CCF Spring Offensive. The other unit to be noted is the Military Missions Commission. The men in these units (whatever their function) continue to have a proclivity for getting captured.

Because so many different U.S. divisions contributed units to the defense of the Kumsong River Salient, it is difficult to identify which of the casualties over the next six days were the result of combat in that battle. Clearly, the 3rd Division, the 45th Division and the 187th RCT were major participants. Although the 5th RCT's 555th FA Battalion was in the middle of it, the RCT itself had relatively few casualties. Some units from the 40th Division were also reported to have participated, but casualties in that division were also comparatively small.

The chronology lists 242 KIA and 718 WIA in the action. Table 130 shows a summary of losses in all U.S. Army units during the six days this battle continued. Also shown at the bottom of the table is a sum of all losses in the listed period of the battle.

Table 130 — Kumsong River, 3rd and 45th Divisions and All Other Units

	KIA	WIA	POW Returned	POW Died	MIA Returned	MIA Died	Unit Total
3rd Infantry Division							
15th Inf, 3rd Inf Div	30	122				2	154
65th Inf, 3rd Inf Div	17	39					56
64th Tank Bn, 3rd Inf Div	2	5				4	11
Other 3rd Div Units (4)	1	9					10
Total 3rd Division	50	175				6	231
45th Infantry Division							
180th Inf, 45th Inf Div	87	13	6		1	5	312
179th Inf, 45th Inf Div	8	38					46
279th Inf, 45th Inf Div	8	22					30
Other 45th Div Units (4)	1	10					11
Total 45th Division	104	283	6		1	5	399
2nd Infantry Division	33	154	3				190
7th Infantry Division	6	42					48
40th Infantry Division	3	25					28
187th RCT	23	60					83
5th RCT	2	24					26
Other Units (11)	4	13					17
Total 07/15–07/20/53	225	776	9		1	11	1022
Total 07/13–07/20/53	263	976	88		4	42	1373

Without more information concerning what units were involved and when, it is really impossible from these data either to confirm or reject the casualty figures for this battle listed in the chronology. One member of the 3rd Division earned the Medal of Honor for his valor and self sacrifice in this battle.

MEDAL OF HONOR: CHARLES F. PENDLETON

Awarded to: Corporal Charles F. Pendleton, Ft. Worth, TX, U.S. Army, Company D, 15th Infantry Regiment, 3d Infantry Division. Near Choo Gung-Dong, Korea, 16 and 17 July 1953.

Cpl. Pendleton, a machine gunner with Company D, distinguished himself by conspicuous gallantry and indomitable courage above and beyond the call of duty in action against the enemy. After consolidating and establishing a defensive perimeter on a key terrain feature, friendly elements were attacked by a large hostile force. Cpl. Pendleton delivered deadly accurate fire into the approaching troops, killing approximately 15 and disorganizing the remainder with grenades. Unable to protect the flanks because of the narrow confines of the trench, he removed the machinegun from the tripod and, exposed to enemy observation, positioned it on his knee to improve his firing vantage. Observing a hostile infantryman jumping into the position, intent on throwing a grenade at his comrades, he whirled about and killed the attacker, then inflicted such heavy casualties on the enemy force that they retreated to regroup. After reorganizing, a second wave of hostile soldiers moved forward in an attempt to overrun the position and, later, when a hostile grenade landed nearby, Cpl. Pendleton quickly retrieved and hurled it back at the foe. Although he was burned by the hot shells ejecting from his weapon, and he was wounded by a grenade, he refused evacuation and continued to fire on the assaulting force. As enemy action increased in tempo, his machinegun was destroyed by a grenade but, undaunted, he grabbed a carbine and continued his heroic defense until mortally wounded by a mortar burst. Cpl. Pendleton's unflinching courage, gallant self-sacrifice, and consummate devotion to duty reflect lasting glory upon himself and uphold the finest traditions of the military service.

Another Medal of Honor was awarded for gallant action during this period, but it is not clear whether or not the action took place specifically in the battle for the Kumsong River Salient.

MEDAL OF HONOR: GILBERT G. COLLIER

Awarded to: Sergeant (then Cpl.) Gilbert G. Collier, Tichnor, AR, U.S. Army, Company F, 223d Infantry Regiment, 40th Infantry Division. Near Tutayon, Korea, 19–20 July 1953.

> Sgt. Collier, a member of Company F, distinguished himself by conspicuous gallantry and indomitable courage above and beyond the call of duty in action against the enemy. Sgt. Collier was pointman and assistant leader of a combat patrol committed to make contact with the enemy. As the patrol moved forward through the darkness, he and his commanding officer slipped and fell from a steep, 60-foot cliff and were injured. Incapacitated by a badly sprained ankle which prevented immediate movement, the officer ordered the patrol to return to the safety of friendly lines. Although suffering from a painful back injury, Sgt. Collier elected to remain with his leader, and before daylight they managed to crawl back up and over the mountainous terrain to the opposite valley where they concealed themselves in the brush until nightfall, then edged toward their company positions. Shortly after leaving the daylight retreat they were ambushed and, in the ensuing fire fight, Sgt. Collier killed 2 hostile soldiers, received painful wounds, and was separated from his companion. Then, ammunition expended, he closed in hand-to-hand combat with 4 attacking hostile infantrymen, killing, wounding, and routing the foe with his bayonet. He was mortally wounded during this action, but made a valiant attempt to reach and assist his leader in a desperate effort to save his comrade's life without regard for his own personal safety. Sgt. Collier's unflinching courage, consummate devotion to duty, and gallant self-sacrifice reflect lasting glory upon himself and uphold the noble traditions of the military service.

From the casualty levels shown in Figure 34, it is apparent that combat for U.S. Army units continued at fairly active levels right through the end of the war. The last major battle listed in the chronology is the 31st Infantry defense of two outposts, Westview and Dale, on July 26 and 27. Obviously, these dates are wrong. The 31st reported no casualties on the 26th and very few on the 27th. On the 22nd, 23rd and 24th, however, they reported a high proportion of KIA, which is usually an indication of a tough defensive battle. On those three days, the 31st reported 32 killed, 51 wounded and 1 captured. These are most likely the days of the outpost defense referred to in the chronology.

The chronology also mentions a 3rd Division battle on Sniper Ridge, east of Triangle Hill, on July 24 to 26. The 15th Infantry of the 3rd Division did report somewhat higher casualties on the 25th and 26th, but fatalities were minimal.

Table 131 is a summary of all U.S. Army casualties in the last seven days of the war.

Table 131 — Final Seven Days, All U.S. Army Units

	KIA	WIA	POW Returned	POW Died	MIA Returned	MIA Died	Unit Total
2nd Infantry Division	2	26					28
3rd Infantry Division	14	93					107
7th Infantry Division	42	99	1				142
40th Infantry Division	7	41				1	49
45th Infantry Division	16	72					88
11th Airborne Division	5	24					29
5th RCT	7	27					34
Other Units (17)	11	25					36
Total 07/21–07/27/53	93	382	1			1	477

Table 132 is a summary of all U.S. Army casualties in the period of the last outpost battles.

Table 132 — Outpost Battles III, All U.S. Army Units

	KIA	WIA	POW Returned	POW Died	MIA Returned	MIA Died	Unit Total
2nd Infantry Division	42	215	3				260
3rd Infantry Division	80	390	3			12	485
7th Infantry Division	241	1136	12			76	1465
25th Infantry Division	22	99	2			1	124
40th Infantry Division	17	113	1			3	134
45th Infantry Division	157	471	8		1	6	643
11th Airborne Division	32	100					132
5th RCT	12	79	49		2	20	162
Other Units (37)*	34	159	27		1	11	232
TOTAL 06/28–07/27/53	637	2762	105		4	129	3637

*Most of these casualties were sustained in the first two days at the Kumsong River. The difference in totals here and in Table 129 is because the 555th FA Battalion was included as a non-divisional unit in Table 129 and as a divisional unit here.

The 1st Marine Division also ended the war engaged in some fierce outpost battles. Figure 35 shows the distribution of U.S. Marine fatalities during the last month of the war.

The chronology identifies three outpost battles in the 1st Marine Division sector during the final days of the war. The first was a battle over outposts Berlin and East Berlin on July 7 and 8. It is clear from Figure 35 that these dates should be July 8 and 9. The second, on July 19 and 20, was a reprise of the fight over Berlin and East Berlin. The third was the battle of Boulder City (Hill 119) on July 24 to 26.

The first Berlin/East Berlin battle was reported to have cost the Marines 21 KIA and 126 WIA. The database records 38 fatalities, three of which were reported miss-

III. The War of the Hills 183

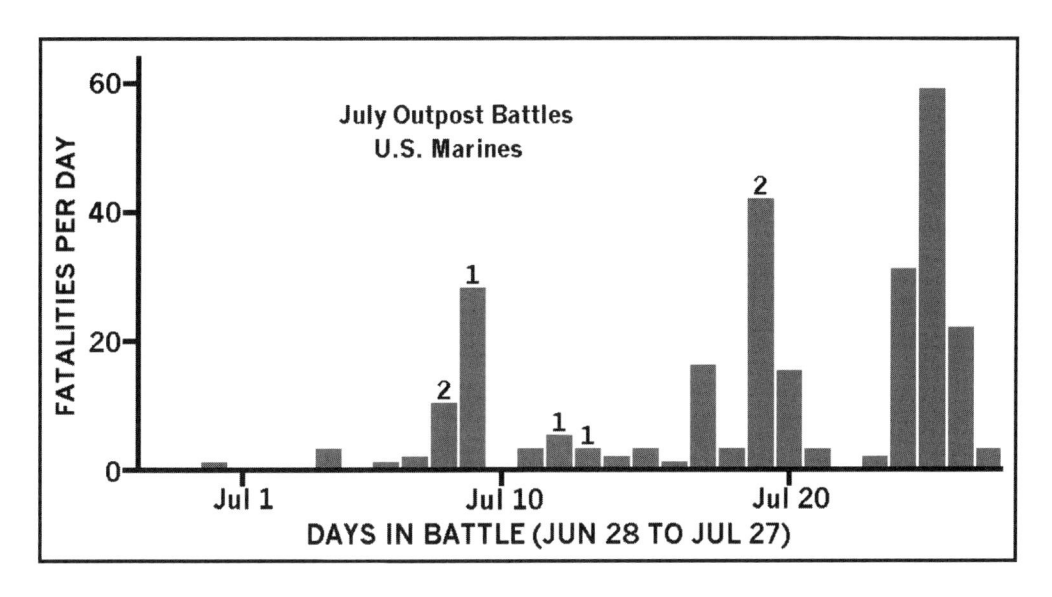

Figure 35. Daily fatalities for U.S. Marine Corps units in the July Outpost Battles. The numbers over the bars on some dates indicate the number of presumed Navy corpsmen killed on those days.

ing and never found. The chronology reported the Marine losses in second Berlin/East Berlin battle to be 6 KIA, 86 WIA, 44 MIA and 12 POW. The database records 56 fatalities, nine of which were reported missing and never found. The battle of Boulder City was reported to have cost the Marines 43 KIA and 316 WIA. The database records 112 fatalities on these dates, three of which were reported missing and never found.

One of the Marine participants in the Battle of Boulder City was awarded the Medal of Honor for his valorous acts in the operation.

MEDAL OF HONOR: AMBROSIO GUILLEN

Awarded to: Staff Sergeant Ambrosio Guillen, El Paso, TX, U.S. Marine Corps, Company F, 2d Battalion, 7th Marines, 1st Marine Division (Rein.). Near Songuchon, Korea, 25 July 1953.

> For conspicuous gallantry and intrepidity at the risk of his life above and beyond the call of duty while serving as a platoon sergeant of Company F in action against enemy aggressor forces. Participating in the defense of an outpost forward of the main line of resistance, S/Sgt. Guillen maneuvered his platoon over unfamiliar terrain in the face of hostile fire and placed his men in fighting positions. With his unit pinned down when the outpost was attacked under cover of darkness by an estimated force of 2 enemy battalions supported by mortar and artillery fire, he deliberately exposed himself to the heavy barrage and attacks to direct his men in defending their positions and personally supervise the treatment and evacuation of the wounded. Inspired by his leadership, the platoon quickly rallied and engaged the enemy in fierce hand-to-hand combat. Although critically

wounded during the course of the battle, S/Sgt. Guillen refused medical aid and continued to direct his men throughout the remainder of the engagement until the enemy was defeated and thrown into disorderly retreat. Succumbing to his wounds within a few hours, S/Sgt. Guillen, by his outstanding courage and indomitable fighting spirit, was directly responsible for the success of his platoon in repelling a numerically superior enemy force. His personal valor reflects the highest credit upon himself and enhances the finest traditions of the U.S. Naval Service. He gallantly gave his life for his country.

There were seven reported Navy ground losses in this period, which are presumed to have been corpsmen attached to the Marines. Two of them were reported missing and never found. Other Navy losses in the period are summarized in Table 133.

Table 133 — Outpost Battles III, U.S. Navy

Fixed Wing Crash Over Land	
Pilot, Killed in Action	5
Pilot, Died while Missing	1
Aircrew, Died while Missing	2
Fixed Wing Crash At Sea	
Non-Aircrew, Died while Missing	1
Total 06/28–07/27/53	9

U.S. Air Forces losses in the last month of the war are summarized in Table 134.

Table 134 — Outpost Battles III, U.S. Air Force

Fixed Wing Crash Over Land	
Pilot, Killed in Action	10
Pilot, Died while Missing	9
Aircrew, Killed in Action	7
Aircrew, Died while Missing	3
Non-Aircrew, Killed in Action	4
Non-Aircrew, Died while Missing	1
Total 06/28–07/27/53	34

IV

THE END OF HOSTILITIES

The cease-fire ending hostilities in Korea began at 10:00 P.M. on July 27, 1953. On that day, prior to the cease-fire, the database records 20 U.S. Army KIA and 117 wounded. The U.S. Marines reported three KIA and the U.S. Air Force lost three pilots in fixed-wing crashes over land.

The chronology reports total losses from hostile action in the war as follows: 33,741 KIA, 103,284 WIA and 7,140 captured. Non-hostile deaths were reported to be 2,827. There is no way to substantiate or refute from the databases the numbers for WIA or POW, because the Marine Corps, the Navy and the Air Force reported only fatalities. However, the total number of fatalities from the databases differs by several hundred from the number listed in the chronology. This may be due to the fact that the Marine Corps casualty section recently updated the numbers for that service. The total number of fatalities in all services for which a name is currently available is 33,985.

In Table 135, all Korean War casualties for the U.S. Army are summarized. As much as possible an attempt was made to include figures for every unit that had significant numbers or patterns of casualties. With almost 600 units reporting casualties in the war, of course, only a relative few could be included.

Table 135 — U.S. Army Casualties — Korean War Totals

	KIA	WIA	POW Returned	POW Died	MIA Returned	MIA Died	Unit Total
1st Cavalry Division							
5th Cav, 1st Cav Div	1122	3965	72	35	37	107	5338
7th Cav, 1st Cav Div	990	4151	75	12	25	75	5328
8th Cav, 1st Cav Div	774	2906	286	119	27	226	4338
8th Engr Bn, 1st Cav Div	49	223	9	3	2	9	295
61st FA Bn, 1st Cav Div	34	161	6	3	2	1	207
99th FA Bn, 1st Cav Div	39	106	19	4	0	21	189
16th Recon Co, 1st Cav Div	54	135	0	0	1	3	193
77th FA Bn, 1st Cav Div	51	128	1	0	0	3	183
6th Tank Bn, 1st Cav Div	11	82	17	3	0	1	114
71st Med Tk Bn, 1st Cav Div	18	34	1	0	0	1	54

(continued on next page)

Table 135 (*cont.*)

	KIA	WIA	POW Returned	POW Died	MIA Returned	MIA Died	Unit Total
82nd FA Bn, 1st Cav Div	8	47	0	0	0	0	55
HHB, 1st Cav Div Fld Arty	10	12	1	0	0	0	23
Other 1st Cav Units (14)	15	103	3	1	3	1	126
Total 1st Cavalry Division	3175	12053	490	180	97	448	16443
2nd Infantry Division							
38th Inf, 2nd Div	1505	5090	453	263	66	266	7643
9th Inf, 2nd Div	1369	4579	282	306	28	266	6830
23rd Inf, 2nd Div	1323	4443	243	56	64	91	6220
2nd Engr Bn, 2nd Inf Div	134	381	100	149	0	64	828
38th FA Bn, 2nd Inf Div	70	152	120	146	3	37	528
503rd FA Bn, 2nd Inf Div	67	120	126	138	1	50	502
82nd AAA Bn, 2nd Inf Div	76	195	99	95	4	25	494
15th FA Bn, 2nd Inf Div	119	191	45	86	5	41	487
72nd Tank Bn, 2nd Inf Div	63	287	8	6	0	3	367
2nd RP Co, 2nd Inf Div	64	240	2	0	8	8	322
37th FA Bn, 2nd Inf Div	52	213	4	9	0	9	287
2nd Recon Co, 2nd Inf Div	54	138	5	4	1	6	208
HHB, 2nd Inf Div Fld Arty	6	16	5	9	0	1	37
2nd Med Bn, 2nd Inf Div	10	8	3	4	0	3	28
Other 2nd Div Units (15)	26	113	9	3	0	7	158
Total 2nd Infantry Division	4938	16166	1504	1274	180	877	24939
3rd Infantry Division							
15th Inf, 3rd Inf Div	685	2777	24	1	0	44	3531
7th Inf 3rd Inf Div	536	2218	67	21	1	84	2927
65th Inf, 3rd Inf Div	487	2098	50	1	2	121	2759
10th Engr Bn, 3rd Inf Div	44	180	1	0	0	7	232
64th Tank Bn, 3rd Inf Div	21	101	2	0	0	4	128
3rd Recon Co, 3rd Inf Div	17	76	4	2	0	1	100
39th FA Bn, 3rd Inf Div	17	64	2	2	0	0	85
58th FA Bn, 3rd Inf Div	11	70	3	0	0	4	88
3rd AAA Bn, 3rd Inf Div	10	58	0	0	0	0	68
10th FA Bn, 3rd Inf Div	11	43	2	0	0	1	57
Other 3rd Div Units (13)	16	61	3	0	0	6	86
Total 3rd Infantry Division	1855	7746	158	27	3	272	10061
7th Infantry Division							
31st Inf, 7th Inf Div	967	3324	178	47	2	298	4816
17th Inf, 7th Inf Div	874	3552	34	4	4	101	4569
32nd Inf, 7th Inf Div	858	3068	76	27	5	298	4332
57th FA Bn, 7th Inf Div	89	196	36	17	0	95	433
13th Engr Bn, 7th Inf Div	62	210	2	1	0	6	281
49th FA Bn, 7th Inf Div	26	97	7	5	0	1	136
48th FA Bn, 7th Inf Div	21	73	1	2	0	5	102
7th Recon Co, 7th Inf Div	22	61	0	1	0	1	85
31st FA Bn, 7th Inf Div	10	63	1	0	0	0	74
15th AAA Bn, 7th Inf Div	11	56	0	0	0	0	67
73rd Tank Bn, 7th Inf Div	8	56	0	0	0	0	64
HHC, 7th Inf Div	9	12	1	0	0	0	22
7th Med Bn, 7th Inf Div	4	4	2	2	3	4	19
Other 7th Div Units (15)	23	70	3	0	7	2	105
Total 7th Infantry Division	2984	10842	341	106	21	811	15105

(continued on next page)

Table 135 (*cont.*)

Unit							
24th Infantry Division							
19th Inf, 24th Inf Div	1324	3617	283	132	27	102	5485
21st Inf, 24th Inf Div	729	2041	191	177	16	43	3197
34th Inf, 24th Inf Div	563	749	64	112	57	84	1629
3rd Engr Bn, 24th Inf Div	102	170	6	8	2	20	308
70th Med Tk Bn, 24th Inf Div	26	158	2	1	2	4	193
52nd FA Bn, 24th Inf Div	32	112	10	8	6	1	169
63rd FA Bn, 24th Inf Div	44	44	24	27	25	5	169
11th FA Bn, 24th Inf Div	40	81	5	2	2	2	132
13th FA Bn, 24th Inf Div	21	103	4	1	2	1	132
26th AAA Bn, 24th Inf Div	27	86	3	0	2	4	122
24th Recon Co, 24th Inf Div	21	60	0	3	0	2	86
24th Med Bn, 24th Inf Div	8	40	2	0	0	0	50
24th QM Co, 24th Inf Div	7	15	6	2	5	1	36
Other 24th Div Units (11)	38	100	4	3	2	5	152
Total 24th Infantry Division	2982	7376	604	476	148	274	11860
25th Infantry Division							
24th Inf, 25th Inf Div	741	3195	132	126	28	113	4335
27th Inf, 25th Inf Div	728	2700	31	12	9	26	3506
35th Inf, 25th Inf Div	673	2488	166	72	15	89	3503
14th Inf, 25th Inf Div	160	867	10	0	0	7	1044
65th Engr Bn, 25th Inf Div	71	169	25	5	0	6	276
159th FA Bn, 25th Inf Div	29	119	1	1	0	1	151
90th FA Bn, 25th Inf Div	29	109	1	0	2	2	143
8th FA Bn, 25th Inf Div	32	96	1	0	0	3	132
25th Recon Co, 25th Inf Div	23	93	7	3	0	3	129
64th FA Bn, 25th Inf Div	24	73	1	0	5	2	105
89th Tank Bn, 25th Inf Div	13	50	0	0	0	1	64
77th Cmbt Engr Bn, 25th Inf Div	12	42	1	0	1	0	56
Other 25th Div Units (17)	34	181	7	1	0	1	224
Total 25th Infantry Division	2569	10182	383	220	60	254	13668
40th Infantry Division							
223rd Inf, 40th Inf Div	126	493	3	0	0	6	628
224th Inf, 40th Inf Div	99	437	2	0	0	0	538
160th Inf, 40th Inf Div	106	359	6	0	0	8	479
140th Tank Bn, 40th Inf Div	12	65	4	0	0	3	84
Other 40th Division Units (13)	19	106	0	0	0	0	125
Total 40th Infantry Division	362	1460	15	0	0	17	1854
45th Infantry Division							
179th Inf, 45th Inf Div	300	1263	19	0	0	25	1607
180th Inf, 45th Inf Div	290	985	6	0	1	10	1292
279th Inf, 45th Inf Div	170	715	5	0	0	4	894
245th Tank Bn, 45th Inf Div	9	37	0	0	0	0	46
Other 45th Div Units (13)	23	166	3	0	0	0	192
Total 45th Infantry Division	792	3166	33	0	1	39	4031
29th Inf Regt/RCT	424	689	64	7	14	81	1279
5th Regimental Combat Team							
5th RCT	733	3090	151	26	10	44	4054
555th FA Bn, 5th RCT	76	222	76	2	6	28	410
72nd Comb Engr Co, 5th RCT	10	30	0	0	0	0	40
Total 5th RCT	819	3342	227	28	16	72	4504

(*continued on next page*)

Table 135 (*cont.*)

187th Airborne RCT							
187th RCT	416	1613	10	4	5	16	2064
674th FA Bn, 187th RCT	5	20	0	0	1	1	27
Other 187th RCT Units (3)	0	23					23
Total 187th Airborne RCT	421	1656	10	4	6	17	2114
Non-divisional Units							
89th Arm Cav Bn	30	174	5	2	1	6	218
2nd Chem Bn, Mortar	22	114	16	8	1	19	180
15th AAA Bn	24	71	8	4	0	20	127
21st AAA Bn	5	92	0	0	0	0	97
92nd FA Bn	14	74	7	0	0	2	97
1st FA Bn, Obs	11	83	1	0	0	0	95
999th FA Bn	25	62	0	0	0	1	88
70th Arm Cav Bn	17	47	2	0	2	5	73
73rd Arm Cav Bn	10	73	0	0	0	0	83
300th FA Bn	11	60	7	0	1	0	79
461st Inf Bn, Hv Mortars	14	54	5	0	0	4	77
96th FA Bn	13	58	0	0	0	3	74
14th Combat Engr Bn	28	31	0	0	0	1	60
196th FA Bn	12	47	0	0	0	0	59
17th FA Bn	6	51	1	0	0	0	58
176th FA Bn	12	29	4	0	0	1	46
2nd FA Bty, 5 in	8	25	9	1	0	0	43
937th FA Bn	14	26	0	0	0	0	40
Hq 10th Corps	5	9	0	0	2	14	30
159th FA Bn	10	18	0	0	0	1	29
76th Engr Bn, Construction	15	14	0	0	0	0	29
235th FA Bn, Obs	5	13	7	0	0	1	26
377th Transp Co, Truck	3	9	5	1	1	1	20
1st Ranger Company	37	57	6	6	2	1	109
2nd Ranger Company	14	47	0	0	0	0	61
3rd Ranger Company	6	35	0	0	0	0	41
4th Ranger Company	5	53	3	0	0	0	61
5th Ranger Company	12	65	0	0	0	1	78
8th Ranger Company	5	37	0	0	0	0	42
8213th Misc Units (8th Ranger Co)	5	27	0	0	0	8	40
8202nd Mil Missions Comm	5	27	16	14	1	4	67
8668th Mil Missions Comm	3	5	6	5	0	0	19
Other Non-div Units (354)	278	1157	36	11	12	37	1531
Total Non-divisional Units	684	2744	144	52	23	130	3777
Total U.S. Army	22005	77422	3973	2374	569	3292	109635

Among the 4,610 Marine Corps records in the database, 109 of them have occurrence dates after the end of hostilities and could not be used in the calculations of losses during the war. It is apparent from those calculations that two categories of casualty were grossly underrepresented in the data; those that were captured and died in captivity and those that were missing and never found. It is possible that some, if not most, of the 109 unusable records actually represented marines that were captured or missing. It may be that the date in the record that was supposed to be the occurrence date was actually the disposition date, the date on which the record was closed. In addition,

IV. The End of Hostilities

a number of other records had little or no information on the specifics of the casualty; i.e., type and disposition. Some of these could also have represented MIAs or POWs.

However, although not all of the records could be used to assign specific losses to specific battles, each record in the database represents a fallen marine and all records can be used to account for the total number of marine fatalities in the war. Table 136 shows how those fatalities were distributed among the several causes and dispositions in the database.

Table 136 — U.S. Marine Corps Fatalities — Korean War Totals

Air Casualties	
Fixed Wing Crash At Sea	
Pilot, Killed in Action	10
Fixed Wing Crash Over Land	
Pilot, Killed in Action	115
Pilot, Died while Missing	7
Pilot, Died of Wounds	3
Ground Casualties	
Aircraft Loss	
Killed in Action	21
Small-arms Fire	
Killed in Action	1764
Died of Wounds	274
Died while Missing	15
Died in Captivity	1
Artillery/Rocket	
Killed in Action	226
Died of Wounds	31
Died while Missing	26
Other Weapon	
Killed in Action	8
Died of Wounds	2
Explosive Device	
Killed in Action	328
Died of Wounds	41
Died while Missing	20
Multiple Fragmentation Wounds	
Killed in Action	714
Died of Wounds	108
Died while Missing	13
Died in Captivity	2
Drowned/Suffocated	
Killed in Action	10
Died of Wounds	1
Died while Missing	1
Burns	
Killed in Action	4
Died of Wounds	1
Accident	
Killed in Action	1
Died of Wounds	1
Unknown	
Killed in Action	59
Died of Wounds	17
Died in Captivity	2
Unknown	
Killed in Action	434
Unknown	350
Marine Corps Total	**4610**

In general, records for Navy personnel in the database tended to be more complete than those for the marines. However, there were still a few missing dates and some records were incomplete. For the most part, the numbers and types of Navy casualties presented here should be reasonably accurate. Table 137 summarizes U.S. Navy losses in the war by cause and disposition.

Table 137 — U.S. Navy Fatalities — Korean War Totals

Fixed Wing Crash At Sea	
Pilot	
Killed in Action	7
Died while Missing	3
Aircrew	
Killed in Action	4
Died while Missing	6
Non-Aircrew	
Died while Missing	2
Fixed Wing Crash Over Land	
Pilot	
Killed in Action	73
Died of Wounds	1
Died while Missing	40

(continued on next page)

Table 137 (*cont.*)

Fixed Wing Crash Over Land (*cont.*)		Burns	
Aircrew		Killed in Action	1
Killed in Action	18	Unknown	
Died while Missing	18	Killed in Action	4
Non-Aircrew		Died while Missing	3
Killed in Action	1	**Sea Casualty**	
Died while Missing	1	Artillery/Rocket	
Helicopter Crash Over Land		Killed in Action	2
Pilot		Died of Wounds	1
Killed in Action	1	Small-arms Fire	
Died while Missing	1	Killed in Action	2
Non-Aircrew		Explosive Device	
Died while Missing	1	Killed in Action	93
Ground Casualty		Died of Wounds	1
Small-arms Fire		Died while Missing	35
Killed in Action	97	Multiple Fragmentation Wounds	
Died of Wounds	9	Killed in Action	2
Died while Missing	9	Died of Wounds	1
Artillery/Rocket		Drowned/Suffocated	
Killed in Action	2	Killed in Action	3
Died of Wounds	1	Died while Missing	3
Other Weapon		Burns	
Killed in Action	1	Killed in Action	1
Explosive Device		Vehicle Crash	
Killed in Action	9	Died while Missing	2
Died of Wounds	1	Misadventure	
Multiple Fragmentation Wounds		Killed in Action	2
Killed in Action	3	Unknown	
		Died in Captivity	1
		Total U.S. Navy	**466**

Table 138 — U.S. Air Force Fatalities — Korean War Totals

Fixed Wing Crash At Sea		Died while Missing	307
Pilot		Died in Captivity	11
Killed in Action	2	Non-Aircrew	
Died while Missing	6	Killed in Action	20
Aircrew		Died of Wounds	1
Killed in Action	1	Died while Missing	75
Died while Missing	9	Died in Captivity	1
Non-Aircrew		**Ground Casualty**	
Killed in Action	1	Small-arms Fire	
Died while Missing	5	Killed in Action	3
Fixed Wing Crash Over Land		Died of Wounds	1
Pilot		Died in Captivity	1
Killed in Action	114	Other Weapon	
Died of Wounds	7	Killed in Action	1
Died while Missing	555	Multiple Fragmentation Wounds	
Died in Captivity	9	Died of Wounds	1
Aircrew		**Unknown**	
Killed in Action	63	Died in Captivity	2
Died of Wounds	4	**U.S. Air Force Total**	**1200**

Air Force records in the database, like those of Navy casualties, appear to fairly accurately represent the actual numbers and causes of the fatalities the service experienced in the war. Table 138 summarizes those losses by cause and disposition.

Operation Big Switch

The chronology lists Operation Big Switch as the last major unfinished business in the aftermath of the Korean War. This was the final exchange of prisoners between the UN and the communists. According to the chronology, the last of 3,597 U.S. prisoners were released on September 6, 1953. The database confirms that, by that date, all but two U.S. Army POWs had been released. Of the two that remained, one was reported released on October 21, 1953 and the other on January 1, 1954. Either or both of these could be recording errors.

The database records a total of 3,970 U.S. Army personnel captured and ultimately released to military control. However, as was mentioned earlier in the recap of the war in 1950, a number of these were very likely not actually POWs. According to the database, 642 reported U.S. Army POWs were released between the beginning of the war and October 24, 1951. Most of these had been "in captivity" for only a short time. Then, after that October date and until the end of hostilities, 355 American GIs were reported captured and ultimately released. Of these only four were released before Operation Little Switch in April of 1953, all of them in captivity for only a short time. It seems unlikely that over 600 POWs were actually released by their captors in the middle of some of the fiercest fighting in the war. More likely, they either escaped or they were never really POWs at all, but rather reported as captured when, in fact, they were actually just missing.

Database records indicate that, beginning on August 5, 1953, and daily for the next month, American POWs were released until a total of 3,194 U.S. Army POWs had been returned to military control. No information is available on how many prisoners from the other services were returned in this operation.

Remembering the Missing

All losses in war are tragedies, but none are more tragic than those that are reported missing, never found and declared dead. For the U.S. Army in the Korean War, a total of 3,292 individuals were recorded in this category, 3 percent of all Army casualties. For the 1st Marine Division, the percentage was probably similar. It was that kind of ground war.

For the airmen of the Marine Corps, Navy and Air Force, the percentages were greater. Air crashes have an indescribable finality to them. Of air crashes reported by the U.S. Marines, 7 of 135 fatalities (5 percent) were missing and never found. The U.S. Navy reported that 72 of 177 fatalities in air crashes (41 percent) were missing and declared dead. In air crashes reported by the U.S. Air Force, 957 of 1191 fatalities (80 percent) were airmen that were reported missing and never found.

V

SUMMARY STATISTICS

Among the data recorded in the databases, several additional items of personal information can be used to help complete the history of the Korean War from the perspective of its casualties. Every record in the AGCF (U.S. Army) database includes the Military Occupation Specialty (MOS) of the individual described in the record. A summary of casualties by MOS provides an interesting picture of the kinds of assignments that were most likely to put these GIs in harm's way. Of course, the front-line rifleman was at the greatest risk, but some other jobs were a lot more hazardous than one might expect. Table 139 shows a summary of casualties among enlisted men by MOS. A number of the descriptions in this table are identified by more than one MOS code. This is because the U.S. Army decided to change its way of coding enlisted MOSs right in the middle of the Korean War.

Table 139 — Total U.S. Army Casualties by
Military Occupational Specialty (MOS) — Enlisted

MOS Code	Description	KIA	WIA	POW Returned	POW Died	MIA Returned	MIA Died	MOS Total
4745	Lt Wpns Infantryman	10400	37086	1674	875	264	1484	51783
1745/2745	Lt Wpns Inf Ldr	3338	13197	442	151	27	402	17557
2812/4812	Hvy Wpns Crwmn	1387	4199	289	129	70	298	6372
3729/5729	Cmbt Const Spec	513	1480	100	89	11	112	2305
4844/3844	Fld Arty Cannoneer	359	1283	185	171	23	127	2148
0657/0666/3666	Aidman	431	1380	87	44	17	50	2009
0345/4345	Lt Veh Driver	303	1099	102	61	22	67	1654
0060/0062/3060	Cook	330	873	94	80	10	79	1466
3795/4795	Tank Crewman	206	1078	35	15	8	18	1360
74745	Lt Wpns Infantryman*	212	751	4	4	3	12	986
0641/4641	Field Wireman	203	595	60	43	10	47	958
1812	Hvy Wpns Inf Ldr	171	696	16	4	0	12	899
4602	AAA Wpns Crewman	97	442	32	31	8	25	635
1844	Fld Arty Chief	91	369	84	8	3	24	579
0014/4014	Wheel Veh Mech	104	363	35	37	3	28	570
1795	Tank Leader	84	434	5	6	1	6	536
0733/4733	Arm Recon Crewman	119	338	9	6	5	12	489
1729	Cmbt Const Foreman	95	357	12	8	1	8	481

(continued on next page)

Table 139 (*cont.*)

MOS Code	Description	KIA	WIA	POW Returned	POW Died	MIA Returned	MIA Died	MOS Total
1666	Chief Med Aidman	93	370	5	0	0	10	478
5704	Fire Dir & Liaison Op	81	183	32	36	4	25	361
0761/4761	Inf Recon Scout	86	215	18	19	2	10	350
0409/4123	Med Tech	60	219	24	18	3	17	341
0677/4677	Mil Policeman	71	235	14	8	2	9	339
0821/1821	Supply NCO	66	197	14	17	1	9	304
0055/4055	Clerk, General	55	195	11	5	3	5	274
0861/2861	Surg Tech	44	166	24	11	2	6	253
71745	Lt Wpns Inf Ldr*	58	189	2	0	0	2	251
0667/4667	Sig Msg Clerk	52	139	12	23	1	10	237
0405/4405	Clerk-Typist	48	134	8	7	3	8	208
	Other Specialties†	1578	5410	340	319	48	255	7950
	Total Enlisted	20735	73672	3769	2225	555	3177	104133

*The initial "7" in this MOS code identifies these individuals as "Parachutist."
†The number of MOS codes included in this category is virtually impossible to estimate because a number of classifications were represented by more than one code.

The MOS codes for officers and warrant officers remained unchanged throughout the war. Table 140 provides a summary of officer/warrant officer casualties by MOS.

Table 140 — Total U.S. Army Casualties by Military Occupational Specialty (MOS) — Officer/Warrant Officer

MOS Code	Description	KIA	WIA	POW Returned	POW Died	MIA Returned	MIA Died	MOS Total
1542	Infantry Unit Commander	772	2393	92	56	6	64	3383
1193	Fld Artillery Unit Cmdr	77	181	21	24	2	8	313
1203	Tank Unit Commander	43	181	7	5	0	1	237
1189	Fwd Obs, Artillery	46	128	13	3	1	6	197
1622	Unit Off, Trng Ctr	36	112	3	2	0	1	154
1331	Combat Engr Unit Cmdr	34	61	3	3	0	0	101
2162	Op & Trng Staff Officer	20	50	5	3	1	2	81
1204	Armored Recon Unit Cmdr	14	42	2	1	0	1	60
2123	Unit Administrator*	10	35	6	3	1	3	58
1174	AAA Auto Wpns Unit Cmdr	13	34	2	4	0	2	55
0200	Communications Officer	8	29	5	1	0	4	47
2110	Adj or Adj General	16	22	4	1	0	0	43
1510	Parachute Inf Unit Cmdr	5	30	1	1	0	2	39
0600	Motor Transport Officer	13	19	4	0	1	0	37
1981	Air Observation Pilot	11	20	1	2	0	2	36
9301	Intelligence Staff Officer	9	20	0	3	0	0	32
4010	Supply & Evac Staff Officer	9	20	0	2	0	0	31
3100	Medical Officer, General	4	15	4	3	0	0	26
1172	AAA Gun Unit Cmdr	2	17	0	1	0	1	21
2120	Administration Officer	5	13	1	1	0	0	20
5310	Chaplain	7	8	0	3	0	1	19
2136	Unit Officer, Non-tactical	6	10	0	1	0	1	18

*All of these individuals were Warrant Officers.

(*continued on next page*)

Table 140 (*cont.*)

MOS Code	Description	KIA	WIA	POW Returned	POW Died	MIA Returned	MIA Died	MOS Total
1183	Recon & Survey Officer	6	8	2	0	0	1	17
2900	Hq Co Commander	1	10	4	0	0	1	16
1620	Mech Cav Unit Cmdr	2	13	0	1	0	0	16
4000	Supply Officer, General	1	13	1	0	0	0	15
	Other Specialties†	98	267	23	25	2	15	429
	Total Officer & Warrant Officer	1268	3751	204	149	14	116	5502

†The majority of these casualties were represented by 137 valid MOS codes. An additional 53 different MOS codes, representing 64 individual casualties, were not identifiable as valid codes and were possibly typographical errors.

At the time they became casualties, all members of the U.S. military had achieved some specified rank in their assigned organizations. These ranks (or pay grades) identify what kinds of duties and levels of responsibility each of these individuals carried at the time. Table 141 summarizes the distribution of casualties among U.S. Army enlisted men by their rank and pay grade.

Table 141 — Total U.S. Army Korean War Casualties by Rank/(Grade) — Enlisted

Rank/Grade	KIA	WIA	POW Returned	POW Died	MIA Returned	MIA Died	Total by Grade
Private (E1)	110	448	13	7	1	18	597
Private (E2)	5209	17617	781	463	151	763	24984
Pvt 1st Class (E3)	8321	29307	1451	841	241	1302	41463
Corporal (E4)	4018	15016	823	510	106	675	21148
Sergeant (E5)	1751	6584	394	216	33	257	9235
Sgt 1st Class (E6)	951	3445	211	135	18	113	4873
Master Sergeant (E7)	374	1247	95	53	5	48	1822
No Grade Listed	1	8	1	0	0	1	11
Total Enlisted	20735	73672	3769	2225	555	3177	104133

Table 142 shows a similar summary for U.S. Army officer and warrant officer personnel.

Table 142 — Total U.S. Army Korean War Casualties by Rank/(Grade) — Officers & Warrant Officers

Rank/Grade	KIA	WIA	POW Returned	POW Died	MIA Returned	MIA Died	Total by Grade
Warrant Officer (W2)	13	46	6	1	0	4	70
Warrant Officer (W?)	1	4	0	4	1	0	10
2nd Lieutenant (O1)	399	1361	49	9	6	38	1862
1st Lieutenant (O2)	606	1721	83	67	5	41	2523
Captain (O3)	187	465	45	39	2	25	763
Major (O4)	44	98	17	20	0	7	186
Lt. Colonel (O5)	14	50	3	7	0	0	74
Colonel (O6)	2	6	0	2	0	1	11
Brig. General (O7)	2	0	1	0	0	0	3
Total Officer & WO	1268	3751	204	149	14	116	5502

V. Summary Statistics

In the databases used to document casualties in this book, the age of the individual is identified only for fatalities. In the AGCF database (U.S. Army), only the year of birth is provided in these records. This limitation makes it impossible to determine the exact age of each U.S. Army fatality, but a reasonable estimate can be calculated by assuming that everyone in the list was born on July 1st of the birth year specified in his record. Using this estimate, no one in the following summaries will be placed in an age category that is off by more than six months.

Table 143 shows all Korean War fatalities of U.S. Army enlisted men by age and by pay grade.

Table 143 — U.S. Army Korean War Fatalities by Age and Grade — Enlisted

Enlisted Grade

Age	E1	E2	E3	E4	E5	E6	E7	Total By Age
16	0	1	2	0	0	0	0	3
17	2	219	219	22	0	0	0	462
18	12	1000	1081	220	22	9	1	2345
19	24	998	1703	597	149	30	5	3506
20	21	895	1774	827	237	69	10	3833
21	20	1003	1548	765	238	80	14	3668
22	16	956	1470	721	274	84	16	3537
23	9	536	1057	636	257	98	14	2607
24	4	277	523	342	168	70	16	1400
25	7	176	314	210	148	62	14	931
26	4	100	213	193	91	68	19	688
27	5	60	136	114	90	67	26	498
28	1	33	72	84	79	75	34	378
29	2	29	54	78	67	68	27	325
30	2	16	39	61	61	60	41	280
31	2	24	36	56	63	63	35	279
32	0	12	25	53	67	63	39	259
33	1	12	29	34	34	41	31	182
34	0	11	18	28	38	27	19	141
35	0	6	13	32	25	33	18	127
36	0	9	15	21	19	31	18	113
37	0	6	13	18	12	21	16	86
38	0	7	8	16	10	17	23	81
39	0	2	6	12	11	15	13	59
40	0	3	4	10	7	15	3	42
41	2	0	6	6	10	7	7	38
42	0	1	5	4	5	5	4	24
43	0	2	1	2	4	4	1	14
44	0	2	2	4	5	5	2	20
45	0	1	1	0	3	0	6	11
46	0	0	0	3	2	3	3	11
47	0	2	0	0	1	2	0	5
48	0	0	0	0	2	0	0	2
49	0	0	1	0	1	0	0	2
55	0	0	0	0	0	1	0	1
61	0	0	1	0	0	0	0	1
None Listed	1	44	92	40	26	7	1	211
Total by Grade	135	6443	10481	5209	2226	1200	476	26170

Table 144 provides a similar summary for U.S. Army officers and warrant officers.

Table 144 — U.S. Army Korean War Fatalities by Age and Grade — Officer/Warrant Officer

Officer/Warrant Grade

Age	Unk	W2	W?	O1	O2	O3	O4	O5	O6	O7	Total By Age
19	0	0	0	1	0	0	0	0	0	0	1
20	2	0	0	3	4	0	0	0	0	0	9
21	0	0	0	26	13	0	0	0	0	0	39
22	0	0	0	47	41	0	0	0	0	0	88
23	0	0	0	94	72	1	0	0	0	0	167
24	0	0	0	90	69	1	0	0	0	0	160
25	0	0	0	58	62	4	0	0	0	0	124
26	0	0	0	29	75	13	1	0	0	0	118
27	0	0	0	20	60	14	0	0	0	0	94
28	0	1	0	19	52	14	2	0	0	0	88
29	0	1	0	15	63	26	2	0	0	0	107
30	0	0	0	12	42	28	1	0	0	0	83
31	0	2	0	6	33	20	5	0	0	0	66
32	0	3	0	7	36	23	11	1	0	0	81
33	0	2	0	10	29	24	7	0	0	0	72
34	0	1	0	3	16	21	6	3	0	0	50
35	0	0	0	0	17	11	5	1	0	0	34
36	0	4	0	1	6	7	5	2	2	0	27
37	0	2	2	0	4	12	2	2	0	0	24
38	0	0	2	0	4	7	8	1	0	0	22
39	0	1	0	0	1	7	6	3	0	0	18
40	0	1	0	0	3	4	4	2	0	0	14
41	0	0	0	0	2	5	0	1	0	0	8
42	0	0	1	0	0	2	1	0	0	0	4
43	0	0	0	0	0	2	1	1	1	0	5
44	0	0	0	0	1	3	0	1	1	0	6
45	0	0	0	0	0	0	0	2	0	0	2
46	0	0	0	0	0	0	1	1	0	0	2
47	0	0	0	0	0	1	0	0	0	0	1
48	0	0	0	0	0	0	1	0	1	0	2
56	0	0	0	0	0	0	0	0	0	1	1
None Listed	0	0	0	6	11	2	2	0	0	1	22
Total by Grade	2	18	5	447	716	252	71	21	5	2	1539

The KCCF database (fatalities in the U.S. Marine Corps, Air Force and Navy) provides an exact birth date for the servicemen recorded in the file, so the age of each individual can be calculated unequivocally. Because the ranks associated with each pay grade tend to differ with each of these services, only the pay grade will be identified in each of the following summaries.

Tables 145 and 146 summarize all U.S. Marine Corps fatalities by age and by pay grade, for enlisted men and for officers/warrant officers, respectively.

V. Summary Statistics

Table 145 — U.S. Marine Corps Korean War Fatalities by Age and Grade — Enlisted

Enlisted Grade

Age	Unk	E1	E2	E3	E4	E5	E6	E7	Total By Age
17	0	1	8	0	0	0	0	0	9
18	0	17	228	18	2	0	0	0	265
19	1	28	524	131	22	0	0	0	706
20	0	20	503	212	44	1	0	0	780
21	0	18	488	192	74	11	0	0	783
22	0	11	310	109	49	6	0	0	485
23	0	3	116	67	45	9	0	0	240
24	0	3	65	31	43	9	3	0	154
25	0	2	44	26	30	14	4	1	121
26	0	0	24	12	23	11	4	0	74
27	1	0	14	14	7	9	3	3	51
28	0	1	8	14	12	11	3	4	53
29	0	2	6	5	15	7	5	6	46
30	0	0	5	6	3	5	7	7	33
31	0	0	3	4	2	3	2	3	17
32	0	0	3	4	4	4	2	3	20
33	0	0	0	0	1	4	3	2	10
34	0	0	0	0	2	1	1	1	5
35	0	0	1	1	0	1	1	0	4
36	0	0	1	1	0	1	1	1	5
37	0	0	0	0	0	0	0	1	1
38	0	0	1	0	0	1	0	0	2
39	0	0	0	0	1	1	0	0	2
40	0	0	0	0	0	1	1	0	2
43	0	0	0	0	1	1	0	0	2
46	0	0	0	0	0	1	0	0	1
47	0	0	0	0	0	0	1	0	1
None Listed	0	7	187	69	34	13	21	3	324
Total by Grade	2	113	2539	916	414	125	62	35	4206

Table 146 — U.S. Marine Corps Korean War Fatalities by Age and Grade — Officer/Warrant Officer

Age	W1	W2	W3	O1	O2	O3	O4	O5	O6	Total By Age
20	0	0	0	1	0	0	0	0	0	1
21	0	0	0	8	2	0	0	0	0	10
22	0	0	0	22	2	0	0	0	0	24
23	0	0	0	31	10	3	0	0	0	44
24	0	0	0	17	4	0	0	0	0	21
25	0	0	0	7	8	1	0	0	0	26
26	0	0	0	5	15	4	0	0	0	24
27	0	0	1	3	15	6	2	0	0	27
28	0	0	0	3	7	17	2	0	0	29
29	0	0	0	1	12	22	4	0	0	39
30	0	0	0	1	7	15	7	0	0	30
31	0	0	0	0	3	17	5	0	0	25
32	0	0	0	1	2	5	9	6	0	23
33	0	0	0	0	1	6	3	0	0	10

(continued on next page)

Table 146 (*cont.*)

Age	W1	W2	W3	O1	O2	O3	O4	O5	O6	Total By Age
34	0	1	0	0	0	1	2	1	0	5
35	0	0	0	0	0	1	2	0	0	3
36	0	1	0	0	0	1	2	1	1	6
37	0	0	0	0	0	0	1	1	2	4
38	0	0	0	0	0	0	0	1	0	1
39	0	0	0	0	0	0	0	1	1	2
42	0	0	0	0	0	1	1	0	0	2
45	0	0	0	1	0	0	0	0	0	1
None Listed	1	0	0	17	8	14	3	4	0	47
Total by Grade	1	2	1	128	96	114	43	15	4	404

Tables 147 and 148 show similar summaries for U.S. Navy personnel.

Table 147 — U.S. Navy Korean War Fatalities by Age and Grade — Enlisted

Enlisted Grade

Age	E1	E2	E3	E4	E5	E6	E7	Total By Age
17	2	2	0	0	0	0	0	4
18	3	5	3	0	0	0	0	11
19	7	21	5	0	0	0	1	34
20	8	27	29	3	0	0	0	67
21	6	25	20	1	0	0	1	53
22	1	23	8	2	2	0	1	37
23	1	4	6	3	4	0	0	18
24	0	2	8	1	2	0	0	13
25	0	1	4	2	2	0	0	9
26	0	2	0	2	8	0	0	12
27	0	0	3	2	4	0	0	9
28	0	0	0	0	1	1	0	2
29	0	0	1	0	3	1	0	5
30	0	1	0	0	3	3	0	7
31	0	0	0	1	1	2	0	4
32	0	1	0	0	2	0	0	3
33	0	0	0	0	3	3	0	6
34	0	0	0	0	0	1	0	1
36	0	0	0	0	0	1	0	1
37	0	0	1	0	1	1	0	3
39	0	0	0	0	0	1	0	1
40	0	0	0	0	1	0	0	1
41	0	0	0	0	1	0	0	1
43	0	0	0	0	0	1	0	1
46	0	0	0	0	0	1	0	1
Total by Grade	28	114	88	17	38	16	3	304

V. Summary Statistics

Table 148 — U.S. Navy Korean War Fatalities by Age and Grade — Officers

Age	O1	O2	O3	O4	O5	Total by Age
20	1	0	0	0	0	1
21	5	0	0	0	0	5
22	14	3	0	0	0	17
23	11	1	0	0	0	12
24	5	12	0	0	0	17
25	2	14	0	0	0	16
26	5	11	2	0	0	18
27	1	12	3	0	0	16
28	0	5	8	0	0	13
29	1	0	7	1	0	9
30	0	0	7	1	0	8
31	1	0	3	3	0	7
32	0	0	5	2	0	7
33	0	0	3	2	0	5
34	0	0	1	1	2	4
35	0	0	0	0	2	2
36	0	0	0	0	1	1
38	0	0	0	1	0	1
39	0	0	0	0	1	1
None Listed	1	0	1	0	0	2
Total	47	58	40	11	6	162

Tables 149 and 150 show similar summaries for U.S. Air Force personnel.

Table 149 — U.S. Air Force Korean War Fatalities by Age and Grade — Enlisted

Age	E1	E2	E3	E4	E5	E6	E7	Total By Age
18	0	0	7	3	0	0	0	10
19	1	1	15	13	2	0	0	32
20	1	0	13	12	8	0	0	34
21	1	1	16	12	9	2	0	41
22	0	0	10	5	7	2	0	24
23	0	0	3	2	8	1	1	15
24	0	0	1	3	6	4	0	14
25	0	1	0	3	17	2	2	25
26	0	0	1	1	6	2	4	14
27	0	0	0	1	9	5	1	16
28	0	0	2	1	5	0	1	9
29	0	0	0	2	3	2	4	11
30	0	0	1	0	5	1	4	11
31	0	0	2	1	5	1	1	10
32	1	0	0	0	2	2	2	7
33	0	0	0	0	5	0	2	7
35	0	0	0	0	3	0	1	4
36	0	0	0	0	1	0	0	1
37	0	0	0	0	1	0	0	1
38	0	0	0	2	1	0	0	3
42	0	0	0	0	1	0	0	1
Total by Grade	4	3	71	61	104	24	23	290

Table 150 — U.S. Air Force Korean War Fatalities by Age and Grade — Officers

Officer Grade

Age	O1	O2	O3	O4	O5	O6	Total by Age
20	0	1	0	0	0	0	1
21	2	2	0	0	0	0	4
22	18	52	0	0	0	0	70
23	14	55	1	0	0	0	70
24	18	67	3	0	0	0	88
25	5	47	13	1	0	0	66
26	3	47	31	0	0	0	81
27	2	50	33	1	1	0	87
28	1	38	36	3	0	0	78
29	1	22	40	8	3	0	74
30	0	25	44	6	1	0	76
31	0	7	36	10	4	1	58
32	1	11	26	3	3	0	44
33	0	11	21	6	2	1	41
34	0	5	11	11	3	3	33
35	0	3	8	5	0	0	16
36	0	0	4	4	1	2	11
37	0	0	1	1	1	0	3
39	0	1	0	0	0	0	1
40	0	0	0	0	0	3	3
45	0	0	1	0	0	0	1
46	0	0	0	0	0	1	1
None Listed	1	2	0	0	0	0	3
Total by Grade	66	446	309	59	19	11	910

Finally, to complete the summary of Korean War losses by the personal attributes of individual participants, Table 151 summarizes all U.S. Army casualties by race. In this table, the race categories listed are those that were used at the time to identify individual service members and that were coded as such in the database.

Table 151 — U.S. Army Korean War Casualties by Race

Race	KIA	WIA	POW Returned	POW Died	MIA Returned	MIA Died	Unit Total
Caucasian	18898	64963	3385	1945	510	2726	92427
Negro	2145	9252	427	395	45	383	12647
Chinese	19	30	0	1	0	1	51
Japanese	102	255	27	4	3	20	411
Hawaiian	26	59	3	3	3	10	104
American Indian	77	180	10	5	0	4	276
Filipino	56	118	21	5	3	12	215
Puerto Rican (Caucasian)	187	910	16	1	1	86	1201
Puerto Rican (Negro)	23	61	2	0	0	0	86
Puerto Rican (other)	206	635	33	2	1	10	887
Mongolian	73	240	3	0	0	3	319
Malayan	30	126	3	0	0	4	163
Other	77	194	32	12	1	16	332
None Listed	86	399	11	1	2	17	516
Total	22005	77422	3973	2374	569	3292	109635

APPENDIX—DATA SOURCES

Two databases listing Korean War casualties were acquired from the National Archives. One was the Adjutant General's Korean War Casualty File—U.S. Army (AGCF), listing all U.S. Army Korean War casualties, fatal and non-fatal. The other was the Korean Conflict Casualties File (KCCF), listing fatal Korean War casualties for all services. Following is my appraisal of these databases after analysis and reconciliation of the data in them.

The Adjutant General's Korean War Casualty File (AGCF)

Descriptive information accompanying the AGCF database indicated a total of 109,975 records, of which "27,727 are records for Army personnel who died and 82,248 are records of nonfatal Army casualties." The description further suggested that "the records for deceased casualties are coded to indicate 25,308 hostile casualties and 2,419 nonhostile casualties."

This database is reasonably comprehensive, and with the repair of its more obvious errors and the acquisition of appropriate code files, it yields significant useful information about each casualty, including personal data, date, place (N or S Korea), date and type of casualty, date and type of disposition, MOS and unit.

Although this database contains 109,975 records, only 109,933 of them reflect identifiable Korean War casualties. The last 13 records in the list are nonsense (all 9's), one record contains no data and 26 records are duplicates of other records in the database. Two records report the deaths of a pair of Lt. Colonels in Formosa on September 3, 1954. In addition, 298 of the casualties in this database use two separate records to describe the circumstances. All of these records report instances in which the individual was wounded and then was either captured or reported missing on the day the wounds were sustained. Subsequently, when they were either found or repatriated, one record was used to report the date the individual was returned to military control and the second record was used to report the date and disposition relative to the wounds.

Almost 600 different Army units have been specifically identified as the assigned units of personnel in this database. Most of the casualties, of course, occurred among personnel assigned to the various infantry regiments. Within the regiments, no further subdivision of units was coded.

Two different code files had to be used to identify the MOS of the enlisted personnel in the database, because the army decided to change the way it coded MOSs during the war. Using both code files, most MOSs could be identified unambiguously.

The Korean Conflict Casualties File (KCCF)

Information accompanying the KCCF database indicates that it contains "a universe of all U.S. military personnel who died by hostile means as a result of combat duty in the Korean Conflict." The file contains 33,642 individual records.

This database is far less comprehensive than AGCF and, in fact, provides many fewer data than its accompanying record layout suggests. In addition, as my reconciliation of this database with AGCF (see below) demonstrates, the data in general are far less reliable.

Of the 33,642 deaths recorded in this database, 27,709 represent Army personnel, 4,207 were Marines, 1,200 were Air Force personnel and 466 were from the Navy. The fields that record the date and the cause of casualty in this database are more comprehensive for the Marines, Air Force and Navy than they are for the Army, because records of Army fatalities confuse the casualty date and disposition date, and the field for cause of casualty is blank in all Army records. Clearly, the records for U.S. Army fatalities in KCCF are of minimal value for compiling casualty statistics. However, they did prove useful for cross-checking records of Army fatalities in the AGCF database, as indicated below.

Reconciliation

A procedure to match the records for fatal casualties in AGCF and the records for Army personnel in KCCF yielded a total of 27,701 record matches. The most significant thing about this result is what is does to the National Archives' suggestion that only 25,308 of the 27,727 Army deaths represented in AGCF were hostile deaths, while at the same time suggesting that all of the 27,709 Army deaths recorded in KCCF were from hostile action. In fact, the reconciliation of the two databases suggests rather clearly that all deaths listed in both files were originally recorded to be the result of hostile action.

The difference between the 27,701 records matched between the two databases and the number of casualty death records they each contain can be reconciled as follows: Both contain records for the two mystery Lt. Colonels who died in Formosa. These need to be eliminated. KCCF contains two duplicate records and AGCF contains 16 duplicate records of Army fatalities. This leaves 27,709 in AGCF and 27,705 in KCCF. There are 4 records in KCCF that were not found in AGCF and 8 records of fatalities in AGCF that were not found in KCCF. This accounts for all the records that were not matched.

The National Archives presumption of non-hostile casualties in AGCF undoubtedly resulted from their misinterpretation of a casualty disposition code in the database that is termed "died, non-battle." There are, in fact, 2,419 casualties in the database with that disposition code. However, a careful appraisal of the total record in these cases shows that, when this code was used, the casualty itself was very much the result of hostile action, although the ultimate fatality was not necessarily the direct result of the casualty. For example, the casualty type in a record might be "captured" and the ultimate disposition "died, non-battle." It would be a bit hard to argue that this death was not attributable to hostile action.

The reconciliation of these two databases was no small task. It required comparing several different common markers in the two files and then direct inspection of a significant number of individual records. The reason for the difficulty was the high percentage of data-entry errors in the KCCF file. In almost all cases, when records differed between the two sources, it was obviously the KCCF record that was in error.

Conclusions

Given the fact that the U.S. Army casualties in common between the two databases are essentially identical, and the useful data available in the KCCF file are so limited, there is no good reason to depend on that database as a significant source of casualty data for Army personnel. The AGCF database has proved to be a highly reliable alternative resource for that purpose. However, there is no alternative source listing casualty data for the other services. KCCF is all we have.

Fortunately, the U.S. Marine Corps portion of that database has been modified recently by the Marine Corps Casualty Section. A number of new records have been added and many others have been corrected, particularly casualty dates. The original KCCF database contained 4,207 records. Now, 413 new records have been added to bring the total to 4610, and the number records with unusable casualty dates has been reduced by two-thirds to about two percent of all records.

Records in KCCF for U.S. Navy and U.S. Air Force personnel were the most reliable in the original database. That database remains the only source of data for these services and appears to provide reasonably dependable information.

Index

Abrell, Charles G. (MOH) 107
Adams, Stanley T. (MOH) 81
Andong 75

Barber, William E. (MOH) 64
Barker, Charles H. (MOH) 172
Baugh, William B. (MOH) 65
Benfold, Edward C. (MOH) 146
Bennett, Emory L. (MOH) 108
Berlin 182–183
Black Tuesday 127
Bleak, David B. (MOH) 137
Bloody Ridge 112–113
Body armor 153, 163
Boulder City 183
The Bowling Alley 30
Brittin, Nelson V. (MOH) 88
Brown, Melvin L. (MOH) 17
Bunker Hill 144–145
Burke, Lloyd L. (MOH) 125
Burris, Tony K. (MOH) 123

Cafferata, Hector A., Jr. (MOH) 65
Carson 168
Champagne, David B. (MOH) 133
Charette, William R. (MOH) 169
Charlton, Cornelius H. (MOH) 103
Chipyong-ni 79–81
Chochiwon 6
Chonghyon 50
Chorwon 89, 136, 161, 165
Chosin Reservoir 55, 63
Christianson, Stanley R. (MOH) 35
Chup'a-ri 115
Collier, Gilbert G. (MOH) 181
Collier, John W. (MOH) 38
Commiskey, Henry A., Sr. (MOH) 34
Coursen, Samuel S. (MOH) 42
Craig, Gordon M. (MOH) 18
Crump, Jerry K. (MOH) 116

Dale 181
Davenport, Jack A. (MOH) 121
Davis, George Andrew, Jr. (MOH) 135
Davis, Raymond G. (MOH) 67
Dean, William F. (MOH) 7
Desiderio, Reginald B. (MOH) 58
Dewert, Richard David (MOH) 91
Dewey, Duane E. (MOH) 132
Dodd, Carl H. (MOH) 77
Duke, Ray E. (MOH) 95

East Berlin 182–183
Edwards, Junior D. (MOH) 74
Essebagger, John, Jr. (MOH) 94

Faith, Don C., Jr. (MOH) 56
Flak jackets *see* Body armor

Garcia, Fernando Luis (MOH) 147
George, Charles (MOH) 160
Gilliland, Charles L. (MOH) 95
Gomez, Edward (MOH) 120
Goodblood, Clair (MOH) 93
Guillen, Ambrosio (MOH) 183

Hadong 8, 9
Hammond, Francis C. (MOH) 168
Hammond, Lester, Jr. (MOH) 143
Han River 33, 84
Handrich, Melvin O. (MOH) 13
Hanson, Jack G. (MOH) 105
Hartell, Lee R. (MOH) 113
Harvey, Raymond (MOH) 88
Heartbreak Ridge 112, 114, 122–123, 144
Henry, Frederick F. (MOH) 22
Hernandez, Rodolfo P. (MOH) 103
Hill 101 164
Hill 303 14–15
Hill 355 *see* Little Gibralter
Hill 598 *see* Triangle Hill

205

Index

Hill 749 118
Hill 1179 *see* Taeusan
Hoengsong 79, 83
The Hook 157, 172
Hudner, Thomas Jerome, Jr. (MOH) 69
Hungnam 63
Hyesan 50

Imjin River 70
Inchon 32–33, 35, 40
Ingman, Einar H., Jr. (MOH) 84
Iron Triangle 89

Jamestown 124
Jane Russell 153
Jecelin, William R. (MOH) 37
Johnson, James E. (MOH) 68
Jordan, Mack A. (MOH) 128

Kaesong 40
Kanell, Billie G. (MOH) 117
Kaufman, Loren R. (MOH) 25
Kelly, John D. (MOH) 133
Kelso, Jack William (MOH) 152
Kennemore, Robert S. (MOH) 63
Kilmer, John E. (MOH) 145
Kimpo Airfield 33
Knight, Noah O. (MOH) 129
Koelsch, John Kelvin (MOH) 110
Koto-ri 57
Kouma, Ernest R. (MOH) 20
Krzyzowski, Edward C. (MOH) 114
Kum River 6
Kumhwa 89, 178
Kumsong River Salient 178–182
Kunsang 44
Kunu-ri 54
Kwaksan 139
Kyle, Darwin K. (MOH) 82

Lee, Hubert L. (MOH) 78
Libby, George D. (MOH) 7
Little Gibralter 163
Littleton, Herbert A. (MOH) 96
Long, Charles R. (MOH) 80
Lopez, Baldomero (MOH) 32
Loring, Charles J., Jr. (MOH) 162
Lyell, William F. (MOH) 115

Martinez, Benito (MOH) 143
Masan 75
Mason 9
Matthews, Daniel P. (MOH) 170
Mausert, Frederick W., III (MOH) 118
McGovern, Robert M. (MOH) 77
Mclaughlin, Alford L. (MOH) 147
Mendonca, Leroy A. (MOH) 109
Millett, Lewis L. (MOH) 82
Mitchell, Frank N. (MOH) 63
Miyamura, Hiroshi H. (MOH) 94

Mize, Ola L. (MOH) 174
Monegan, Walter C., Jr. (MOH) 33
Moreland, Whitt L. (MOH) 106
Moyer, Donald R. (MOH) 101
Munsan-ni 86
Murphy, Raymond G. (MOH) 164
Myers, Reginald R. (MOH) 66

Naktong Bulge 12
Naktong River 9, 11, 12, 30
Nevada cities 164, 168, 172
The Notch 9

Obregon, Eugene Arnold (MOH) 34
O'Brien, George H., Jr. (MOH) 158
Old Baldy 136, 140, 142, 149, 165–167
Operation Big Switch 73, 191
Operation Commando 124–125
Operation Counter 136
Operation Dauntless 89
Operation Detonate 102
Operation Killer 84–85
Operation Little Switch 171, 191
Operation Nomad 125
Operation Piledriver 102
Operation Polar 125
Operation Ripper 85–89
Operation Rugged 89
Operation Showdown 153–156
Operation Smack 160, 161
Operation Summit 118
Operation Thunderbolt 76–84
Operation Tomahawk 86
Osan 5
Ouellette, Joseph R. (MOH) 21
Outpost Bruce 144–145
Outpost Harry 173
Outpost Kelly 149

Page, John U. D. (MOH) 60
Panmunjom 2, 135, 165
Pendleton, Charles F. (MOH) 180
Phase Line Kansas 89
Phase Line Missouri 125
Phase Line Utah 89
Phillips, Lee H. (MOH) 48
Pikes Peak 153
Pililaau, Herbert K. (MOH) 115
Pittman, John A. (MOH) 54
Pohang 75
Pomeroy, Ralph E. (MOH) 156
Pork Chop 165–167, 170, 172, 175
Porter, Donn F. (MOH) 144
Poynter, James I. (MOH) 49
Punchbowl 105, 109
Pusan 8–11, 26, 32, 33
Pusan Perimeter 11–32, 36–38, 45, 72, 93, 179
Pyonggang 89
Pyongyang 40, 41, 42, 44, 46

Index

Ramer, George H. (MOH) 119
Red Cloud, Mitchell, Jr. (MOH) 50
Reem, Robert Dale (MOH) 49
Reno 165, 168
Rodriguez, Joseph C. (MOH) 101
Rosser, Ronald E. (MOH) 131

Schoonover, Dan D. (MOH) 177
Schowalter, Edward R., Jr. (MOH) 155
Sebille, Louis J. (MOH) 11
Seoul 5, 33–36, 70, 85, 92, 151, 166
Shea, Richard T., Jr. (MOH) 177
Shuck, William E., Jr. (MOH) 141
Simanek, Robert E. (MOH) 146
Sinchon 78
Sinuiju 47
Sitman, William S. (MOH) 80
Sitter, Carl L. (MOH) 66
Skinner, Sherrod E., Jr. (MOH) 157
Smith, David M. (MOH) 24
Sniper Ridge 182
Sondong 75
Speicher, Clifton T. (MOH) 138
Spud Hill 161
Stone, James L. (MOH) 129
Story, Luther H. (MOH) 23
Suchon 44, 45
Sudong 47, 50
Sudut, Jerome A. (MOH) 117
Sukchon 42
Sunchon 42

T-Bone 161
Taegu 8, 9, 30
Taejon 6–8, 44
Taeusan 109
Tanchon 40
Thompson, William (MOH) 28
Triangle Hill 153, 155, 182
Turner, Charles W. (MOH) 24
Twin Tunnels 78

Unson 47, 50
USS *Brush* 40
USS *Lewis* 159
USS *Magpie* 40
USS *Mansfield* 40
USS *Pirate* 46
USS *Pledge* 46
USS *St. Paul* 134
USS *Sarsi* 148
USS *Walke* 107

Van Winkle, Archie (MOH) 48
Vegas 165, 168
Vittori, Joseph (MOH) 120

Walmsley, John S., Jr. (MOH) 122
Watkins, Lewis G. (MOH) 152
Watkins, Travis E. (MOH) 22
West, Ernest E. (MOH) 150
Westview 181
Wilson, Benjamin F. (MOH) 104
Wilson, Harold E. (MOH) 97
Wilson, Richard G. (MOH) 43
Windrich, William G. (MOH) 68
Woegwan 9
Womack, Bryant E. (MOH) 132
Wonsan 46, 159

Yalu River 47, 50
Young, Robert H. (MOH) 41